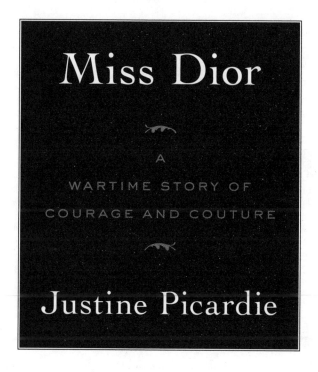

Miss Dior

A

WARTIME STORY OF
COURAGE AND COUTURE

Justine Picardie

Picador • Farrar, Straus and Giroux • New York

Picador
120 Broadway, New York 10271

Illustration credits can be found on pages 434–438.

The Library of Congress has cataloged the Farrar, Straus and Giroux
hardcover edition as follows:
Names: Picardie, Justine, author.
Title: Miss Dior : a story of courage and couture / Justine Picardie.
Description: First American edition. | New York : Farrar, Straus and Giroux, 2021 |
    Includes bibliographical references and index.
Identifiers: LCCN 2021022274 | ISBN 9780374210359 (hardcover)
Subjects: LCSH: Dior, Catherine, 1917–2008. | Dior, Christian—Family. | World War,
    1939–1945—Underground movements—France—Biography. | France—Biography.
Classification: LCC CT1018.D57 P53 2021 | DDC 929.7/4—dc23
LC record available at https://lccn.loc.gov/2021022274

Paperback ISBN: 978-1-250-85884-9

Our books may be purchased in bulk for promotional, educational, or business use.
Please contact your local bookseller or the Macmillan Corporate and Premium Sales Department
at 1-800-221-7945, extension 5442, or by email at MacmillanSpecialMarkets@macmillan.com.

For book club information, please visit facebook.com/picadorbookclub or
email marketing@picadorusa.com.

picadorusa.com • instagram.com/picador
twitter.com/picadorusa • facebook.com/picadorusa

1   3   5   7   9   10   8   6   4   2

Frontmatter illustrations:
Page i: Drawing by René Gruau for 'Miss Dior'
Page ii: Lillian Bassman, *Black – with one white glove, Barbara Mullen, dress by Christian Dior*, 1950
Page vi: Miss Dior vintage bottle
Page viii: Lithograph by René Gruau

For my husband Philip

For four years, we worked, we searched, like alchemists in pursuit of the philosopher's stone. And then Miss Dior was born . . . Because, you see, for a perfume to 'hold', it must first be held for a long time in the hearts of those who created it.

CHRISTIAN DIOR

Contents

Catherine Dior in her garden in Provence.

Into the Rose Garden

This is the story of a ghost who walked into my life on a sunlit Sunday morning in early summer, and would not let go of me, however much I might wish, at times, to be free of her. Her name is Catherine Dior, and she arrived as I wandered through the garden of La Colle Noire, her brother Christian's graceful château in the hills of rural Provence; a place she often visited, and a house where she lived for a while, after his sudden death of a heart attack at the age of fifty-two, in 1957.

Catherine was twelve years younger than Christian – he was born in 1905, the second son of a prosperous family; she was the youngest of five children, born in 1917, just before their eldest brother, Raymond, began his service in the French army during the First World War. But thoughts of war were far from my mind during that enchanting day at La Colle Noire. Instead, I was seduced by the exquisite beauty of the house, bought and restored by Christian Dior with the proceeds of the successful brand that he had created in 1946.

His debut collection, shown in Paris on 12 February 1947, had been christened the New Look by Carmel Snow, the editor of *Harper's Bazaar* (a position that I, too, have been privileged to hold). But despite the name, it was as much a nostalgic reimagining of the Belle Epoque, the golden years before the Great War. This was the era of Christian's early childhood, growing up in the secure surroundings of the Dior family home in Granville, on the coast of Normandy. His mother, Madeleine, had dressed in the romantic, sweeping gowns of the period, and it was these that inspired Dior's creation of swishing full skirts and a rounded hourglass silhouette, achieved with a corseted waist and padded bust.

Yet equally important to Dior's conception of 'flower-like women' that emerged in his couture salon in Paris was his mother's love of gardening. Madeleine's passion – which she passed on to Christian and Catherine – had found expression in the expansive garden she established at Granville, a miracle of hope and desire, built on a rocky outcrop overlooking the churning sea, several hundred feet below.

Her husband, Maurice Dior, had inherited the family fertiliser business, and on days when the wind was blowing in the wrong direction, the stench of his factories would drift across the town, although seldom as far as Les Rhumbs. But for all its unsavoury connotations, the guano industry paid for Madeleine's magical creation on a barren cliff top: tender flowerbeds protected from the salt-laden storms by hardy conifer trees, and most importantly of all, the roses that were (and remain) the centrepiece of the garden.

Roses continue to bloom everywhere at La Colle Noire, too: tumbling over pergolas and climbing up the outside walls, their tendrils gently tapping at the windows; luxuriant even on the patterned floral wallpaper and chintz furnishings within. And beyond the terraces and herbaceous borders is a meadow of a thousand rose bushes, whose flowers are still gathered (just as they have been since the field was planted to Christian Dior's original specifications) to produce an essential ingredient for his perfumes. The first of these, and closest to Christian's heart, was launched alongside the New Look collection, and named in honour of his beloved sister Catherine: Miss Dior.

Catherine outlived her brother by five decades, and died in June 2008, not far from La Colle Noire, at her home in the neighbouring village of Callian. Here she too cultivated roses, both for her own pleasure and to be distilled as an essence for Dior's perfume manufacturers in nearby Grasse. She had been a loyal and loving sister throughout her brother's life, and continued to be so after his death, honouring his legacy in many ways, including her consistent support for the Christian Dior museum that was eventually established in Granville.

But while Christian became one of the most famous Frenchmen in the world – a celebrated name alongside Charles de Gaulle – the remarkable story of Catherine Dior has never been fully explored. The little I knew of her life I had gathered from the Dior archives before I first visited La Colle Noire: she had lived with Christian in Paris in the late 1930s, and shared a small farm with him during the war, on the outskirts of Callian, where they grew vegetables, as well as roses and jasmine. Then she joined the French Resistance, and was captured by the Gestapo, before being deported to Ravensbrück, a German concentration camp for women.

One of the Dior archivists, Vincent Leret, had come to meet me at La Colle Noire on this particular Sunday morning, to discuss the possibility of me writing a new biography of Christian Dior. Yet as we spoke, I found myself asking him more and more questions about the mysterious Catherine, who appeared to have rarely referred to her involvement in the Resistance, nor her time in Germany. Vincent had known Catherine – before moving to his job at the Dior archives in Paris, he worked for the museum in Granville – and they corresponded, whenever he had queries that she could answer about her brother. But she gave nothing away of her wartime experiences, and he said that he felt it would have been impolite to press her for more information. As for the other writers who had previously chronicled the life of Christian Dior, few were particularly interested in Catherine, or even aware of her deportation to Ravensbrück. It was as if the hermetic world of haute couture had no concern for a woman such as Catherine Dior, or for the suffering that she had endured; nor even as to whether her experiences had played a part in her brother's legendary vision of fashion and femininity.

I wrote some notes, and then walked down to the meadow of roses, where butterflies danced about the petals, accompanied by a chorus of birdsong and bees. All was peaceful, caressed by gentle sunlight; yet as I stood there, I wished with all my heart that I had met Catherine before her death, a decade previously. And it was then, in that instant, that the seed was sown within me; a desire more akin to obsession – even possession –

that I would tell the story of this silent woman and her unknown comrades, who had somehow survived Ravensbrück and returned to France; but to a France where many of their compatriots preferred simply to forget the war years and disregard the shame of collaboration.

I did not hear Catherine's voice; the blue skies did not open. But the scent of the roses seemed to contain within it a question: was it conceivable that so much beauty had arisen from the ashes of the Second World War? And if so, what message might Catherine Dior have for us today, even if she never said another word.

Catherine Dior aged thirty, in 1947.

The Dior family in their garden, *c.*1920.
Catherine sits in the middle, between her parents. Behind them, left to right,
Christian, Jacqueline, Bernard and Raymond.

The Garden Maze

A soft rain is falling over the midsummer roses that are blooming in the garden of Les Rhumbs, and a sea mist is gathering, veiling the solid lines of the house. This substantial late-nineteenth-century villa, positioned high above the Normandy town of Granville, overlooking the English Channel, was the childhood home of Christian Dior. Hence the decision to turn it into a museum that cherishes his heritage, while the surrounding garden, created by his mother, has become a park open to the public. It is surprisingly quiet this morning in the grounds, perhaps because of the damp weather, although the museum has several dozen visitors who have come to see a new exhibition, dedicated to Princess Grace of Monaco, and displaying clothes designed for her by Christian Dior.

I've just been given a guided tour of the exhibition, each section staged in a different room that had been lived in by the Dior family in the early decades of the twentieth century, and I can't help feeling a strange blurring of time. For while I am admiring Princess Grace's outfits from the 1950s, and watching her glide on continuous loops of film, wearing the same couture gowns that are now preserved, inanimate, in glass vitrines, I am also searching for any clues about Catherine Dior that might be hidden in the fabric of the building. The dead princess walks through her palace in Monaco on the video screens, beckoning towards her lost life, as if in an uncanny fairytale. But I do not want to be distracted by this ghostly presence, nor by her silken sartorial relics.

Instead, I'm hoping to discover an earlier era, when Catherine was a child. She seems absent, however, even in the small bedroom that had been hers, where a short text explains her role in the story of Christian Dior:

Catherine was Christian's favourite sister, and when he introduced his first perfume in 1947, he christened it Miss Dior for her, and described it as 'the fragrance of love'. So it seems appropriate that I should be wearing the same scent on my trip to Granville. The original formula is classed, in the specialist terminology of perfumery, as a 'green chypre', blending complex notes of galbanum (a distinctive-smelling plant resin), bergamot, patchouli and oakmoss, with the warmth of jasmine and rose at its floral heart. And just for a moment, standing in Catherine's former bedroom, I become aware of this unmistakable scent; not on my own skin, but emanating from some other, unseen source . . . perhaps the huge flagon of perfume presented to Princess Grace by Christian Dior, on show in a nearby gallery?

None of the rooms in Les Rhumbs is furnished. Instead, they are lined with museum cabinets for the display of artefacts, drawings and photographs; on this occasion, relating mostly to Princess Grace's wardrobe. Yet for all the poignancy of these objects – in particular, the image of a youthful Grace Kelly, wearing an ethereal white Dior gown at the ball celebrating her engagement to Prince Rainier in 1956, unaware that she would die before growing old – Les Rhumbs remains a monument to a more distant past. For this is the place where Maurice and Madeleine Dior moved at the beginning of the century and raised their five children. They had married in 1898, when Madeleine was a beautiful nineteen-year-old girl; Maurice Dior, at twenty-six, was already an ambitious young man, intent on expanding the fertiliser manufacturing business that his grandfather had set up in 1832. By 1905, Maurice and his cousin Lucien were running the flourishing company together, and its growing success was reflected in their social ascendancy. Lucien Dior would become a politician, and remained in parliament until his death in 1932, while a rivalry developed between his wife Charlotte and Madeleine, apparently arising from their competitive aspirations to be the most fashionably dressed chatelaines of the wealthiest households.

I have brought my battered paperback copy of Christian Dior's memoir, with his evocative memories of Les Rhumbs, and the exterior remains just as he described it: 'roughcast in a very soft pink, mixed with grey gravelling . . . these two shades have remained my favourite colours in couture.' But the elaborately decorated interiors that he described in such detail have vanished: gone are the china shepherdesses, glass bon-bon dishes, and all the other ornaments that Christian remembered in such detail. I have read and reread his autobiography many times but for some reason, it is only today that I realise he does not mention his brothers or sisters by name. Indeed, he only refers to one brother – and then only briefly – and to his beloved Catherine. It is as if Raymond and Jacqueline never existed. Yet here in the entrance hall of the museum, the siblings remain gathered together in a family photograph: Raymond, the eldest, born on 27 October 1899; then Christian, who was born on 21 January 1905 (the same year that his father bought Les Rhumbs); followed by Jacqueline on 20 June 1908, Bernard on 27 October 1910, and seven years later, the baby of the family, Catherine, on 2 August 1917.

Les Rhumbs has a spectacular setting, standing proud on a granite headland, with a magnificent view across the bay. It had been built by a ship-owner, and its name comes from a nautical term referring to the points on the face of a compass, traditionally known as the 'rose of the winds', which is itself a symbol that appears on an original mosaic floor inside the villa. Today, the sky is a gentle grey – Dior grey – and the sea merges into the horizon. After my tour of the exhibition, I have been granted permission to spend the remainder of the day writing in what was the Dior children's playroom in the garden. It is set some distance away from the house, hidden at the end of a path, out of sight of onlookers – yet once inside, the view from the windows is unexpectedly dramatic. Two sides of the room are glazed, and it seems to be constructed on a sheer drop, with a vista of the jagged rocks below. The tide is out, and the sand bars exposed, the beach deserted, as gulls fly overhead, their melancholy cries calling across the waves.

The Dior family home, Les Rhumbs, in Granville, on the Normandy coast.

How might such an outlook have shaped the hopes and dreams of the Dior children? Clearly, it was very much on the mind of Christian Dior, when he wrote his memoir in 1956, the year before his sudden death. 'Our house at Granville,' he observed, 'like all Anglo-Norman buildings at the end of the last century, was perfectly hideous. All the same I look back on it with tenderness as well as amazement. In a certain sense, my whole way of life was influenced by its architecture and environment.'

Christian's earliest memories were rooted at Les Rhumbs, which remained the family's primary residence, although they also spent some time in Paris. In 1911 Maurice Dior bought an apartment in the opulent 16th arrondissement of the city; but during the First World War, they lived entirely at Granville, thereafter returning to Paris in 1919, to a larger apartment on Rue Louis-David, in the same district, when Christian was a teenage schoolboy at the nearby Lycée Gerson. Catherine, meanwhile, was educated at home by a governess, and at a girls' school in Granville; the Dior archives contain several evocative photographs of her playing on the beach as a child. Certainly, she felt sufficiently strongly about Les Rhumbs to have supported the initiative that it should become a museum, attending its opening ceremony in 1997, and serving as its honorary president from 1999 until her death. It was thanks to her recollections of the past that the garden was restored as closely as possible to its original design, and the wrought-iron conservatory at the front of the villa filled with a selection of palms and ferns, just as it had been under her mother's stewardship. Catherine continued to correspond with the museum curators, providing concise answers to their questions about the planting of the garden; she remembered it as 'a verdant fortress' protected from the wind by ramparts of trees, and shored up with great mounds of earth that had been transplanted to the headland upon which the house was built. Her brother Christian, she recalled, had trained roses, honeysuckle and wisteria to climb a white wooden pergola; and together they would watch the goldfish that swam beneath the water lilies in the pond. As for their mother, Catherine described her as 'a remarkable botanist', with a profound understanding of the Granville climate and soil. And despite Madeleine Dior's strictness with the children, Catherine made a brief yet intriguing reference to her mother 'closing her eyes' and giving them the freedom to create two flowerbeds, one in the shape of a tiger, and the other a butterfly.

Christian's surviving writing also provides a sense of the emotional resonance and powerful influence of the landscape. The young trees that were planted, as he described them in his memoir, 'grew up, as I did, against the wind and the tides. This is no figure of speech, since the garden hung right over the sea, which could be seen through the railings, and lay exposed to all the turbulence of the weather, as if in prophecy of the troubles of my own life . . . the walls which encompassed the garden were not enough, any more than the precautions encompassing my childhood were enough, to shield us from storms.'

For this is a home built on the very edge of France, where the land gives way to the sea. The original iron railings and stone walls still enclose the garden – although they are not sufficiently high to conceal the cemetery adjoining the property. And for all the bourgeois respectability of the house, and the care that has gone into planning and maintaining the garden, the sea and the sky are so vast that any human endeavour to create stability might seem reckless. Yet the Diors had lived and prospered in Granville for many generations; their wealth based on the enterprise of Christian's great-grandfather, who imported guano from South America into Normandy, to supply raw materials for the fertiliser industry. 'L'engrais Dior, c'est d'or!' proclaimed the company's publicity ('Dior fertiliser is gold!'). But Christian declared himself horrified on his few visits to the family's foul-smelling factories – 'they have left appalling memories,' he declared in his memoir, establishing in him a 'horror of machines' and a 'firm resolve' never to work in such an unpleasant environment.

Instead, like his sister Catherine, he preferred to stay at home and help their mother in the garden, away from the malodorous Dior factories.

Christian went so far as to learn by heart the names and descriptions of flowers in the illustrated seed catalogues that were delivered to Les Rhumbs, while Madeleine Dior's love of roses was inherited by her youngest child, Catherine, who made it her life's work to grow and nurture them. If the Dior children regarded their parents as distant figures of authority – as is suggested by Christian's biographer, Marie-France Pochna, who noted that they were raised in an era 'when open demonstrations of affection were considered likely to weaken the character and strictness was the norm' – it might also be possible that the way to their mother's heart was through her cherished garden.

Aside from the garden, the place that Christian felt safest in was the linen-room, where 'the housemaids and seamstresses . . . told me fairy stories of devils . . . Dusk drew on, night fell and there I lingered . . . absorbed in watching the women round the oil-lamp plying their needles . . . From that time I have kept a nostalgia for stormy nights, fog-horns, the tolling of the cemetery-bell, and even the Norman drizzle in which my childhood passed.'

These, then, were the shadows of devils and the dead that were kept at bay during the gilded age of the Belle Epoque, when Les Rhumbs had not yet been touched by the threat of war or financial ruin. But what of Catherine, born when the battles of the First World War were raging? Her birth certificate gives her name as Ginette Marie Catherine Dior; family lore has it that it was her brother Bernard who first chose to call her Catherine, rather than Ginette, when she was still a baby. Pictures of her at Les Rhumbs show a solemn little girl, dressed in starched white cotton and lace; her parents are stern, somewhat remote, Christian a more gentle-looking figure standing behind them.

I close my eyes, searching for Catherine, trying to envisage her as a small child in the garden, just outside, playing hide and seek. *Catch me if you can*, whispers the imaginary child, and then her voice is gone, and I can hear only the sound of the wind murmuring in the chimney, sighing in the empty fireplace beside me.

The Dior family album. This page, clockwise from top left: Catherine on the beach at Granville; Catherine and friends; Catherine; Catherine and Bernard; Catherine, 1920; the Dior children. Opposite page, clockwise from top left: Raymond; Christian, Bernard and Jacqueline with their governess Marthe Lefebvre, 1916; Jacqueline, Christian and Raymond; Madeleine Dior; Catherine; Christian.

The Dior family album. This page, clockwise from top left: Christian at Raymond's wedding, 1925; Raymond and his bride; Maurice and Madeleine Dior at the wedding; Madeleine Dior; Les Rhumbs. Opposite page, clockwise from top left: the clifftop garden of Les Rhumbs; Madeleine and Maurice Dior; Les Rhumbs; Madeleine's mother, Marie-Juliette Surosne; Christian (left) and Raymond in the garden; Catherine.

Through the windows, I notice two tiny figures walking along the beach in the distance, an adult and a child; as the rain becomes heavier, they disappear out of sight. The grey sea mist is thickening; the daylight seems to be dissolving into the fog; the glass of the playroom's windows is darkening, the wind growing wilder. And I feel a glimmer of understanding as to why Christian and Catherine felt such an attachment to Les Rhumbs, yet chose not to return to live here, even when they had the means to do so in adulthood. For this is a place where journeys begin, a starting point that could never be entirely forgotten; the restless waves and soaring seabirds a constant reminder of what might lie beyond the house on the headland.

There is something about the view of unyielding granite cliffs and rocks that might reflect the severity that Catherine attributed to her mother. As she said in a rare interview with Marie-France Pochna, in 1993, Madeleine Dior was a disciplinarian: 'My mother was severe with the boys, and even more so with the girls.' But such maternal sternness is not enough to explain the character of Catherine, or to understand the haunting atmosphere of this garden built on stone. So I decide to brave the rain, and leave the warmth of the playroom for a brief excursion. The brisk sea breeze is cold, buffeting the roses, their bruised, delicate petals falling to the damp earth, like confetti after a wedding.

Just along the path, I find a maze made out of privet hedges, and remember that one of the curators in the Dior archives told me that Catherine, in old age, had described this to him as an important feature of the garden in her childhood. I am tall enough to be able to see over the hedges, but a little girl, running through the green labyrinth, would have to know it very well to find her way out. *I know my own way*, comes a whisper in my head, though I cannot be sure whether it is mine, or a memory of my lost sister's voice, when we played together in the secret gardens of our own childhood.

If the ghost of Catherine is indeed here, she is not inclined to speak to me, in this, her private domain. The playroom is usually closed to visitors; it has been unlocked for me today as a special dispensation. And why should an adult sit alone in a playroom? I cannot envisage Madeleine Dior approving of this, nor encouraging much in the way of playfulness. As Christian himself wrote in his memoir: 'My early years were those of a very good, very well-brought-up little boy, watched over by vigilant *fräuleins*, and seemingly quite incapable of mingling in the hurly-burly of life.'

As I reread his words in my well-thumbed copy of his memoir, I am struck, for the first time, by the reference to German governesses, and wonder what became of them during the First World War. The answer comes a few pages later: 'The outbreak of war caught us by surprise at Granville . . . At first our *fräulein* refused to go, since she thought, as everyone did, that the cataclysm was impossible. She lived completely as one of the family, but when war broke out, she declared to our terrified amazement that she was ready, if needs be, to go "bang-bang" at the French soldiers . . .' As a consequence, a twenty-five-year-old French governess, Marthe Lefebvre (soon known affectionately as 'Ma'), was employed by the Diors in 1915, and she was to remain with them for the rest of her life.

Long after Christian discovered the delights of the capital city, he remained devoted to the family home in Granville, and to the grounds in which he had spent so much time as a small boy. In 1925 – when he was supposed to be hard at work in Paris as a student of political science, having been refused permission by his parents to study architecture – Christian found the time to design a new garden feature at Les Rhumbs, with arched trellises covered by roses surrounding a pool of water, complete with a small fountain.

This seems almost like an act of bravado, when one considers the vast expanse of ocean on the other side of the railings; but even so, there are pictures of Christian standing beside his water garden. The expression on his face is inscrutable; like his younger sister, he had the ability to present an enigmatic look to the world. Yet the roses that continue to flourish where once he stood – thanks to the instructions of Catherine, who oversaw their replanting here – are irresistibly beautiful, each new bud opening to reveal its own untouched perfection. The salt winds may blow and the rain pour down, but these roses seem bred to survive in the most challenging conditions.

The tide is coming in, and the sound of the sea is growing louder. If I had expected anything of this visit, it was to feel a sense of peace. Instead, I am aware of something more uncomfortable, and a growing unease. It may be that in such an eerie place – where the veil between the living and the dead is translucent; where ghosts are not confined to the glass cabinets that contain their old clothes; where their whispers are carried across the waves – a search for calm is misguided. After all, the Dior family was not safe here forever, nor did the protective buttresses of wealth remain intact. Sadness, madness, death and misfortune were not kept at bay; and the long shadow cast by the First World War reached Granville, as well as the rest of France. Roughly one third of France's male population between the ages of eighteen and twenty-seven died in the war. Raymond Dior, who had volunteered for the army soon after his eighteenth birthday in October 1917, was the only member of his platoon not to be killed in battle. And like so many other survivors, his psychological suffering continued long after the Armistice. What the British called 'shell shock' was perhaps more eloquently described by the French as a *crise de tristesse sombre* (an attack of dark sorrow). In the words of one of the army's leading commanders, Marshal Philippe Pétain, young soldiers would return from the front with expressions that 'seemed frozen by a vision of terror; their gait and their postures betrayed a total dejection; they sagged beneath the weight of horrifying memories . . .' By the spring of 1918, his British counterpart, Field Marshal Sir Douglas Haig, reported that Pétain himself 'had a terrible look. He had the appearance of a commander who was in a funk and has lost his nerve.'

Raymond Dior, who served in an artillery regiment on the battlefront, endured months of intense bombardment, as well as explosions of

Raymond Dior in his military uniform, at Les Rhumbs in 1918,
during the First World War.

Top, from left to right: Bernard, Maurice, Jacqueline, Catherine (sitting on Christian's lap) and Madeleine Dior. Above: Bernard.

poisonous mustard gas. In the years that followed the war, Raymond found it hard to readjust to civilian life. He married, and joined his father's business for a time, as was expected of him, but became periodically estranged from the family, including his siblings. As an aspiring writer, he expressed his rage in angry essays denouncing the evils of capitalism, but his fury alternated with despair and at least one suicide attempt.

Meanwhile, Bernard, the youngest of the three Dior brothers, began to display symptoms of a psychiatric disorder in 1927, when he was seventeen; having failed his school exams, he sank into a state of mute depression. According to Christian's memoir: 'My brother was struck down with an incurable nervous disease, and my mother, whom I adored, suddenly faded away and died of grief.' Several family photographs show Madeleine in the latter years of the 1920s looking desperately unhappy, her eyes cast to the ground, her mouth narrowed, her face turned away from the camera. Raymond's wife, who was also named Madeleine, told Marie-France Pochna that her mother-in-law was 'proud, ambitious and authoritarian'; yet the woman captured in these pictures appears to have become more fragile.

Christian's memoir contains only three mentions of his mother: her passion for flowers, her death, and her slenderness, which set her apart from the rest of the household. 'All the family was of Norman blood, except for the drop of "*douceur angevine*" brought in by my mother, the only thin person with a small appetite in our clan of good livers and hearty eaters.' (The *douceur angevine*, or 'sweetness of Anjou', is a traditional phrase in the region, and an oblique reference to Madeleine's origins; her father was a lawyer from Angers who died when she was fourteen, and her mother came from Normandy.) Frédéric Bourdelier, the director of the Dior archives, once memorably described Madeleine Dior to me as 'the Madame Bovary of Granville'; not that he was indicating she had doomed love affairs, but because of her longing for exaltation and elegance, and the disparity between her romanticised view of the world and the staid realities of bourgeois life.

Christian Dior in the garden at Les Rhumbs.

In the spring of 1931, Madeleine Dior was admitted to a clinic near Paris for an urgent operation, from which she did not recover. She died of septicaemia on 4 May at the age of fifty-one, and was buried in the family vault in the Granville cemetery, close to her garden at Les Rhumbs. 'Looking back on it now I see that it was fortunate that her death came when it did, although it marked me for life,' wrote Christian in his memoir. 'My mother left us before she knew of the perilous future unfolding before us.' For just a few months afterwards, Maurice Dior lost his entire fortune, having invested his capital in what proved to be a ruinous venture into real estate. And in the midst of this catastrophe, Bernard's condition worsened after his mother's death; he suffered delusions, suicidal thoughts and hallucinations, and was eventually diagnosed with schizophrenia in 1932. After failed attempts to treat him by doctors in Paris and Brussels – who speculated that he had an 'Oedipus complex', a term that revealed the growing influence of Freudian psychoanalysis – Bernard was sent to a mental asylum in Normandy. He remained incarcerated within the forbidding walls of L'Hospice de Pontorson from January 1933 until his death at the age of fifty in April 1960.

All of these disasters, believed Christian, were foreshadowed in an ominous event that occurred at Les Rhumbs in 1930. 'At the end of the holidays came a portent which alarmed me more than the bank crash. In our empty house, a mirror came unhooked by itself and smashed on the floor in a thousand smithereens.' Rereading his words at Les Rhumbs, an echo of that bad omen seems to reverberate; and as the wraith-like fog rolls in from the sea, obscuring the horizon, I imagine the compass of Les Rhumbs spinning again, pointing towards an unknown destination . . .

Catherine Dior reading in her family's Paris home, c.1922.

Through the Looking Glass

I am sitting at my desk, surrounded by piles of photocopied papers gathered from a dozen different archives, and it feels as if they are shards of broken glass, the wreckage of the shattered mirror in Granville; almost impossible to piece together to create a reflection of Catherine Dior as a young woman in the 1930s. The sense of fragmentation in Catherine's life, and that of her family, is heightened by the wider chaos of the era: first and foremost, the cataclysmic effects of the Wall Street Crash that set in motion the ruin of Maurice Dior. Then came the Great Depression, whose long shadow was cast over the Dior family, its darkness obliterating the certainties and conventions that had once defined their upbringing in the prosperous Belle Epoque.

When Madeleine Dior died in 1931, the family's way of life seemed to die with her. Gone were the stately rituals of the social seasons, moving between Paris and Granville; vanished like the wealth that had sustained Les Rhumbs, with its housemaids and gardeners. Catherine was thirteen at the time of her mother's death, and everything was collapsing around her. Her three brothers were deeply troubled: Raymond was still traumatised by his experiences as a soldier in the First World War, while Bernard showed no signs of recovering from his breakdown. (According to a cousin who visited him in mental hospital in 1934, Bernard did not even recognise members of his own family.) Christian, too, had been battling depression, after the failure of his business ventures in Paris. Thanks in part to his father's investment, in 1928 Christian had established an avant-garde gallery with a friend, Jacques Bonjean, showing work by emerging artists including Max Jacob and Christian Bérard, alongside more established modern masters such as Picasso, Matisse and Dufy. When this fell apart soon after Maurice Dior's bankruptcy, Christian joined another gallerist friend, Pierre Colle, giving Alberto Giacometti his first ever solo show in Paris, and championing Salvador Dalí, with a series of notable exhibitions. But despite the prescience of their aesthetic choices, Colle and Dior had little commercial success; for example Dalí's masterpiece *The Persistence of Memory* (depicting melting clocks and swarming insects) sold for a modest $250. Selling art in the wake of the Wall Street Crash was, as Dior observed in his memoir, 'an incredibly difficult task in those panic-stricken times. Paintings which today would be worth millions of francs hardly fetched a few tens of thousands . . . we went on from losses [to] organising surrealist abstract exhibitions by which we chased away the last private collectors.'

As for Catherine, she had no choice but to accompany her father on his downward spiral. For he had lost almost everything: his substantial fortune, his cherished wife, his good reputation, his social position, his sizeable apartment in Paris, and finally the splendid home in Granville (which did not find a private buyer, and ended up in the hands of the town council). Only the steadily loyal Marthe Lefebvre remained with the diminished Dior family, as Catherine's governess. For reasons that remain obscure, it was Marthe who suggested that a small farmhouse in a remote region of Provence might be a suitable refuge, far away from Maurice Dior's native Normandy, and any disapproving Parisian acquaintances or angry creditors. When they moved there in 1935, the property, called Les Naÿssès, had no electricity and only the most rudimentary plumbing; a stark contrast to the bourgeois comforts of Les Rhumbs.

It is little wonder that Catherine was lonely and unhappy in her newly enforced isolation at Les Naÿssès; she was just eighteen, and although she would grow to love the Provençal landscape, she had no friends of her own age in the area, nor any prospects of a social life or further opportunities beyond the confines of home. The following year, she left to join Christian in Paris, as soon as he offered her an escape route.

Christian had been leading a peripatetic existence since the family's disintegration – sleeping on friends' sofas, travelling to the island of Ibiza to recover from a severe bout of tuberculosis, and visiting Les Naÿssès. A photograph shows him sitting on the terrace there, pencil in hand, absorbed in his drawing, with a serious expression on his face. By this point, he had been forced to give up his dreams of a career as a successful art dealer and was teaching himself to produce fashion illustrations. After months of painstaking practice, he began to sell sketches to magazines as a means to support his destitute father and sister.

When Catherine and Christian returned to Paris in 1936, they lived together at the Hôtel de Bourgogne, close to the Place du Palais Bourbon. At the time, staying in hotels provided a loophole from paying tax, which may explain why so many artists and writers – including the philosopher Jean-Paul Sartre and his lover Simone de Beauvoir – chose this way of life. A fellow resident at the Hôtel de Bourgogne was Georges Geffroy, a dilettante designer-turned-decorator; having befriended the Diors, he introduced Christian to a rising star of Paris couture, Robert Piguet, who bought some of his sketches. Thus began Christian's career as a freelance fashion designer, producing work for various milliners and couturiers, including Edward Molyneux, whom he greatly admired.

Despite the age difference of twelve years, Christian and Catherine remained the closest of the Dior siblings, continuing to share the love of flowers and gardening that they had inherited from their mother, and a mutual passion for art and music. Both had suffered from the traumatic events that tore apart their family, and yet they had also learned to be resourceful, now that their mother was dead and their father impoverished. No longer in the traditional role of a powerless daughter, supported by her father's wealth until she married, Catherine discovered the independence of earning her own wages, encouraged by Christian, who helped find her a job in a *maison de mode*, selling hats and gloves. One of the most memorable photographs that I have ever seen of Catherine was taken during this period of happiness in Paris, when she was

Portrait of Christian Dior as a young man, painted by his friend Paul Strecker, 1928.

Photograph of Catherine Dior before the Second World War.

living with her brother. She is smiling warmly, her face alight with the energy of youth, her hair pinned up, a brooch attached to her tailored jacket. Whenever I think of this carefree episode in Catherine's youth, I am reminded of the story that she told Christian's biographer, Marie-France Pochna, in 1993: 'My brother loved designing costumes,' she said. 'I remember a Neptune costume he made for me, with a raffia skirt covered with shells, and another skirt, painted with a Scottish motif . . .'

Catherine is more conventionally dressed in the five pictures that I have of her in Paris from the late 1930s. All are black and white, so it is impossible to discern the colour of the jewellery that she is wearing, but she is clearly well dressed, her hair coiffed, her eyebrows arched. The Dior archivists believe that the photographs were taken at the Hôtel de Bourgogne in 1937, when Catherine was twenty, with her playing the role of a model for Christian's earliest designs. In two of the images, she is sitting on a chair, wearing a chic long-sleeved black dress and a decorative necklace. She looks to the side in one of these pictures, showing her distinctive profile; in the second, her dark eyes face the camera, meeting mine. The same direct gaze is evident in the other photographs: standing with her arms raised in front of drawn curtains that provide a makeshift backdrop, and seated behind a desk, a hat perched on the back of her head, three strands of pearls around her neck, and a necklace bearing a crescent moon.

These portraits are the only surviving visual clues to Catherine's life in Paris with Christian. But I feel sure that she must have understood by then that her brother was gay; they shared a home, after all, and a bohemian circle of friends. Paris was already renowned for its gay and lesbian subcultures – homosexuality had been decriminalised in 1791 at the time of the French Revolution – and Catherine and Christian were both working in the fashion business, a milieu that celebrated talented gay men. Many were well known to Christian: Edward Molyneux, for example, and Georges Geffroy, who began his career at the couture *maison* of Jean Patou before turning to interior design. Unlike his openly gay

Photographs of Catherine aged twenty,
while she was living in Paris with Christian.
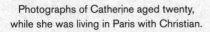

friends Jean Cocteau and Christian Bérard, Dior tended to be discreet about his private life – a consequence, perhaps, of his Catholic upbringing – but his sister was an integral part of it. When he fell in love with an urbane young man named Jacques Homberg, he did not keep the relationship secret from Catherine. Jacques was closer in age to Catherine – he was born in 1915 – and they remained friends long after his initial romance with Christian had become one of platonic affection.

Together the siblings explored the pleasures and freedom of Paris; and after Christian was offered a full-time job at Robert Piguet's couture house in 1938, he rented an apartment on Rue Royale, which was large enough for Catherine to have a room there. At the same time, Christian's vision of a youthful, idealised femininity was developing in his work. If the photos of Catherine modelling her brother's designs are suggestive of an early version of Miss Dior, as a modern Parisienne, then another variation seems to emerge in the form of Christian's first significant success at Piguet: a dress named 'Café Anglais', made of houndstooth trimmed with lace. According to Christian himself, this design was inspired by a popular children's book, *Les Petites Filles modèles*, written by the Comtesse de Ségur, and originally published in 1858; its heroines were a pair of pretty little sisters, Camille and Madeleine de Fleurville, whose adventures reveal that virtue is its own reward. But I sometimes wonder if the creation of the Café Anglais dress is part of the DNA of Christian's imaginary Miss Dior: a nostalgic representation of an adorable young girl, framed by a pastoral landscape of flower-filled gardens.

Such was the acclaim he received for 'Café Anglais' that he was introduced as its talented creator to Marie-Louise Bousquet, the Paris correspondent of *Harper's Bazaar*, who in turn arranged for him to meet the magazine's all-powerful editor, Carmel Snow. 'I really began to think that I had arrived,' wrote Dior in his memoir. 'What had in fact arrived even more surely than I had, was the fatal year of 1939. It made its appearance in a burst of follies, which always seem to precede a catastrophe. Paris had rarely seemed more scintillating. We flitted from ball to ball . . . Fearing the inevitable cataclysm, we were determined to go down in a burst of splendour.'

On 15 March 1939, Hitler's troops invaded and occupied Czechoslovakia, but in the weeks that followed, the Parisian beau monde continued its social life with even more merriment than usual. Diana Vreeland, the celebrated fashion editor of *Harper's Bazaar*, described the couture houses in July as 'jammed with buyers – frantic, amusing, exhausting and glorious'. And as Janet Flanner observed in the *New Yorker*, 'There have been money and music in the air, with people enjoying the first good time since the bad time started in Munich last summer.'

As the high society parties grew wilder and more extravagant – culminating in a circus-themed ball at Versailles, complete with acrobats, clowns and three elephants – Salvador Dalí was working on his Surrealist set design for *Bacchanale*. This was a new production for the Ballet Russe de Monte Carlo, portraying the madness of King Ludwig II of Bavaria, with music by Wagner, the corps de ballet on crutches, and a backdrop dominated by a giant white swan with a gaping hole in its breast.

The delirious frenzy came to a shuddering standstill with the declaration of war on 3 September 1939. Christian was called up for military service (along with all Frenchmen between the ages of eighteen and thirty-five); he saw no action, however, having been dispatched to provide farm labour in Mehun-sur-Yèvre, in rural central France, as part of a unit of army engineers. Catherine was also forced to leave Paris and return to Les Naÿssès; like many other employees of the fashion industry, she no longer had a job. Two of the city's leading couturières, Madeleine Vionnet and Coco Chanel, closed their premises. 'Everyone in my place had someone who was in uniform – a husband, a brother, a father,' said Chanel.

Carmel Snow reported on the remarkable change in the French capital in an article for *Harper's Bazaar* written in early September. 'In the last week it has become, almost overnight, a city deserted. The taxis have disappeared from the streets. All the telephones are cut off . . . When I went about the city to make my farewells at the dressmaking houses, I found evacuation already in process . . .' As the men who worked in the fashion industry were being mobilised, observed Snow, the women she encountered were notable for their composure. 'It is not a moment of mass courage but of individual heroism . . . each accepts the inevitable with a calm that leaves one awed.'

This strange air of calm continued for the eight months of what became known as the *Drôle de guerre* or 'Phoney War', so named because of the comparative lack of action on the Western Front. Jean-Paul Sartre, who had been drafted to undertake meteorological duties for the French army, was posted to a small town north of Strasbourg, close to the German border. 'My work here consists of sending up balloons and then watching them through a pair of field glasses,' he reported in a letter to Simone de Beauvoir. Given the relaxed nature of his military service, Sartre had time to work on a new book, and professed: 'This will be a modern war without slaughter, just as modern painting has no subject, modern music no melody, and modern physics no solid matter.' De Beauvoir herself noted a similar air of vacancy in a diary entry for October 1939: 'What does the word "war" really mean? A month ago, when all the papers printed it boldly across their headlines, it meant a shapeless horror, something undefined but very real. Now it lacks all substance and identity . . .'

Bettina Ballard, the Paris correspondent for American *Vogue*, continued to deliver her dutiful reports on the couture houses, but confessed in her memoir that life appeared to have come to a standstill, and that cynicism was pervasive. 'The word *ennuyeux* came up in every conversation, whether it was with your butcher because he couldn't give you the quality of meat you desired or your dinner partner who couldn't give you the stimulating conversations you expected. Everyone was corroded with boredom, and the abnormal tension of waiting for something, you couldn't imagine what, had a numbing effect.'

A similar ennui was evident on the military front; Major-General Edward Spears, who had served as a liaison officer between the French and the British forces in the First World War, was sent by Winston Churchill to check on the preparations for the forthcoming battle in France. He reported back that there was 'unfathomable, limitless boredom', which was 'horribly depressing'.

Despite Major-General Spears's concern about what he perceived as a dangerous apathy, his French counterparts were still confident that the massive fortifications of the Maginot Line, built at vast expense in the 1930s as a supposedly impregnable defensive front along the border with Germany, would provide sufficient protection. But when the German offensive against the Allied forces began on 10 May 1940, the formidable speed and strength of the Panzer divisions and Luftwaffe units overwhelmed Luxembourg, Belgium, the Netherlands and France in just six weeks. As the British were evacuating their stranded troops from the beaches of Dunkirk, the Germans pushed on towards Paris, with hundreds of thousands of refugees fleeing ahead of them, desperately trying to reach the south.

Amidst rising panic and confusion, immense numbers of terrified people set out on journeys that often had no clear destination, in what would thereafter be called *l'exode*, or the Exodus. Historians estimate that eight million people were on the move in France during this period; six million of them French, out of a total population of 40 million, and two million refugees from the Low Countries. The main roads were soon blocked by vehicles that had broken down or run out of petrol; endless traffic jams formed, but people continued on foot or by bicycle, pushing prams, dragging their possessions on handcarts or wheelbarrows. Railway stations were besieged by huge crowds, while even those who could fight their way onto a train faced lengthy delays and sudden cancellations. Communications lapsed between the national and local goverment, and in the absence of any official information, rumours spread, adding to the mayhem. Food and drink were in short supply, and looting ensued; pregnant women, the sick and the elderly collapsed on roadsides; children became separated from their parents. Hospitals, schools and prisons were evacuated, and the stories of escaped criminals added to the prevailing sense of fear, as did the terrifying threat of being strafed by German planes that flew over the slow-moving columns of refugees.

The chaos also presented insurmountable problems for the Allied forces, whose troops were held up for hours at a time by the immobile traffic. General Alan Brooke, a corps commander in the British Expeditionary Force in France, confronted by the hordes of exhausted, hungry refugees who had brought the roads to a standstill, commented in his notes to his diary: 'One's mind, short of sleep, is continually wracked by the devastating problems of an almost hopeless situation, and on top of it one's eyes rest incessantly on terrified and miserable humanity cluttering the lines of communication on which all hope of possible security rest.'

On 10 June 1940, the day that Italy declared war on France, the government itself abandoned Paris, declaring it to be an 'open city', and thereby allowing the Germans to enter the deserted capital without any opposition on 14 June. Swastika flags were hung from prominent buildings, including the Arc de Triomphe and the Eiffel Tower, providing an appropriate setting for Hitler when he made a brief tour of the city's landmarks on 23 June. The photographer Jacques Henri Lartigue recorded his impression of the atmosphere in the conquered capital: 'Paris is fading away. One can scarcely hear her breathe. She has fainted in her party dress . . . without cars, the avenues, boulevards and roads have become enormous and look like parts of an aerodrome . . . The Germans talk about Paris as if it were a toy they had just been presented with. A large toy full of subtleties which they do not suspect.'

Yet neither Christian Dior nor Catherine was there to witness the shocking subjugation of Paris. After the Armistice with Germany was signed by the defeated French on 22 June – a humiliation referred to by Christian in his memoir simply as 'the debacle' – he was fortunate to

The 'Exodus' of 1940, when millions of refugees tried to escape the approaching German army.

find himself in the so-called Free Zone, which had not yet been occupied by the Nazis. Their elder brother Raymond was unluckier: having been drafted into the army in 1939 he served as a brigadier, but following the fall of France in June 1940, he was taken as a prisoner of war in Vendée, and deported to Stalag X-B, an internment camp in northern Germany that held thousands of Allied POWs. Nearly two million French soldiers were captured during the invasion of their country; about one and a half million of these were transported to Germany. In 1941, Raymond was liberated, thanks to a deal between the German and French authorities concerning the release of First World War veterans, and he returned to Paris.

Meanwhile, towards the end of the tumultuous summer of 1940, Christian was able to make his way back to Provence to join his sister and father in Callian, about twenty-three miles north-west of Cannes, which at this point was also unoccupied by the Germans. Under the leadership of the eighty-four-year-old Marshal Pétain, the French government (having fled first to the city of Tours in the Loire Valley, then onwards to Bordeaux) agreed to a strictly enforced, heavily guarded demarcation line, specified in the terms of the Armistice, dividing the country in two. Paris would submit to Nazi rule, along with the rest of the Occupied Zone that comprised the north and west of the country, including the entire Atlantic coastline. The Unoccupied Zone in the south of the country remained subject to French control, although only for as long as the Germans agreed to this.

On 1 July 1940, the French government moved into the genteel spa town of Vichy in Auvergne (a choice influenced by the large number of comfortable hotels there), where it swiftly ratified the Armistice, abolished the Third Republic and suspended parliamentary democracy, giving full powers to Pétain as head of state, and appointing Pierre Laval as his chief minister. Such was the Vichy regime's willingness to adopt Nazi ideology

Hitler and his staff in Paris, June 1940, with Albert Speer (centre left).

that it introduced anti-Jewish regulations of its own accord at the beginning of October 1940, without any prompting from the Germans.

No such historical details are to be found in Christian Dior's memoir; instead, his account was of a life of tranquil rural isolation. His description of this pastoral episode is all the more surprising when one sees it in the context of the war, with the seismic shockwaves that were crashing across Europe, and the violent political earthquakes in France. In contrast, he describes a bucolic quietude; for despite having been 'rudely torn from my atmosphere of chiffon' as a designer in Paris, he adapted to a new life 'in sabots', working in the fields. 'I quickly forgot couture in that very different atmosphere, for I was once more penniless, having saved nothing from my pre-war earnings. I found myself living for the first time in the depths of the country. I became passionately fond of it and developed a feeling for hard labour on the land, the cycle of the seasons, and the perpetually renewed mystery of germination.'

Rereading his words now, I am struck by Christian's pragmatism, as well as his quiet enthusiasm: after all, someone has to sow seeds and grow food in a time of crisis. Unlikely as it may sound for a former student of political science, he noted simply that his stint of farm duty 'taught me that I had a strong streak of the peasant'. Christian therefore returned to Les Naÿssès ready to take on new agricultural challenges: 'so with my sister I decided to cultivate the little piece of land which surrounded the house. Callian has admirable soil for growing vegetables, and they fetched excellent prices on the market during this period of general restrictions.'

But as he himself confessed, 'My time was not wholly occupied with my runner beans.' Twice a week, he and Catherine went to Cannes together, to sell their vegetables at the local market, and also to see friends, many of whom had fled Paris with the arrival of the Germans, and taken refuge in the south. This group included the illustrator René Gruau (who helped Christian find freelance commissions as an illustrator on the fashion pages of *Le Figaro*) and an aspiring interior designer named Victor Grandpierre. Together, they were soon enlivening the Riviera with parties and amateur theatricals, until their social gatherings were forbidden by Vichy decree, on the grounds that they were scandalous. For amidst this artistic circle of painters, musicians, writers and actors were a number of gay men – Christian among them – who represented the bohemian elements of French artistic life that Pétain's Vichy regime despised.

A revered veteran of the Great War, Marshal Philippe Pétain was a popular choice as leader for the more conservative elements of the French population, and not just as 'The Lion of Verdun' who had finally achieved victory in that most protracted battle, less than a quarter of a century before. Pétain's enthusiastic supporters also welcomed his '*Revolution Nationale*', a campaign to rebuild a 'Good France', shaped by Catholic morality and traditional family values. France's historic republican motto – '*Liberté, égalité, fraternité*' – was changed to '*Travail, famille, patrie*' (work, family, fatherland).

As the figurehead of the French state, Pétain represented patriarchal authority, and he was swift to insist that the decision to collaborate with Germany was a patriotic act. This was made clear following his historic meeting with Hitler at Montoire-sur-le-Loir on 24 October 1940. In Pétain's radio broadcast to the French people on 30 October, he sought to highlight the value of the agreement he had reached with Hitler. 'It is with honour,' he declared, 'in order to uphold French unity – a unity dating back ten centuries – and as part of the active construction of the new European order, that I set forth today on the path of collaboration . . . Follow me: keep your faith in eternal France.'

What seems so extraordinary, at least with the benefit of hindsight, is that people were not only prepared to obey Pétain, as he abolished democracy, but did so with a fervent belief that he was their saviour. The octogenarian marshal became a popular icon, with his image appearing on brooches, bookmarks, medals and scarves, and his photograph given pride of place in shop windows.

Janet Flanner observed this phenomenon with her signature perspicuity, writing in the *New Yorker* about 'the widespread, worshipful cult of

Top: The French leader Marshal Pétain and Hitler in October 1940, when Pétain agreed to collaborate with the Germans. Above: Pétain addresses his supporters at a rally, beneath banners proclaiming '*Travail, famille, patrie*' ('Work, family, fatherland').

A bookmark celebrating Pétain.

the Marshal' that prevailed throughout much of the country, particularly in Vichy France, in the early years of the Occupation. 'To many millions of the French . . . the Pétain mystique became a sort of strange, esoteric state religion. The defeat, the fall, and the cutting up of France had produced in the French people the same sort of profound physical shock that might be experienced by an individual, far from young, who had been cruelly beaten, had had a violent concussion, and had also suffered the agony of amputation. In that shock something French in France came close to dying. Gradually, as they recovered, the people became racked with penitence and fell into a daze in which the Marshal confusedly figured both as a healer who seemed to have saved life and as a holy man whose intercession with the higher powers had saved the soul. Pétain became a sort of spa saint, an image at a sacred watering place. Vichy turned into a kind of political Lourdes . . .'

Integral to the regime's zealous autocracy was the belief that France should be purged and purified from the taint of corruption and immorality. At the same time as initiating its vicious anti-Semitic legislation and extending the 'aryanisation' programme of the Occupied Zone, the Vichy authorities introduced censorship, set up internment camps, banned trade unions and political parties, intercepted postal services, monitored telephone calls, and condemned all forms of cultural modernism, including jazz, and everything else deemed to be an expression of 'indecency' or 'depravity'. In this campaign, they received the unequivocal backing of the fascist French press. Such was the growing fanaticism of the Vichy crusade against 'decadence' and 'degenerate art' that Christian Dior – with his love of modern painting, as well as his sexuality – was personally vulnerable, as Catherine was surely aware.

As the economy worsened and food shortages became ever more severe, Catherine and Christian continued to grow their own vegetables; but life was becoming harder, even in a secluded village such as Callian. The Nazis were requisitioning colossal quantities of French produce – siphoning food back to Germany, along with industrial components, fuel, raw materials, looted art, furniture, and much else besides – while also charging France a hugely inflated fee for the cost of Occupation. Rationing had been introduced in September 1940, and the dwindling supplies of milk, butter, eggs, olive oil and meat led to increasing levels of malnutrition.

At the end of the autumn harvest in 1941, Christian made the reluctant decision to return to Paris, in search of paid work as a designer, while Catherine remained in Callian with their father and Marthe Lefebvre. But soon after her brother's departure, she met the man who would change the course of her life – a hero in the French Resistance named Hervé des Charbonneries.

Shadowland

One of the words most often used about Catherine Dior, by her few surviving friends and relatives, is 'discreet'; and it is telling that even a decade after her death, several of those who knew her still request anonymity when answering my questions about her relationship with Hervé des Charbonneries. All of them give slightly different accounts of the complications that ensued when Catherine and Hervé fell unexpectedly in love in November 1941. But the one thing they do agree on was that it was love at first sight: or in the more powerful French phrase, *un coup de foudre* (a stroke of lightning). And the lightning struck at a time when France seemed shrouded in the darkness of its defeat by Germany and its collaboration with the Nazis.

Born in January 1905, and therefore the same age as Christian, Hervé des Charbonneries was tall, charming, handsome, and already married with three children. He was also politically aware (like Christian, he had studied at the Ecole Libre des Sciences Politiques in Paris) and an early member of the Resistance, as were his mother and his wife Lucie.

When Catherine first encountered Hervé, it was at a radio shop in Cannes where he worked as the manager. Catherine was in search of a battery-operated radio (electricity had still not been installed at Les Naÿssès), in order to follow the progress of the war, and to hear the banned BBC broadcasts by General Charles de Gaulle, the exiled leader of the Free French in London. This was in itself a significant act by Catherine: it was dangerous to listen to de Gaulle, who had embarked on his

Robert Doisneau, *Resistance*, c.1940.

Above: Hervé des Charbonneries, an early supporter of the French Resistance.
Opposite page: General Charles de Gaulle, in London on 25 June 1940, the week after
his first BBC broadcast to Occupied France, calling for the French people to resist.

crusade against the Occupation on 18 June 1940, and was thereafter condemned to death *in absentia* by a French military court in August that year. Anyone discovered tuning in to de Gaulle could be arrested and imprisoned. But the general's inspiring messages, calling for 'the flame of the French resistance' to be kept alight, were vital for the morale of those who opposed the Nazis and the Vichy regime. Hence radio was key to the Resistance – for transmitting information, as well as receiving messages – so Hervé was especially well placed for his work in a network called F2.

Despite Catherine's unwavering support for General de Gaulle – which was shared by Hervé – F2 in fact had closer links with the Polish and British intelligence services. The Resistance was not a single, integrated organisation: it was made up of disparate units, drawn from many different backgrounds and conflicting ideologies; yet they were linked by the conviction that to do nothing in the face of evil was wrong. One of the earliest and most effective of the Resistance groups operating in France, the F2 network had initially been established in July 1940 by three Polish army intelligence officers who had found themselves stranded in Toulouse, behind enemy lines, after the German invasion. They went into hiding and built a radio set, transmitting their first message to exiled Poles in London on 22 August 1940.

Following the German invasion of Poland in September 1939, the Polish intelligence service had established its headquarters in Paris, where it formed a close working relationship with the station chief of the British Secret Intelligence Service, Wilfred Dunderdale, a suave character with a penchant for fast cars who was later reputed to have been the inspiration for James Bond. Nicknamed 'Biffy' by his British colleagues because of his prowess as a boxer, Dunderdale was certainly a friend of Bond's creator, Ian Fleming. In the summer of 1940, after the fall of France, the Polish intelligence service escaped to London, as did Dunderdale, and the links between the two strengthened, with the British SIS offering financial, technical and logistical support to the Poles, who in turn shared the intelligence that they acquired through their extensive network of agents in Europe.

On 6 September 1940, the three founders of F2 were joined by a fourth Polish officer, smuggled into Marseilles with the help of the British secret service: he was a quick-witted naval engineer, Lieutenant Commander Tadeusz Jekiel, who had studied in France before the war and previously been seconded to the French navy, maintaining excellent contacts there. His mission was to recruit French members to strengthen the network across the entire country, and to keep British intelligence informed about Axis military operations. Together with another Polish officer, Leon Sliwinski, Jekiel (under the code name of 'Doctor') built up the network into a resourceful organisation that collected vital information for the Allies. Their reports were dispatched to London by radio operators, or on microfilms that were smuggled out of France via Switzerland, and aboard small boats that sailed at night from Cannes to Gibraltar.

The first Frenchman to be recruited by Jekiel, shortly after his arrival, was a former racing driver, Gilbert Foury (known by the code name of 'Edwin'), who swiftly expanded F2's operations into the port cities of Le Havre, Brest and Bordeaux, to spy on German submarine movements. They were subsequently joined by a senior French naval officer, Jacques Trolley de Prévaux, and his Polish-Jewish wife Lotka, who had worked as a model for Vionnet before the war. By the autumn of 1940, F2 had established itself in Toulon and developed a network along the Mediterranean coastline, in Cannes and Nice. Hervé and Lucie des Charbonneries were both members of this section of the network; their involvement was notably courageous, given that they had three young children to protect. (The couple had married in 1931, and had a son and two daughters.)

Coincidentally, Hervé and Lucie also had an unexpected connection with Christian Dior's close friend René Gruau. The illustrator was still living in Cannes, and in 1941 he drew a portrait of Lucie, which reveals her poise and elegance. She was born Lucie de Lapparent in 1907; several of her family members were involved in the Resistance, including her cousin Hubert de Lapparent, who later became a well-known actor. Some family anecdotes suggest that after Hervé met Catherine, his separation from Lucie was *'en bonne entente'* (in other words, cordial). However, I also know – from a conversation with one of Catherine's surviving friends, who was related to Hervé – that the more traditional members of his family disapproved of the fact that he pursued a relationship with Catherine while still married. Indeed, Hervé and Lucie were never divorced.

Certainly, by falling in love with a married man, Catherine was disobeying a doctrine of her Catholic upbringing, as well as the patriarchal authority of Vichy France, which deemed that a woman's place was at home, as a dutiful wife or docile daughter, subservient to male authority. Women still did not have the right to vote in France: the organised campaign for female suffrage began in 1909, but enfranchisement was not granted until the end of the Second World War. During a period of repression, Catherine's rebellion seems all the more striking; and her refusal to conform to pious conventions in relation to her personal life appears to be reflected in her willingness to resist the Vichy regime and Nazi Occupation. In this sense, Catherine's heartfelt belief in freedom becomes apparent in her actions and choices.

Events moved swiftly. By the end of 1941, Catherine was dividing her time between Callian and the coast, renting an apartment in Cannes to be closer to Hervé and his comrades in the Resistance as the activities of the F2 network became even more perilous. Hervé's code name was 'Eric', Lucie's was 'Coal', and Catherine became known as 'Caro'. Her task was to gather and transmit information on the movements of German troops and warships, and in order to do so, she made frequent and lengthy trips by bicycle to liaise with other F2 agents.

Catherine's dearest friend, Liliane Dietlin, was also in F2; and it is thanks to another of Liliane's friends, the acclaimed Austrian-born investigative journalist Gitta Sereny, with whom I myself worked many years ago, that I know something of what Gitta described as 'the unsung heroism' of these women in the Resistance. General de Gaulle had called for French men – soldiers, sailors and airmen – to join him in the battle against Nazism. Yet just as many women rallied to the cause of freedom, some of them very young and without any military training. As Gitta recalled in a tribute to Liliane, written soon after her death in February 1997: 'I can barely think of Lili as old; to me she was always and remained throughout her life as I saw her when we first met – the epitome of the young Parisienne: small, slim, finely boned, with that very special elegance of speech, behaviour and of course dress that none of us adoptive Parisians could ever emulate.'

Gitta was unaware of the activities of F2 until the early 1970s, when she published her book *Into That Darkness*, about Franz Stangl, the commandant of the Treblinka extermination camp in Poland. It was only then, after three decades of friendship, that Lili 'initiated a conversation about the evil in man, of which I then found she had more experience than most'. Otherwise, Lili was as discreet as Catherine about her time in F2; to such a degree that her own daughter Anne did not know about her mother's experience in the Resistance. Indeed, it was Catherine Dior who finally told Anne; and only when Anne rang Catherine to tell her about her mother's memorial mass. Catherine asked her, 'You will see to it, won't you, that somebody speaks about what she did: that she was a heroine, a great heroine?' This meant nothing to Anne, until Catherine explained that Lili had been 'in the same *réseau* [section] in the Resistance as I, but for much longer'.

Gitta also knew Catherine Dior, and her brief account of their activities in F2 provides a rare insight into the secretive role that these young women played. During the years of Occupation, Lili worked in Paris as a courier for one of the Polish leaders of F2, Stanisław Lasocki, who reported directly to the intelligence services in London. According to Gitta, 'This elite organisation of more than 2,000 agents – which suffered enormous losses – was later credited as one of the most dynamic intelligence movements in Europe.' Records show that by the end of the war, F2 had about 2,500 agents, of whom 23 per cent were women; and at least nine hundred of the network's members were interned, deported or killed. Yet in spite of the terrible risks that she and Catherine faced on a daily basis, Lili downplayed her time in the Resistance. When Gitta asked her what she would have done if she'd been captured by the Gestapo, 'she answered lightly, patting my hand as if to console me retrospectively. Eaten a *"gentille petite pille que j'avais"* – a nice little pill. The incredible courage this veritable slip of a girl showed, the incredible things she did for her country.'

After the defeat of France in June 1940, Gitta became a volunteer nurse for a charity in the Loire Valley, looking after children who had lost their parents. (Such was the chaos at the time, as vast numbers of refugees fled the advancing German army, that many families were separated for months on end.) Gitta seldom came to Paris, but when she did, on one occasion in the winter of 1941, she arranged to meet Lili at a café. 'I questioned her choice of meeting place – the Right Bank was full of Germans, the Champs-Élysées worst of all. "The safest places in Paris are those where they congregate," she said in her light voice.'

Lili had arrived at the café on her bicycle, 'on which she virtually lived during those years. She wore wool stockings, a straight dark skirt with one seam undone to give her space for riding her bike, a short fur jacket that had seen better days, passed on to her by her mother, and a knitted cap that hid her dark hair. She was twenty-nine then, but looked eighteen, and there wasn't a male eye that didn't follow her when she came through that terrace door and hugged me, rather tightly I thought.'

It wasn't until thirty-five years later that Lili told Gitta more about the terrifying circumstances: 'she had carried four messages, three to individuals in the morning and one to a group meeting that afternoon; eight people had been arrested that day, two in the morning and the six others that afternoon, just as Lili had turned into the streets on her bicycle. All would be executed, mostly hanged after being tortured. "A bad day," she remembered. Were there many like that? She shrugged, "*Ah oui . . .*"'

Gitta's fond homage to her friend – the beautiful, brave girl on a bicycle – seems to reflect the archetypal portrait of Resistance heroines, playing their part in the fight against the Nazis, in stories that were already a mainstay of popular culture during my childhood. 'What was so wonderful about her was that she made it all seem so easy, almost fun,' said another former member of F2, Pierre Heinrich, quoted by Gitta, 'and you know, in the midst of all that horror and, yes, all the risks, she never stopped laughing.' Gitta also wrote that Lili was known as '*une petite fleur*', a phrase that might equally be applied to Catherine Dior, or Lotka de Prévaux, or any other of their youthful, idealistic comrades. And a scene in which Gitta described bidding farewell to Lili in Occupied Paris – not knowing if they would ever meet again – evokes a memorably cinematic atmosphere: 'she wore a wide cotton skirt that day and a brilliantly white short-sleeved blouse I had watched her ironing that morning, no stockings, but sandals with, I think, wooden soles. After a brief hug, she cycled away from us across the Pont de la Concorde. Her shiny hair blowing in the gentle wind of that day, she raised her arm goodbye . . .'

As I reread Gitta's words, and then close my eyes, I see fleeting images of other spirited young women in the Resistance, disappearing across a bridge into the distance; I think of their courage, their innocence, and the suffering of those who did not survive the war. Each of them deserves her own accolade; yet they remain forever unknowable . . . as elusive as Miss Dior.

★

In the course of researching this book, I have been fortunate to meet Liliane's son, Nicolas Crespelle, who was the much-loved godchild of Catherine Dior. We met in Paris for tea one day, at a café in the same street as the Dior archives, and he appeared to me as quintessentially Parisian as his mother did to Gitta: distinguished-looking, urbane and

Portrait of Catherine Dior.

entirely unruffled, despite having arrived by bicycle. Nicolas was very generous in sharing what he knew, while also emphasising how much had been kept secret from the post-war generation. He was born in February 1947, in the same week as the launch of the New Look collection, and his sister Anne in 1945. 'No one told us about the war,' said Nicolas. 'Catherine only talked to me about it on one occasion, when she said she had been in a camp in Germany.' All he knew about his mother's role, at least while she was still alive, was that she had ridden a bicycle during the war; but whenever she started to talk about why she had spent so much time on these cycling expeditions, his father would say that it 'wasn't interesting'.

Why was that? I asked Nicolas.

'I think my mother was in love with one of the Polish guys in F2. He died during the war, she was left alone, and then my parents met.' Nicolas wondered if his father was jealous of Lili's love affair with another member of the Resistance before they met, or whether it was simply that people of his parents' generation avoided discussing the German Occupation of France. Nevertheless, he could see the powerful bond that existed between his mother and Catherine, which led to Catherine being chosen as his godmother. The two former resistants continued to spend much time together, for though Nicolas and his sister went to school in Paris, his parents had a holiday home in Provence, in a village close to Catherine's home in Callian. 'Catherine and my mother trusted each other completely,' said Nicolas. Their attachment was based on their shared wartime experience in F2, and because Catherine's own silence had been responsible for saving Lili's life.

The enduring strength of their relationship also arose out of the fact that they were in a surprisingly small minority of the French population who resisted the Germans. Estimates based on the records of wartime intelligence services suggest that for most of the period of Occupation, there were no more than a hundred thousand active members of the Resistance. It was not until after the Allied invasion of Normandy in

June 1944, when it was becoming clear that Germany was likely to lose the war, that the number of resistants approached four hundred thousand: about 1 per cent of the population.

This, then, is the context of Catherine's proud service in F2, the facts of which emerge from the few surviving manuscripts outlining its formation and activities, in the archives of the Resistance. These reveal Catherine's tireless activities within the organisation in gathering information and compiling intelligence reports to send to the British secret services in London. She wrote up the reports on a typewriter that she continued to use for correspondence throughout her later life.

A dossier in the military files of the Resistance notes that Catherine performed a vital role in the operation of the Cannes office, not only by transporting reports for Hervé des Charbonneries and Jacques de Prévaux, but also hiding this incriminating material from the Gestapo during a raid, before delivering it safely to another key member of the F2 network, thereby proving her 'composure, decisiveness, and sang-froid'. Other Resistance archives show that she worked closely with one of the original leaders of the network, Gilbert Foury, covering the entire Mediterranean zone. Their clandestine operations included making surveys of the coast around Marseilles and drawing maps with details of German infrastructure, fortifications and landmines, all of which were transmitted to the intelligence services in London.

At this point, F2's southern command post was based in Nice, its agents active along the Mediterranean coast; but the network had also spread across much of France, with each of its four sub-groups given female names: Anne, Cécile, Madeleine and Félicie. It had couriers, cipher officers and radio operators; printers to forge convincing identity cards, permits and travel documents; and a maritime team, with boats travelling at night, delivering equipment, picking up reports and evacuating compromised agents.

Yet for all the careful planning and security measures that were in place, F2 was under constant threat from informers, and the danger had intensified in November 1942 when the Germans crossed the demarcation line and extended their Occupation into the zone of Vichy France. The German military intelligence service, the Abwehr, set up units in Nice, Toulon and Grasse (the latter less than fifteen miles from Callian), while the Gestapo established its headquarters at the Hôtel Hermitage in Nice, with a unit for interrogation and torture nearby at the Villa Trianon. One indication of local support for the Nazis was the response to a Gestapo commandant's request for forty female informants in Nice: no fewer than three hundred Frenchwomen applied. Denunciations were widespread during the Occupation – in the form of anonymous letters sent to the authorities, naming Jewish neighbours or those with sympathies for the Resistance, or supplied by informers who could receive large sums of money if their evidence led to arrests. The Milice, a fascist French militia created by the Vichy regime at the beginning of 1943, and led by Joseph Darnand, a First World War veteran, was also increasingly active in southern France. Darnand, a close associate of Pétain and Pierre Laval, had further demonstrated his allegiance to Hitler by joining the Waffen-SS.

In July 1943, Georges Makowski, Jacques de Prévaux's Jewish right-hand man in Nice, was warned that he had been betrayed by an informer. Rather than attempting to escape, he went home in order to destroy all the paperwork that might compromise other members of F2. As the door to his fifth-floor apartment was battered down by the Gestapo, Makowski had just finished burning the last of the compromising documents – but before he could be seized, he leapt from an open window, killing himself in the fall, believing that suicide was preferable to being captured and tortured.

Despite his sacrifice, more arrests were to follow: on 29 March 1944, Jacques de Prévaux himself was apprehended by the Gestapo in Marseilles, along with several other important members of F2. That same day, his wife Lotka was captured at their home in Nice (her parents had already been deported from Paris to Auschwitz the previous year). When the Gestapo arrived at their apartment, Lotka had just enough time to entrust the couple's baby daughter into the care of their nanny, who safely hid her for nine months before taking her to Jacques's brother and sister-in-law in Paris after the Liberation.

Both Jacques and Lotka were kept in solitary confinement, and repeatedly interrogated and tortured at Montluc prison in Lyons, which was run by the notorious SS officer Klaus Barbie. On 19 August – four days after the Allies had landed on the Mediterranean coast – they were executed by a firing squad, part of a group of twenty-four resistants murdered there during the final atrocities of the Occupation. A few days later, the Germans abandoned Montluc, and Lyons was liberated on 3 September 1944.

In a further sign of the remarkable silence that reigned for so long in France on the subject of the war, Jacques and Lotka's baby daughter Aude – who was adopted after their death by her father's brother and sister-in-law – was told nothing about her real parents' identity and their heroic service in the Resistance. It was only a chance encounter, when she was twenty-three, that finally led to her discovering the truth.

The effect of the de Prévauxs' arrest was calamitous for many others in F2. As soon as Hervé des Charbonneries received the news, he rang Catherine to give her a coded warning: 'We will dine, tomorrow evening, with your brother in Paris.' Cannes was too dangerous for Catherine to stay there; even the isolation of Les Naÿssès was unlikely to keep her safe from the Gestapo. She had to leave immediately, and join Christian in Paris.

A cyclist distributing clandestine leaflets for the Resistance in Paris, c.1944.
Photograph by Robert Doisneau

Rue Royale

As its name suggests, Rue Royale is one of the grandest streets in Paris, running from the monumental Place de la Concorde to L'Eglise de la Madeleine, a church that was originally designed as a magnificent temple to the glory of Napoleon's army. It has long been associated with fashion: as a boy, Christian Dior had accompanied his mother Madeleine to her dressmaker, Rosine Perrault, whose premises were at 13 Rue Royale; he also visited Edward Molyneux's couture house, which was situated at number 5, next door to Maxim's restaurant. The entrance to 10 Rue Royale is as impressive as the rest of the street, but on the other side of the immense gateway there is a warren of staircases and hidden doorways. One of these leads up a narrow flight of steps to a place I have long searched for: Christian Dior's apartment, his home in Paris during the war, and where Catherine stayed in the spring and summer of 1944, having been forced to flee Provence.

The current occupant of the apartment has learned something of its wartime history from an elderly neighbour, an inhabitant of the building since childhood. When I visit, it is a Saturday, and central Paris is unusually deserted – the protests by the Gilets Jaunes against a rise in fuel tax are in full swing, and all of the nearby shops have shuttered their glass windows after the violent rioting a week previously, when Dior and Chanel were among those luxury boutiques that were ransacked. Such demonstrations are a reminder of the city's history of insurgency; after

German military personnel, off duty, on Rue Royale during the Occupation.
Photograph by André Zucca

the revolution of 1789 came a series of uprisings and insurrections, and in 1871, during the radical days of the short-lived Paris Commune, an enormous barricade was constructed across Rue Royale as a rampart in the street battles with the French army.

Once I step inside the inner courtyard, the wailing police sirens become less insistent, and within the apartment itself there is a sense of quiet. But knowing, as I do, that Catherine Dior was being hunted by the Gestapo when she sought refuge here in 1944 casts the apartment in a different perspective. Looking out of its windows, across the rooftops of Paris, it becomes evident that there is only one way in and out; so while you could feel safe, you might equally be trapped, with no effective escape route.

The man who lives here now is kind-hearted; after showing me around, he says I am welcome to spend some more time alone, and perhaps get a sense of the atmosphere, while he goes back to work in his study. 'Which room should I be in?' I ask him. He beckons me to follow him, and we go into the smallest room, with a single bed in it, and a wooden stepladder to a little windowless attic that would be invisible to anyone looking up at the apartment from the street below. 'This one,' he says. 'This is where the ghosts are . . . Sometimes, when I sleep here, I hear the ghosts in the attic just above – it used to be a hiding place for Catherine and her friends in the Resistance during the war.'

He smiles, gently, then touches the green leaves of a houseplant that stands beside the bedroom window, and gestures to another by the door. 'These are for Catherine,' he says. 'I think that she would want to have plants kept in this room.'

'And the butterflies?' I ask him, looking at the delicate insects that have been mounted and framed, and are hanging on the walls.

'Ah, those,' he says; 'those are a reminder of a very strange day in the history of Rue Royale, in the mid-nineteenth century, when thousands of butterflies landed on the street and covered all the buildings. But the butterflies also remind me of Catherine. And I feel that having winged creatures here will keep the nightmares at bay.'

Typing pamphlets for the Resistance in Paris.
Photograph by Robert Doisneau

'Your nightmares?' I ask, a little confused.

'No, not mine; Catherine's nightmares,' he says. 'Can you understand why?' And silently, I nod my head.

★

It was to Rue Royale that Christian Dior returned at the end of 1941, having finally made the decision to leave Provence, after being offered a job by his former employer, Robert Piguet. Christian had hesitated for several months before undertaking the journey. 'I disliked intensely the idea of returning to a humiliated and beaten Paris,' he wrote in his memoir. 'And my new countrified mentality disliked the thought of the intrigues and labours of studio life. I also had to consider the future of our agricultural venture if it was left under the sole supervision of my sister.' He does not explain what, exactly, gave him the impetus to resume his work as a couturier; but in any event, Piguet had already filled the position by the time Christian eventually came back from the south of France. Instead he found a job at another couture house, that of Lucien Lelong, who was also the president of the Chambre Syndicale de la Haute Couture, the official trade federation for the industry, and as such, responsible for negotiating with the Nazi authorities in Paris.

There are many different ways of viewing the activities of Lelong and his colleagues during the Second World War. According to Dior himself, 'the couture houses had reopened their workshops, as much to provide employment for thousands of workers as out of patriotic pride . . . Such an apparently frivolous and futile occupation risked earning the displeasure of the Germans: but somehow we managed to exist until the day of Liberation.'

In fact, the Germans took a close interest in the Paris fashion business, and proposed that it should be moved to Berlin; indeed, as early as August 1940, Nazi officials had visited Lelong and told him that the decision had been made to transfer the couture ateliers to Germany, where they would operate under the direct rule of the Third Reich. In November 1940, Lelong travelled to Berlin, determined to defend French interests, while simultaneously basing his calculations on a shrewd understanding that a certain amount of co-operation with the Germans would be necessary to ensure the survival of the couture houses in Paris. His arguments were sufficiently persuasive for the Germans to abandon their plan to centralise the fashion industry in Berlin.

Some collaboration with the Germans was inevitable for couturiers such as Lelong who continued to work under the Nazi regime, even though there were those who saw the survival of Paris fashion as a sign that French culture remained invincible in the midst of defeat. The author and journalist Germaine Beaumont, writing in the winter of 1942, observed that a couture dress was 'such a little thing, so light and yet the sum of civilizations, the quintessence of equilibrium, of moderation, of grace . . . because a Paris gown is not really made of cloth, it is made with the streets, with the colonnades . . . it is gleaned from life and from books, from museums and from the unexpected events of the day. It is no more than a gown yet the whole country has made this gown . . .'

But for all the romance of the notion that couture represented a quintessentially Parisian art, it was governed by the strictly enforced rule of the German authorities, with dozens of precise regulations controlling everything from textile rationing to the ownership of the ateliers. Jewish proprietors had their businesses confiscated, losing their possessions, their liberty and in many cases their lives. For example, Lotka de Prévaux was the daughter of a milliner, and her parents had a haberdashery shop in Paris that was seized by the authorities before their deportation to Auschwitz. Lotka's sister and brother-in-law fared no better: having lost their successful fur business, they were forced to flee Paris in August 1942, slipping across the demarcation line to the Unoccupied Zone, but once there they too were tracked down and sent to their deaths in Auschwitz.

Overleaf: Swastikas hanging over Rue de Rivoli. Photograph by André Zucca

Wholehearted French support for the 'aryanisation' of the fashion industry was by no means uncommon, as a feature of the 'cleansing' activities imposed by the Third Reich and the Vichy regime. 'France will be saved and will be rebuilt by elements that are intrinsically her own; the essentials are French blood and the French brain,' declared the writer François Ribadeau Dumas in November 1940, the same month that the Jewish couturier Jacques Heim was forbidden to do business in Paris. 'The moment . . . the more than questionable Jewish houses disappear, the atmosphere of the Parisian luxury trade will be purified!'

This, then, was the environment in which Christian Dior found himself when he joined Lucien Lelong in Paris, a city that had been conquered by the Nazis, and a business that was subjugated to the will of the Third Reich. From 1940 onwards, Otto Abetz, the German ambassador to Paris, and his French wife Suzanne ruled over the new version of high society from their palatial embassy, the Hôtel Beauharnais on Rue de Lille, entertaining senior military staff, diplomats, politicians, industrialists, actors, artists, authors and couturiers. One of Abetz's closest friends was Jean Luchaire, a journalist and leader of the French collaborationist press. The two men had known each other for a decade, and Suzanne Abetz had previously been Luchaire's secretary. Another of the regular guests, the virulently anti-Semitic French writer Louis-Ferdinand Céline, referred to Abetz as 'King Otto I' and France as 'the kingdom of Otto'. In this realm – adorned with art looted from the mansions of the Rothschilds and other Jewish families – several couturiers flourished under the patronage of Otto and Suzanne Abetz. These included Marcel Rochas, who reportedly crossed the street to avoid his former clients once they had been marked out as Jewish, and Jacques Fath, who attended soirées at the German embassy with his elegant wife Geneviève, herself a celebrated model and former employee of Coco Chanel. Fath more than trebled his staff numbers, from seventy-six employees in 1942 to 240 by 1944, while Rochas presented a private show of designs to German dignitaries in November 1940.

Suzanne Abetz was a frequent customer of Elsa Schiaparelli's couture salon, and almost as powerful as her husband. Indeed, when another notable client, Elisabeth de Rothschild, moved seats at a Schiaparelli show so as to avoid sitting next to Mme Abetz, she was arrested the next day and deported to Ravensbrück concentration camp, where she died in March 1945. Elisabeth had been born into an aristocratic French Catholic family, and made the tragic mistake of assuming that she would be safe in Paris, even after her estranged husband Philippe de Rothschild had escaped to join General de Gaulle's forces in London.

Hermann Goering's second wife Emmy, a former actress, was another highly placed couture client; her husband, the commander-in-chief of the Luftwaffe, visited Paris twenty-five times between 1941 and 1942, helping himself to enormous quantities of looted art, as well as ordering gowns and jewellery for his wife. Indeed, according to Sir Francis Rose, an expatriate English artist who knew the Goerings, the Reichsmarschall was just as likely to wear the jewels himself: 'he had to be the most obvious and most glamorously attired male in any place. Jewels, especially huge stones and massive gold trinkets, suited him . . . instead of Emmy wearing [a new set of diamonds], he appeared in a suit of his favourite blue at Maxim's with coat and waistcoat buttons and tie pin made out of them.'

But to assume that the couture houses were simply supplying the wives of German dignitaries in Paris would be wrong; of the twenty thousand 'couture ration cards' issued in 1941, a mere two hundred were reserved for Germans. Josée Laval, the daughter of the Vichy leader Pierre Laval, was already a customer at Chanel and Lelong before the war. In 1935, she married Comte René de Chambrun, a lawyer who would go on to represent Coco Chanel. Josée's passion for couture was matched only by her conviction that her father was a visionary politician. Her wartime diary reveals that she was a regular client at Lanvin, Lelong, Schiaparelli and Balenciaga. Similarly, Jean Luchaire's daughter Corinne, a minor film star, was always dressed in the latest fashions, most often designed by her favourite couturier, Marcel Rochas.

Then there were the women known as the 'BOFs', the wives and daughters of the flourishing black marketeers, nicknamed after the initials of the increasingly scarce food products that had enriched their families: *beurre, oeufs, fromages.* With these and other newly rich clients, business soared for the couture houses: revenue rose from 67 million francs in 1941 to more than 463 million francs in 1943.

Christian Dior's friend and colleague at Lelong, Pierre Balmain, gives a vivid account in his memoir of the customers they were obliged to see, and Dior's own sardonic response. 'The clientele at Lelong during the Occupation consisted mainly of wives of French officials who had to keep up appearances, and of industrialists who were carrying on business as usual. Apart from Madame Abetz, the French wife of the German Commissioner, few Germans came to us. Nevertheless, there was still a somewhat unreal, strange atmosphere about the showings. I remember I was standing with Christian Dior behind a screen, scanning the audience awaiting the first showing of 1943, the women who were enjoying the fruits of their husbands' profiteering. "Just think!" he exclaimed. "All those women going to be shot in Lelong dresses!"'

As it happened, both Balmain and Dior had an opportunity to leave France in September 1942, when Lelong obtained permission from the German authorities for his designs to be displayed at an international fashion exhibition in Barcelona. According to Balmain, 'Christian suggested that I should go as I was more familiar than he with installing the stand and dressing the wire dummies with our display models.' Before Balmain left for the neutral territory of Spain, 'Lelong made me give my word that I would return to Paris and continue my work with him; and consciousness that I shared the responsibility of maintaining the livelihoods of the numerous employees dependent on the firm stifled my desire to use the opportunity to flee to London or New York.'

However, while he was in Barcelona, Balmain was out of touch with anyone in Paris. 'Some friends thought I had either been killed or arrested. Mother had far more glamorous ideas. She thought her son had gone to London to join the Free French Forces and would be returning in triumph to liberate France.' In fact, as Balmain later confessed in his autobiography, 'I was on a wild shopping spree, restocking my wardrobe with fourteen suits, forty-five shirts, eighteen pairs of shoes, three coats and a vast number of useless objects which were unobtainable in France. The future in those days seemed such an uncertain affair. Money meant little . . . I like clothes, and so I took the opportunity of buying them.'

Balmain also provides a memorable description of Christian Dior's Paris apartment, where they often retreated together in the evening. They always avoided Maxim's, just across the road, since the restaurant was too expensive for them, as well as being frequented by Germans and French collaborators. Despite its position in the heart of Nazi-controlled Paris, Dior's apartment provided a safe haven from the reality of the Occupation. At a time when French street signs had been replaced by ones in German, the clocks reset in accordance with the Greater Reich and swastikas hung from every public building, Dior had created a nostalgic version of his childhood home before the First World War. According to Balmain, it was 'a large bourgeois type of apartment furnished in the style of the Second Empire. There was a black grand piano in the salon, and what I regarded as a remarkable number of seemingly worthless trinkets: photographs of elderly ladies in plush velvet frames, small gilded goats drawing mother-of-pearl shells mounted on wheels, opaline fruit dishes, and, dominating all, a larger-than-life full length portrait of a woman dressed in the style of 1880. She bore such a striking resemblance to Christian . . .'

Balmain remained grateful to Dior for his friendship – 'Christian was gentleness and kindness itself' – and even with the restrictions of the curfew, 'there were peaceful, happy occasions in Paris.' Thanks to Dior, Balmain was introduced to a fashionable social circle, including the artist Christian Bérard, the writer Jean Cocteau, the interior decorator Georges Geffroy and the musician Henri Sauguet. The latter happened to encounter Catherine Dior at her brother's apartment in June 1944,

while she was staying there. Sauguet was perturbed to be a witness to what he described as her 'comings and goings' with several other members of the Resistance, and he subsequently admitted in his memoir that he was beset with anxiety as to how he might explain this to the Gestapo, if they were ever to question him.

By sheltering his sister and her comrades, Christian was certainly putting himself at risk, and expressing his tacit support for the Resistance. But some of his friends and acquaintances in Paris society did not share Catherine's courage or her convictions. Philippe de Rothschild has a devastating line in his memoir, when he quoted 'a smart Parisienne' as saying: 'It was so much more chic to collaborate.' He does not name the woman, but her words could have been spoken by any number of society hostesses. Take, for instance, Marie-Louise Bousquet, the influential Paris correspondent for *Harper's Bazaar* and widow of the playwright Jacques Bousquet, who had long been known for the salons that she held every Thursday evening at her home on the Place du Palais Bourbon. These continued throughout the Occupation, and she welcomed pro-Nazi French intellectuals alongside German officers whom she considered cultured, including Ernst Jünger and Gerhard Heller. Jünger was a highly regarded author as well as a soldier decorated for his actions during the First World War, and he worked with Heller at the German censorship office in Paris. Heller was tasked with banning books by Jewish and anti-fascist writers on a lengthy list drawn up by Otto Abetz, while Jünger's role involved reading letters written by German soldiers, and checking French newspapers and other publications for signs of insubordination.

Despite enjoying Mme Bousquet's hospitality and appreciating the beautifully bound books in her library, Jünger seems to have had some reservations about her, confessing in his diary to treating her 'with the same caution that a chemist exercises when handling questionable

Christian Dior at home in his Rue Royale apartment. Photograph by Frank Scherschel

compounds'. Heller, however, described Bousquet's home as a 'sanctuary' from his daily censorship duties. He had joined the Nazi party in 1934, yet was an enthusiastic Francophile and approved the publication in 1942 of Albert Camus' novel *L'Etranger* (translated, after the war, as *The Outsider* in London and *The Stranger* in New York). When Heller read the manuscript of *L'Etranger*, Camus was not yet famous – he was an obscure Algerian-born journalist suffering from tuberculosis. A former student of literature, Heller deemed the novel not only acceptable but 'highly original'. In an interview after the war, Heller explained that he thought the censorship system worked very well during his time in Paris: 'I concluded a pact with editors and publishers: they could produce what they liked as long as paper was available, except on a few themes, like war or security, and no works by Jews, and nothing anti-German. Auto-censure was best.' It remains unclear whether Heller was aware of Camus' subsequent role, from the end of 1943 onwards, as editor of the Resistance underground paper *Combat*, but the moral ambiguities of the situation were symptomatic of the grey areas in what became known as 'the Dark Years' of Occupation.

Meanwhile, another of Marie-Louise Bousquet's regular guests, Jean Cocteau, a self-professed pacifist and intermittent opium addict, seemed happy to socialise with Otto Abetz. It may be equally surprising that the German ambassador was willing to entertain Cocteau, given his unorthodox lifestyle would have been declared 'degenerate' by both the Vichy government and the Nazi regime. Bousquet also introduced Cocteau to Ernst Jünger, and the two men became well acquainted. On 23 November 1941, Jünger wrote in his diary that Cocteau was 'amiable and at the same time, ailing, like someone who dwells in a special, but comfortable, hell'. Cocteau came up with his own whimsically surreal description of living with the enemy: 'Paris has swallowed the German army, just as an ostrich stomach swallows a pair of scissors.' The ostrich can reputedly digest anything, as well as being known for burying its head in the sand, and Cocteau proved himself a similarly adaptable creature, with his infamous remark about the Occupation: 'Long live the shameful peace . . .'

Jünger also met Picasso at Marie-Louise Bousquet's gatherings, and several leading French literary figures, including Pierre Drieu la Rochelle and Marcel Jouhandeau, both of whom were openly fascist and anti-Semitic, and who both accepted Goebbels's invitation to visit a writers' congress in Germany in October 1941. And it was thanks to Bousquet that Jünger was introduced to one of her closest friends, the immensely rich socialite Florence Gould, who entertained German officers and French writers at her own salon. An American military intelligence report into Gould's activities in France during the Occupation stated that she and Bousquet provided sexual entertainment as well, by procuring women who were prepared to offer their services to high-ranking German officers. Bousquet herself was alleged to have had an affair with Colonel Arnold Garthe, who ran the Abwehr in Paris, while Gould's wartime lovers were said to have included Helmut Knochen, the head of the Gestapo and senior commander of security in the city.

Thus these queens of the beau monde were at the forefront of carnal collaboration, as well as encouraging Franco-German social gatherings. On one such occasion, in March 1942, Jünger recorded in his diary that he was enjoying vintage champagne with Gould, along with her friends Gerhard Heller and Marcel Jouhandeau, at Le Bristol hotel, when an air-raid alarm went off. 'Conversed about death during all of this,' he continued. 'Madame Gould had some good observations on this subject, namely that the experience of death is one of the few that no one can take from us . . . She mentioned the fundamental premise of any correct political attitude: "Have no fear." On a tropical evening, she once saw a butterfly land on the back of a gecko in the light of a garden lamp. For her that symbolized great safety.'

Although Jünger would become fond of Florence Gould, some of the French intellectuals that he encountered in the elegant salons of Paris struck him as being far more vehemently anti-Semitic than he was

Ernst Jünger, the German author and soldier, on horseback in Paris, *c.*1941.

himself. In his diary entry of 7 December 1941, Jünger described listening to Céline, who was a doctor as well as an eminent writer, complain that the Germans were not acting with sufficient speed against the Jewish population in France. 'He spoke of his consternation, his astonishment, at the fact that we soldiers were not shooting, hanging, and exterminating the Jews – astonishment that anyone who had a bayonet was not making unrestrained use of it . . . "If I had a bayonet, I would know what to do."'

On 29 May 1942, Jewish people were ordered to wear a yellow star embroidered with the word *Juif,* under a law that had already been introduced in Germany and Poland. Textile coupons, which were part of the widespread rationing, had to be exchanged for these stars; Jews who refused to wear them were arrested, as were non-Jews who wore them in sympathy. Less than a fortnight after the introduction of the yellow star, on 8 June, Ernst Jünger lunched at Maxim's with the French novelist and Vichy diplomat Paul Morand, and Morand's elegant wife Hélène. Afterwards, wrote Jünger, 'On Rue Royale I encountered the yellow star for the first time in my life. Three young girls who were walking past arm in arm were wearing it . . . I then saw the star more frequently that afternoon. I consider things like this, even in my own personal history, a significant date. Such a sight is not without consequence – I was immediately embarrassed to be in uniform.'

Presumably the Morands felt no such discomfiture: their fascist friends included Céline, and they shared his anti-Semitism. Philippe de Rothschild, who encountered the Morands as he was attempting to find a way to leave France after the German invasion, observed that 'Madame Hélène launched into a tirade. Was I mad? What was wrong with me? The Germans were perfect people with perfect manners. The decadence into which Europe had declined was entirely due to the corrupt Jews . . . The Nazis were the only ones who had the solution.'

Soon after Jünger's lunch with the Morands at Maxim's, detailed plans were made in Paris for the arrest and deportation of all Jews to German extermination camps. The SS officer Adolf Eichmann arrived in the city on 1 July 1942 to discuss arrangements, and René Bousquet, the Vichy Prefect of Police, offered his men for the task, while Pierre Laval ensured that four thousand children under the age of sixteen were included in the arrests. Laval had not been asked to do so by the Germans, but later claimed that it had been a 'humanitarian' measure on his part, to keep Jewish families together during deportation. In fact, many of the children were separated from their parents before being sent to the camps. On the night of 16 July, and into the following morning, nearly nine hundred teams of French policemen seized more than thirteen thousand men, women, children and newborn babies in the *Grande Rafle* ('the Great Raid') and incarcerated them in the Vélodrome d'Hiver, an indoor sports arena. There was no food, no running water, no sanitation, and in these merciless conditions people began to die (pregnant women were among the victims). Those that survived the five days of imprisonment in the Vélodrome were sent to an internment camp in the north-eastern Paris suburb of Drancy – again, under the direction of French gendarmes – and from there deported by train to Auschwitz. Ernst Jünger wrote in his diary: 'Yesterday a large number of Jews were arrested here in order to be deported – first of all the parents were separated from their children, so that their crying could be heard in the streets. Not for a single moment can I forget how I am surrounded by wretched people, human beings in the depth of torment.'

Did the sight of the yellow stars and the cries of the children reach as far as Christian Dior's apartment on Rue Royale? Certainly, Pierre Balmain describes how, whenever he and Christian saw the Germans marching down the Champs-Elysées, they turned away: 'with sickness in our hearts [we] became ostensibly absorbed in a window display.'

Top: Two Jewish girls wearing the compulsory yellow star in Paris.
Below: A young supporter of Marshal Pétain selling badges with the insignia of the French leader, 1 May 1941, Paris. Photograph by Pierre Jahan

As for Cocteau, in his diary entry of 2 July 1942, he recorded a conversation at dinner with the new head of the Paris municipal police, whom he found to be 'a charming young man': 'He speaks of Hitler with great esteem and without any pomposity and without any narrow-mindedness. Like me, he thinks that it would be disastrous to prevent someone like him from achieving his objectives, to limit him en route. Maps of the "new Europe" are ready at the prefecture . . . No more customs. No more frontiers.' Three weeks later, when the Jewish detainees were being held in appalling misery at Drancy, Cocteau again mentioned Hitler in his diary. 'Hitler has studied Napoleon's mistakes and wants to combine his genius as a soldier with the [diplomatic] methods of Talleyrand. This is the reason the public fails to understand his greatness and his shifts of policy.'

By the end of 1943, Cocteau could have been in no doubt about the reality of Hitler's anti-Semitic regime. His friend Max Jacob, a Jewish-born poet and painter who had converted to Catholicism before the First World War, wrote a letter to Cocteau in December, telling him that his brother had been deported to Germany, that his sister had died of a broken heart, and that he himself lived in fear of being arrested at any moment. On 20 January 1944, Jacob contacted Cocteau once more, writing that another of his sisters had been arrested after the death by torture of her husband, and asking him to intervene on her behalf. She later died in Auschwitz, and Max Jacob himself was arrested on 24 February 1944. Cocteau wrote to Gerhard Heller and Otto Abetz, requesting their help in freeing his friend, but without success: Jacob died of pneumonia less than two weeks later at the Drancy internment camp. The convoy that he was supposed to be on left Drancy for Auschwitz with 1,601 Jews on board, 170 of whom were children.

Christian Dior had also been a friend and admirer of Jacob since 1928, when he had exhibited the artist's work at his gallery. In his memoir, Christian made no mention of Jacob's death, but instead described the close-knit group of young men that had regarded him as 'our master and friend', including Georges Geffroy, Christian Bérard and Henri Sauguet. They were united, he wrote, in 'affection for Max' and their 'worship of frivolity'. Together, in their carefree youth, they would stage charades, dress up in lampshades and curtains, with Max as their merry leader, dancing in red stockings. It was these games of charades, continued Christian, which taught him, many years later, how to act the role of 'Couturier' at public appearances 'with the necessary gusto'.

Aside from a shared fondness for Max Jacob and various other mutual acquaintances, Jean Cocteau and Christian Dior had been part of overlapping artistic circles since the late 1920s. As Christian declared in his memoir: 'dominating every avant-garde effort, the beacon of Jean Cocteau illuminated and revealed all.' But they were also linked in another, more unlikely way. One of Cocteau's former lovers was a talented young author named Jean Desbordes (whose work was admired by Ernst Jünger). Christian remained friends with Desbordes, but it is unclear whether he knew that the brilliant writer was a member of the same Resistance network as Catherine. While Catherine worked for F2 in southern France, Desbordes, under the code name of Duroc, commanded a group in the north, monitoring German submarines and naval movements in the English Channel, and providing secret intelligence reports to London on the fortifications and airfields of Cherbourg.

It seems unlikely that Cocteau, who was notorious for his indiscretion, was aware of Desbordes's role in F2; and in June 1944, when Desbordes was forced into hiding in Paris, he sought refuge with another friend, Georges Geffroy. This brought him perilously close to the German authorities: Geffroy's apartment was at 248 Rue de Rivoli, just a few steps away from Le Meurice, the luxurious hotel that had been requisitioned as the military headquarters, and marked as such by the vast swastika flags that hung above its entrance. Geffroy's own war record is ambiguous; there were stories, possibly apocryphal, that he enjoyed secret sexual liaisons with German officers. Whatever the truth of these rumours, Desbordes (who had married Madeleine Peltier, a young pharmacist, in 1937) was

Max Jacob, *Vision of the War*, c.1943.

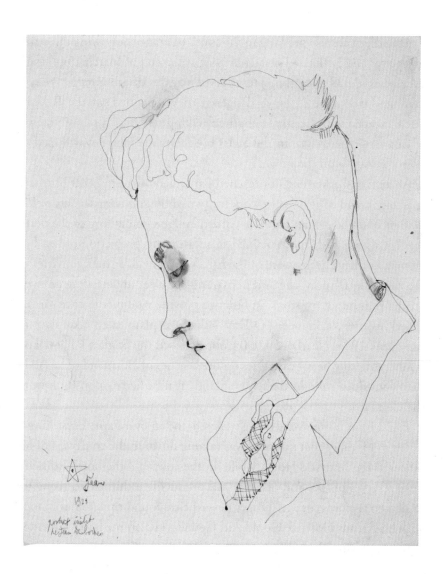

Jean Cocteau, drawing of Jean Desbordes, 1928.

facing increasing threats as the Gestapo stepped up their surveillance of the F2 network in Paris.

The risks were also growing in the south of France, following the arrest of Jacques and Lotka de Prévaux in Nice at the end of March 1944; their colleagues in F2 – including Hervé and Lucie des Charbonneries – knew that they would be in grave danger if they remained on the Riviera. Lucie escaped with her three children, taking refuge in a remote region of eastern France, close to the Swiss border, while Hervé was forced to keep constantly on the move.

As soon as Catherine Dior reached Paris, she moved into her brother's apartment, and continued to work for two of the surviving leaders of F2, Gilbert Foury and Stan Lasocki. Christian knew something of the perils that his sister faced, and remained steadfast in his protection of her, but he may not have been aware of the full extent of Catherine's activities in the network. By now, she and her colleagues were undertaking an even greater number of missions, in order to provide vital intelligence for the Allied invasion of France – D-Day – that was planned to take place in early June 1944. Nearly 160,000 troops crossed the English Channel on 6 June, suffering heavy casualties on the beaches of Normandy; the Allies then continued to fight their way inland, against fierce opposition from the Germans.

By 22 June, battles were being waged in the air over Paris. Ernst Jünger noted in his diary that shrapnel was raining down in the courtyard of his offices at the Majestic Hotel, while 'in the course of the bombardment, huge reserves of fuel and oil were hit, producing a thin cloud rising up to darken the heavens . . .' Jünger nevertheless found time to have lunch with his friends Florence Gould and Gerhard Heller; the latter informed them that Céline 'had already fled to Germany. I still find it curious how very much people who callously demand the heads of millions are afraid for their own paltry lives. The two things must be linked.'

Yet the Gestapo and their French collaborators showed no signs of retreating, and as they intensified their investigations into the Resistance, the number of arrests and executions increased. While the Allies fought to gain control of Cherbourg and Caen in northern France, the Gestapo had successfully infiltrated the F2 network in Paris, through a French female informer of the same age as Catherine Dior. Like Catherine, she was involved in a close-knit network of agents that had been formed during the Occupation: but their aims were to support the Germans and annihilate the Resistance, using extreme force and unspeakable brutality.

Rue de la Pompe

There are places in Paris where the opaque veil between the past and the present seems to yield a little at dusk, when ghosts may walk in the shadows between the solid stone edifices that embody the city in all its grandeur. Some of these mysterious spaces are beguiling; others are more sinister. But the one I fear most exists in my mind's eye, just beyond the locked doors of 180 Rue de la Pompe. From the outside, the substantial property looks much like any other, boasting a prime position in the prosperous 16th arrondissement, near the junction with Avenue Foch; yet inside, throughout the summer of 1944, this was the scene of truly terrible crimes against members of the Resistance, including Catherine Dior.

During the Occupation, the German security service had requisitioned so many buildings in and around the impressive surroundings of Avenue Foch that it was referred to as Avenue Boche by Parisians (using a slang word for Germans), although only in a whisper, for the Nazi agents and officers who operated there were feared throughout the city. Theodor Dannecker, the SS officer in charge of Jewish deportations to extermination camps, took up residence at 31 Avenue Foch, while his colleague Helmut Knochen established the Gestapo headquarters at number 72 and extended his empire to include several more buildings on the street, which were commandeered for the use of Nazi counter-intelligence departments. From there, Knochen set out to recruit a private army of French informers, spies, torturers and assassins. Known as the French

A swastika flag hanging from the Arc de Triomphe in Paris, June 1940.

Gestapo (*gestapistes français*), some of these men were career criminals, such as the notorious gangster Henri Lafont, who made a fortune from the black market under Knochen's protection. In return, as part of a mutually beneficial relationship, they procured goods for the Germans on the black market, often in the form of generous 'gifts' (Lafont, for example, presented Knochen with a white Bentley and diamonds). But as the war progressed and Germany's domination of France looked less unassailable, the *gestapistes* were also required to act as so-called 'auxiliaries' to the SS, in clandestine operations against the Resistance and Allied agents in France. Lafont had well over a hundred men working for him, including several former policemen; indeed, his second-in-command, Pierre Bonny, had been a Paris police inspector before the war, jailed for corruption in the late 1930s.

In April 1944, one of the most ruthlessly efficient of these teams moved into a large apartment, occupying three floors of 180 Rue de la Pompe. Its leader was Friedrich Berger, a nefarious figure with a background in espionage and extortion. Born in Saxony, in eastern Germany, in 1911, Berger joined the Foreign Legion in 1934 and subsequently spied for the Abwehr under a number of different aliases, including Franz von Sartorius. In December 1940, Berger was arrested for treason in Vichy France, transferred to Algeria, and sentenced to death in August 1941. But thanks to official German intervention he was released in May 1942 and made his way to Paris. Fluent in French, which he spoke with a slight accent, Berger rapidly became an accomplished operator on the black market.

In an era when many Parisians were constantly hungry, even verging on starvation, due to food shortages and the strict rationing in force, racketeers such as Berger wielded great influence. As Ernst Jünger observed in his diary on 4 July 1942, after dining at the Tour d'Argent, 'In times like this eating – eating well and much – brings a feeling of power.' The Tour d'Argent, along with Maxim's and other prestigious Parisian restaurants, relied on the black market for its supplies. Jünger recognised that the privileged few (presumably including himself) who enjoyed such luxuries were 'looking down from their demonic comfort' like gargoyles gazing from a high tower, while far below them 'the starving eke out their living . . .'

Jünger's friend Florence Gould also made use of the black market, thereby ensuring that vintage champagne and cognac flowed freely at her literary salon. This was held each Thursday at her apartment on Avenue Malakoff, a short stroll away from her admirer Helmut Knochen's headquarters on Avenue Foch. Everything was available for the right price on the black market – including priceless antiquities, such as those acquired by Gould to decorate her home. On 4 March 1943, Jünger recorded in his diary that he and Gerhard Heller had visited Gould for breakfast; her other guests were her confidante Marie-Louise Bousquet, the author Marcel Jouhandeau and the artist Christian Bérard. 'Conversation in front of a vitrine filled with Egyptian artefacts from Rosetta,' wrote Jünger. 'Our hostess showed us ancient unguent jars and tear vials from classical graves. From these, she playfully scratched off the thin dark purplish-blue and mother-of-pearl layer – the accumulation of millennia – letting the iridescent dust swirl in the light . . .'

Thus the black market was associated with power as well as transgression, and its influence spread like a stain throughout Paris, from high society gatherings to lowlife gangs, whose diverse lives were linked by collaboration. The devious relationships between the Gestapo and their auxiliaries often had their origins in black-market transactions, when a judicious mixture of bribery and intimidation applied by an SS officer could turn a local racketeer into a mercenary. In Berger's case, he had already set up what was euphemistically referred to, in the language of Occupied Paris, as a 'purchasing agency' or 'economic bureau', at 14 Rue du Colonel Moll, to deal in a wide variety of products, including food, alcohol, cigarettes, narcotics, textiles and jewels.

At some point in 1943, Berger came to the attention of a German officer, SS-Untersturmführer Karl Kleindienst, who had been posted to

Paris to investigate the black market. Kleindienst offered him a choice: either be prosecuted and punished, or agree to work for the Gestapo. Berger took the latter course, which appeared to benefit him as much as Kleindienst. According to a US intelligence report into Berger's activities: 'From then on, he passed himself off as a purchaser of rationed goods being fraudulently sold and in each case, when the deal was ready to be concluded, revealed himself to be a German policeman and seized the goods. He then took the would-be seller to his offices at 14 Rue du Colonel Moll, and after maltreating him there, brought him to the Rue des Saussaies [another of the Gestapo's premises]; the seller was then obliged to agree to the transaction "proposed" by the Gestapo. Berger set up a gang to help him in these operations . . . the members of this team became a veritable organisation of evil-doers soon to be known as "the Berger band".' The US intelligence report also noted that by August 1943, Berger was in 'direct contact' with a more senior officer, SS-Hauptsturmführer Alfred Wenzel, who was Kleindienst's superior in Paris. Thereafter Berger followed Wenzel's directions, and he and his team 'specialized in seeking out Jews and Resistance networks'.

Berger tended to use the same techniques to recruit his own gang of crooks and opportunists as Kleindienst had applied to him: threatening them first with arrest, and then holding out the prospect of a substantial fee in return for collaboration. And there was just as much profit to be made from the business of hunting down the Resistance as there was on black-market deals. As the writer David Pryce-Jones observes in his book, *Paris in the Third Reich*, 'If someone was ready to sell supplies illicitly, what stopped him from selling his compatriots? Desire for money imperceptibly shaded into treason.'

The forty or so men under Berger's command were not official members of the Gestapo, but they were armed and generously funded by the German secret police, while also adding to their already substantial earnings by looting and stealing from the people they arrested. Wenzel, who was based at Avenue Foch, paid Berger, oversaw his black-market

Friedrich Berger and members of his unit, giving the Nazi salute
as they follow German officers.

operations and worked closely with him, as did Kleindienst and another German SS officer, Dr Walter Kley, a well-spoken former academic at Stuttgart University; all three were regular visitors to Rue de la Pompe. A fourth SS officer, Otto Mayer, was also involved with Berger's activities.

The apartment at Rue de la Pompe was within easy access of the Gestapo offices in Avenue Foch, and the fact that it was made available to Berger is evidence of his value to the SS. The commandeering of what had once been a Jewish family home is yet another indication of the ways in which the civilised landscape of Paris was distorted by the Nazi Occupation. After its Jewish inhabitants had been forced out of their property in the summer of 1940, it was at first assigned to one of the Gestapo's most valued informers, an Austrian countess: such was her success that she was duly rewarded with a large house on Avenue Foch. The spacious residence at Rue de la Pompe contained a magnificent drawing room, with heavy plush purple curtains and furnished with a number of armchairs, sofas and a grand piano; a kitchen and dining room; several bedrooms; a large bathroom; and a basement, reached by an internal staircase. Everything about the apartment looked conventional, comfortable – the epitome of *haute bourgeoisie* – yet under the rule of Friedrich Berger, it was to be twisted into something foul and menacing.

The majority of Berger's team were Frenchmen with a background in the black market; in addition, he employed two expert torturers who were longstanding residents of Paris, but originated from Tbilisi in Georgia. A trio of young Frenchwomen were also associated with the gang: Berger's mistress, Denise Delfau, who worked as a 'secretary', witnessing and making notes during the interrogations carried out at Rue de la Pompe; Denise's elder sister (and Berger's occasional lover) Hélène; and Madeleine Marchand, the girlfriend of a senior member of Berger's unit, Fernand Poupet.

Born in January 1918 in the town of Nogent-le-Rotrou, a hundred miles south-west of Paris, Marchand was just a few months younger than Catherine Dior and, like her, had come to live in Paris in the late

1930s. During the Occupation, she worked first in a fabric shop and then as a secretary and cashier at the Théâtre Édouard VII. In 1943, Marchand became involved with a boyfriend who was the same age as her, Edmond Roger (nicknamed'Cri-Cri'); he was already active in the black market and, following the by now standard process of coercion and inducements, started working for Berger in February 1944. The following month, Marchand transferred her affections to the more powerful Poupet, who often deputised for Berger.

Poupet was ten years older than Marchand, a hard-faced gangster with a dandy's taste for sharp suits. A mechanic by trade, he developed a lucrative illegal sideline as a *passeur*, or guide, smuggling people past the guards that policed the demarcation line, crossing from the German-controlled northern zone into Vichy France. He then turned to dealing on the black market in Paris and, despite some success, was arrested and briefly jailed for these activities. On his release from prison in September 1943, Poupet was recruited by Berger; Marchand was enlisted into the gang the following spring, whereupon she swiftly revealed a talent for duplicity. Like the Delfau sisters, she seemed to be vehemently opposed to the Resistance – denouncing them as 'terrorists' when in the company of other collaborators – but she could also present an entirely convincing appearance of being a trustworthy supporter of the Free French.

I have only one photograph of Marchand, which emerged from the vast cache of documents generated by the judicial investigation into the Rue de la Pompe Gestapo, launched soon after the Liberation of Paris. Madeleine's face stares out at me as I write these words, her dark eyes looking directly into mine. She is pretty, with high cheekbones and softly waved hair; her eyebrows are plucked and painted into narrow arches, in the fashion of the period; she is smiling, and wearing lipstick. Her make-up is carefully applied, though a little too heavily, as if in a mask. The picture is a black-and-white headshot, so I cannot see her complete outfit, but the fabric of her top is a striking print, with a lace-trimmed collar. On the bottom left of the photograph is a circle, a neat hole made so that it could be clicked into a ring file. Its emptiness is distracting: the void is a reminder of all that is unknown about Madeleine Marchand.

There is nothing in the typewritten legal report into her wartime activities that explains why she chose to become involved with the French Gestapo. She is described as coming from a '*bonne famille*'; her life appears to have been unexceptional. And yet by the summer of 1944, Marchand was enjoying the excitement of wielding a revolver, and being paid a salary by Berger for her successful infiltration of the F2 network in Paris. This she had accomplished via one of its agents, a young man named Daniel Poulain, whom she had befriended two years previously at the Théâtre Edouard VII. When she offered to help Poulain on his missions on behalf of F2, he unfortunately saw no reason to question her motives, and the pair travelled together to Amiens, eighty miles north of Paris. Marchand persuaded him that she had family in the area, so it would be a convenient place for her to visit; she also told him that they should pretend to be romantically involved (which makes me wonder if Poulain was flattered by her attention, and by the prospect of a shared adventure).

The city's railway lines had been bombed by Allied aircraft in the second week of June, after the Normandy landings, as they sought to destroy communication links; before then, in February 1944, a daring RAF raid on Amiens jail had resulted in the escape of dozens of resistants who had been imprisoned there. Yet Marchand's incursion into the F2 network, over the course of several trips to Amiens, would prove every bit as destructive in its outcome, as she identified Poulain's closest associates and passed on their names to Berger. In the words of Germaine Tillion, a founding member of another Resistance group, who was herself arrested in Paris in 1942: 'When a traitor penetrated part of the organism, like venom, his ambition was to move up the arteries to the heart. This was only too easy to do and when it happened there was one network less and a few more deaths.' Tillion had been betrayed by a Catholic priest, Robert Alesch, who presented himself as an opponent of the Nazis, yet was in fact in the pay of the German secret police. Madeleine Marchand was similarly treacherous, and the information she provided was essential to Berger's devastatingly effective operations against the Resistance, which would lead to more than three hundred arrests in the summer of 1944.

By early July 1944, Berger's gang was poised to move against the F2 network in Paris. On 5 July, they seized the leader of its northern branch, Jean Desbordes, soon after he had left his friend Georges Geffroy's home on Rue de Rivoli, on his way to the Place de la Madeleine. Desbordes was one of twenty-six members of F2 to be captured over two days of arrests, the last of whom was Catherine Dior. All would be tortured with the utmost savagery at Rue de la Pompe. Desbordes refused to give any information at all, and was beaten to death. He was seen in the basement of the building, mutilated and comatose, by an acquaintance, Dr Charles Berlioz, who had himself been picked up by Berger's men at his cousin Georges Geffroy's home on the night of 5 July. Geffroy was away from Paris at the time, and Desbordes and Berlioz had both been staying in his apartment. Berlioz was not involved in the Resistance and knew nothing about F2, yet was arrested by four men, three of whom were wielding revolvers, another carrying a machine gun. Having been shown the unconscious Desbordes, Dr Berlioz was then attacked with a whip by Berger. Desbordes's wife Madeleine was also arrested and taken to Rue de la Pompe, where she too was beaten savagely by Berger. But Jean Desbordes's sister Eliette, with whom he had left all his microfilms for safekeeping, contacted Jean Cocteau, saying that her brother had disappeared. Cocteau immediately sent a letter to his friend the German ambassador, Otto Abetz, whose secretary replied tersely that if Desbordes were to be shot, Eliette would receive her brother's clothes and any other belongings within five days. In fact, Desbordes had already been killed, and buried under the cover of night in an unmarked grave in a cemetery on the outskirts of Paris. When his body was exhumed after the Liberation, he could be identified only by his teeth.

At 4.30 pm on 6 July, the net finally closed in on Catherine Dior: she was arrested on the Place du Trocadéro by a group of four armed men, who took her bicycle and handbag, forced her into their car, blindfolded her and drove her to Rue de la Pompe. In a witness statement that she gave to the war crimes investigators in 1945, Catherine described her experience as follows: 'When I arrived in the building, I was immediately subjected to an interrogation on my activities for the Resistance and also on the identity of the chiefs under whose orders I was working. This interrogation was accompanied by brutalities: punching, kicking, slapping, etc. When the interrogation proved unsatisfactory, I was taken to the bathroom. They undressed me, bound my hands and plunged me into the water, where I remained for about three-quarters of an hour. [Two of Berger's men] Leclercq and Zulgadar put me through this torture. From time to time, they submerged me completely and immediately afterwards they questioned me . . . Berger would come to see how the operation was progressing. I lied to them as much as I could.'

Towards the end of this horrific ordeal, Catherine managed to convince Berger that she had a rendezvous with the leader of her Resistance network at the Tuileries, and she was driven there, via Christian's apartment at 10 Rue Royale, which was fortunately empty at the time. When no one arrived at the fictitious appointment, Catherine was forced back into Rue de la Pompe. There she saw several other women she knew in F2 who had also been arrested: Anne de Bauffremont, Yvonne de Turenne and Jeanne Van Roey. Together, they were taken to the Gestapo office at Rue des Saussaies, where they were interrogated about their identities (but without the extreme violence used by Berger's gang), and finally transported to the prison at Fresnes.

Two days later, Catherine was picked up from her cell at Fresnes and returned to Rue des Saussaies, where Berger was awaiting her. He drove her to Rue de la Pompe, where she was tortured yet again in the bathroom and submerged in icy water for several hours, until she came close to drowning. On this occasion, Denise Delfau took notes of her interrogation, and the same two men as before, who pushed her under the water, also banged her head against the bathtub. The first of these was a forty-five-year-old Frenchman, Théodore Leclercq, a former metal worker from Lille, who had traded in black-market tobacco and fabrics, then taken up the role of guard and torturer for Berger. The second was Rachid Zulgadar, who was born in Tbilisi in 1909, moved to Paris with his family as a child and worked as a taxi driver before joining Berger's gang. (Zulgadar's brother, in contrast, was a supporter of Charles de Gaulle and a member of the Free French forces.) After the water torture, Catherine was made to kneel on triangular wooden rods, with her hands behind her back, her wrists handcuffed.

More men came to question Catherine, including Jean-Baptiste Zimmer – known in the gang as *le Professeur*, because he had a reputation for being an 'intellectual' and played the piano – and the odious Georges Guicciardini, whose brutish sons, twenty-three-year-old Francis and twenty-one-year-old-Adrien, worked alongside him. Georges Guicciardini also had a background in the black market, and had been arrested for trafficking food coupons in 1943. Berger apparently valued him and his sons, as they were among the best paid of the team, receiving ninety thousand francs for their work in June 1944 alone. Eventually, Georges Guicciardini drove Catherine back to Fresnes, and during the journey lectured her on the excellence of Berger's operation.

This is the bare outline of Catherine's shocking experience. She faced it with exceptional bravery. Despite suffering a series of violent assaults, such as to make it almost impossible to think clearly, she was not broken by the prolonged interrogations. And Catherine's responses to the barrage of questioning evidently protected her colleagues in the Resistance, as well as her brother, for none of them were arrested. As a consequence, she saved the lives of her best friend Liliane Dietlin, her lover Hervé des Charbonneries, his wife Lucie, and the surviving members of F2, including two of its leaders, Gilbert Foury and Stan Lasocki. Her swift thinking also ensured that F2's Paris headquarters, at 28 Rue Lauriston, had been cleared of any compromising material and was empty when the Gestapo inevitably came to search it. As she explained in her statement to the investigating team in 1945, 'I had given instructions for everything I knew was dangerous to be removed as I left for the rendezvous at which I was arrested. In fact I had told them to remove everything from the office if I wasn't back a quarter of an hour after the agreed time.' It is no surprise that Catherine's records in the Resistance archives refer to her 'exemplary courage' when subjected to 'particularly odious' forms of torture. Indeed, one of the Polish leaders of F2 initially reported that Catherine had been tortured to death, and paid tribute to her as 'an extraordinary young patriot'.

Another woman arrested by Berger in the summer of 1944, Marie Bruhat, described the apartment at Rue de la Pompe as '*infernale*'. She had been forced to listen to the agonised cries of her husband Georges Bruhat, a distinguished French academic and brilliant physicist, as he was tortured for refusing to betray a student suspected of being in the Resistance. Others who suffered there said it was 'cruel and grotesque', like a surreal '*roman noir*', 'a museum of horrors', 'a circus'. A nightmarish atmosphere of psychopathic madness seemed to prevail: a four-year-old child could be seen wandering between the naked bodies of unconscious, bleeding victims; Zimmer performed Mozart and Bach on the piano in the drawing room, surrounded by a stack of machine guns, although the music was not loud enough to drown out the sound of screaming. Dr Berlioz noted that the men in Berger's gang carried guns in one hand and glasses of champagne in the other. Berger himself was as keen a consumer of morphine and cocaine as alcohol, and there was no shortage of any of these at Rue de la Pompe. A French barman was employed to keep the drinks flowing, and to buy sufficient ice every day to fill the bath for the purposes of torture, as well as for making cocktails; a French cook served excellent meals, which were sometimes eaten while the torture continued in the dining room; a French shoemaker was on call to craft custom-made leather shoes for the entire gang; and a French doctor, Fernand Rousseau, attended to their various medical needs, providing Berger with morphine injections, as well as being on hand to revive unconscious victims of torture with a phial of camphor, to enable their interrogations to continue. The doctor, like everyone else in Berger's team, could be relied upon for his discretion and loyalty, whatever the circumstances.

If the rest of the gang were obvious miscreants who had been forced to sign a pledge to their 'chief', on pain of death, Dr Rousseau might initially seem a more surprising associate. Born in Paris in 1885, he had served with distinction as a doctor with the French army during the First World War, and was a recipient of the Légion d'Honneur. A specialist in urinary tract surgery, Rousseau first encountered Berger in November 1943, when he was called out in a medical emergency to treat Denise Delfau for appendicitis. At the time, Dr Rousseau and his wife were neighbours of Berger and Delfau on Rue du Colonel Moll, and the two couples stayed in touch after the move to Rue de la Pompe.

Dr Rousseau already enjoyed the privileges afforded to those who collaborated with the Germans in Occupied Paris: he was a member of the Cercle Européen, a private club on the Champs-Elysées, where supporters of the Nazis conversed and dined together. Its other members included leading politicians, such as Pierre Laval and Jacques Doriot, and the couturiers Marcel Rochas and Jacques Fath. Rousseau's wife was as staunch in her support of both Marshal Pétain and Germany's Third Reich as he was: together, they joined Doriot's fascist, anti-Semitic Parti Populaire Français, and served as officials for the party. Dr Rousseau was also affiliated with a notorious series of propagandist broadcasts on the pro-German Radio Paris. When the time came for the couple to leave Paris in August 1944, Mme Rousseau was seen raising her right arm and shouting, '*Heil Hitler.*'

Was it Rousseau's own political views that allowed him, as a doctor who had presumably taken the Hippocratic Oath, to witness with apparent equanimity the atrocities at Rue de la Pompe? When Berger summoned him after Jean Desbordes had been beaten into a coma, Rousseau's only response was to apply camphor oil, a remedy that did not save the dying man. His medical ethics were no more apparent when he was called to Rue de la Pompe to examine another member of the Resistance, Pierre-Paul Schweitzer, who had attempted suicide rather than risk talking under further torture. Yet it would have been impossible for Dr Rousseau – or indeed anyone else who entered the apartment – to remain ignorant of the ghastly crimes that were being committed there. When Rousseau saw Jean Desbordes, he was lying in the bloodstained basement; it seems implausible that the doctor could not have noticed Desbordes's compatriots who were also in the cellar, chained, naked and beaten. Rousseau simply noted that Berger had '*un air ennuyé*' – an annoyed look – at the prospect of having to deal with a dead body on the premises.

Nor did Dr Rousseau seem perturbed by the blood in the bathroom which had been clearly visible to Dr Berlioz when he was dragged in by Berger's men. In fact, Rousseau was himself seen in the bathroom by a senior member of the Polish Resistance as he was being immersed. Even Mme Rousseau was accused by one of Desbordes's colleagues in F2, who had endured the bathroom torture, of having been the note-taker during his interrogation. Dr Rousseau appeared no more concerned at the sight of an elderly man being beaten in the dining room; according to Berger's cook, who happened to enter during the interrogation, it was Dr Rousseau who told her to leave. The cook, Victorine Le Fessant, later spoke to the judicial investigation about this incident: 'The prisoner was in a pitiable state, his face was black from the blows he had endured, you couldn't tell if it was a man or an animal.'

In this and other reports of the scenes of horror at Rue de la Pompe, there is a sense that many of those who worked there no longer regarded the prisoners as human. The cellar contained a couturier's mannequin that the gang used for target practice; on at least one occasion, they indulged in a macabre game derived from the story of William Tell, where they shot at the prisoners instead, to see if they could blow out candles placed on top of their heads. For much of the time, the people hauled into the apartment were treated as commodities, like the vast quantities of black-market products that passed through the hands of Berger's gang. Each prisoner might be of value, if they provided information under torture; if they remained silent or they knew nothing, then they were worthless.

Most of the criminals who worked at Rue de la Pompe were capable of manifest cruelty, and all were greedy. The apartment was filled with pillaged valuables – linen, china, silverware and jewels – that had been stolen during the course of arrests and then sold or distributed to the gang. Denise Delfau was always dressed in expensive clothes and purloined jewellery – except when she was called upon to take notes in the bathroom during the middle of the night, in which case she would appear in her dressing gown. Those who were tortured were especially shocked to see the involvement of Frenchwomen such as Delfau, who seemed to enjoy watching the interrogations.

Jacqueline Bernard, a heroic journalist who worked with Albert Camus at the underground Resistance newspaper and network *Combat*, was arrested less than a week after Catherine Dior and subjected to the same methods of torture. She recalled Delfau's presence in the bathroom clearly; in her statement to the inquiry into Berger and his gang, she described Delfau as appearing 'calm' throughout the interrogation. 'She sat on a stool in the bathroom, writing notes on a pad. One of the torturers asked her if she thought my confession was sincere. She replied, "I don't think so," and the torture continued.' Jacqueline also related how, twenty-four hours after her arrest – when she was about to be taken out of Rue de la Pompe, in an attempt to force her to lead Berger's men to her colleagues at *Combat* – she was escorted upstairs to Delfau's bedroom on the first floor. There, Delfau gave her some clothes to change into, as her own were covered in blood. This was no act of kindness on Delfau's part, but an attempt to make Jacqueline look less noticeable on the street, despite the fact that by now, her face was swollen with bruises and cuts.

It turns out that Delfau herself was beaten and abused by Friedrich Berger, in what appears to have been a sado-masochistic relationship, but she always returned for more. There is a picture of them together with another couple (one of Berger's associates in the black market, François Mauro, and his wife). Berger is pointing a gun beyond the camera. He is wearing a businessman's sober suit and white shirt, but his eyes are deranged. Delfau is just behind her lover's shoulder, with an air of guarded admiration. Her earrings are decorative, her demure blouse has a frilly lace ruff; she does not have the look of a gangster's accomplice, even as she stands next to Berger, glancing in the direction of the gun barrel. If it were not for the weapon in the picture, you might think she was a secretary on a works outing, and indeed she does seem to have regarded herself as the secretary of a business, rather than the chatelaine of a house of torture. Meanwhile, her sister Hélène continued to keep careful records of weekly expenditure and salaries at Rue de la Pompe, like an efficient bookkeeper, and the two women somehow managed to navigate the fact that Hélène was known to be Berger's occasional mistress.

Taboos were constantly violated at Rue de la Pompe; sexual violence was commonplace. Many of the gang's victims were traumatised not only by the torture itself, but also by the realisation that those who inflicted it took pleasure in causing and witnessing pain. Both men and women were sexually assaulted at Rue de la Pompe. One member of the gang, Manuel Stcherbina, who looks like a studious and bespectacled accountant in photographs, was described by several of his victims as being a particularly vicious sadist, especially towards women. Jacqueline Bernard described the ferocity of his attack on a resistant named Yvonne Baratte: spreading her arms apart and tying them to different door handles, in such a way as to crucify her with pain. And while Catherine Dior made no mention of sexual assault in her statements to the judicial investigators, it is possible that she was unable to have children as a consequence of the torture she experienced. When I talked to her godson, Nicolas Crespelle, he recalled a visceral childhood memory of being told by his mother that Catherine could not have a child of her own because of what had happened to her at Rue de la Pompe. 'My mother wanted to protect

Top: Friedrich Berger and Denise Delfau (left), with a black-market associate and his wife.
Above: Berger's identity document.

me from the worst details of the torture, as I was still a young boy, but she said that people had put ice in Catherine's tummy – I suppose she thought that was the best way to explain it to me.'

A week after Catherine's ordeal, on 14 July – traditionally a national holiday in celebration of the unity of the French people – a thirty-three-year-old member of the Polish Resistance, Irène Lewulis, who lived in Paris and had previously been attached to the Polish embassy there, was arrested and taken to Rue de la Pompe. On the way, she was told by one of her captors that it was a '*petit enfer*' (little hell). Irène's husband was also in the Resistance, and they were sheltering five other comrades at their home; she was determined not to betray the network. When she remained silent, Irène was strung up in the drawing room in every conceivable bodily configuration and beaten for two hours by Stcherbina and a tattooed French thug named Raoul Fouchet. Stcherbina also burned her with cigarettes and a blowtorch, and sexually assaulted her. Eventually, after her arms and jaw had been dislocated, she was taken into a bedroom, where Berger reclined on his bed, playing with two poodles. Stcherbina went on beating her as Denise Delfau and another French girl served Berger his dinner, which he shared with his dogs; as ever, there was plenty of alcohol.

Irène would later testify that Berger employed a numerical system to signify various forms of torture. When he said 'Number five', she was made to kneel down; Stcherbina and Fouchet then handcuffed her from behind, the right wrist to the left ankle and the left wrist to the right ankle. 'They tried to keep me chained like this in a kneeling position.' Every time she fell to the floor, she was whipped. Berger, she told the investigating judge, continued to interrogate her from his bed. 'I refused to confess.' Nor did she pass out, explaining: 'I focused all my attention on recording the scenes where I was the victim, saying to myself: I must remember.'

Berger proceeded to offer her a hundred thousand francs for the name of anyone else in the Resistance. 'He declared, "I am an officer, I give you my word of honour."' When Irène did not reply, Berger ordered that she be dragged by her hair from the room. She was kept chained up for a further two hours, 'because the man who had locked the chains hadn't returned with the key'.

Irène somehow survived the night, although when she was taken back to Rue des Saussaies the following day, a German policeman pointed at her and said, 'This time [Berger] has gone too far.' A fellow member of her Resistance network, a fifty-two-year-old Polish diplomat named Wladimir Kaczorowski, did not recover from his torture. In the early hours of the morning, Irène had heard the water running in a room adjoining the corridor, and the voice of Kaczorowski as he implored, '*Non, Monsieur, ne faites pas cela.*' ('No, sir, do not do that.')

There are countless such harrowing testimonies in the judicial archives, relating to the crimes committed by the Rue de la Pompe Gestapo during the Occupation: literally thousands of pages in dozens of folders, with repeated accounts of frenzied brutality. Pregnant women were kicked and kept handcuffed all night; mothers were told that their children would be murdered in front of them. The same phrases – 'hit her', 'punch him', 'flogged with a whip' – appear over and over again like violent, repeated blows. In the end, it becomes unbearable to go on reading these reports, let alone find the right language to explain such atrocities. But perhaps the most telling evidence of all comes from a member of the Resistance who had been interrogated at Rue de la Pompe, and scratched the following words on the cellar wall with his nails: 'We have been tortured by the French people.'

Darkness Falls

All that survives of Catherine Dior's imprisonment in Paris, following her interrogation at Rue de la Pompe, is a slender file of records in the French military archives at Caen: faded pieces of paper, bearing the handwritten dates of her journey from one jail to another. The ink is indelible, the contents are impersonal in their efficiency: she is listed first by her name, secondly by her date of birth, and then she becomes just a series of numbers. Catherine herself falls silent, and it is only by piecing together the words of a few other women, who left journals of their shared experiences, that she does not vanish entirely. Such obliteration was precisely what the Nazis proposed for political prisoners: in December 1941, Hitler had issued a directive called '*Nacht und Nebel*' – 'Night and Fog' – ordering that opponents of the Third Reich should be made to disappear, and never be heard of again by their families. The very uncertainty of their fate was part of the punishment, and a further means to intimidate the population of the occupied countries.

When Catherine Dior was incarcerated in Fresnes prison, on the southern fringes of Paris, in July 1944, it was already filled with members of the French Resistance and agents of the British Special Operations Executive (SOE), who were being held there in appalling conditions. The largest prison in France at the time, Fresnes had been built between 1895 and 1898; its dismal cells were freezing in winter and stifling in summer, and forever infested with vermin and fleas. Many of the prisoners had been tortured before they were locked up

Fresnes prison, c.1945. Photograph by René Saint-Paul

in Fresnes, and others endured further interrogation while they were there.

Agnès Humbert, an art historian and one of the founders of an early Resistance network in Paris, spent two months in solitary confinement at Fresnes in 1942, before being deported to Germany, and her journal bears witness to the terrors of the prison. On 20 January 1942, she wrote: 'Yesterday I heard the screams of a man being tortured. When the screams died down, they were followed by deep, throaty laughter. I don't know which was the more terrible. The laughter, I think . . . There are a lot of suicides.' Yet the resistants incarcerated at Fresnes found ways of communicating with one another, even if they were held in solitary confinement, and in doing so, they strengthened their sense of solidarity and camaraderie. Intricate stratagems were devised to relay messages from cell to cell – codes tapped on the walls, or notes sent via internal pipes and air shafts – and at pre-arranged times, the prisoners would start singing the French national anthem, *La Marseillaise*, in a show of courage and defiance.

Virginia d'Albert-Lake, a young American who had joined the Resistance with her French husband, was arrested not long before Catherine Dior. Like Agnès, Virginia wrote a vivid memoir of her time at Fresnes, in the heat of July 1944. 'It was absolutely forbidden to open the window, already bolted shut . . . Twice a week we were allowed a "*promenade*". We would file down to the ground floor and along a narrow corridor onto which opened a row of little rectangular courtyards . . . we were allowed the "liberty" of a courtyard for twenty minutes; the "liberty" of looking at the sky . . . Sometimes I pressed my face between the bars, which gave me a strange illusion of freedom as I looked out onto the grass and trees beyond. But I could never stay long. Tears soon blinded me.'

At the end of July, Catherine Dior was transferred from Fresnes to Romainville, as part of a larger group of women, including Virginia d'Albert-Lake, who were all members of the Resistance. A fortress on the eastern outskirts of Paris, Romainville was known to be a holding area for prisoners before they were deported to Germany. There the women were kept in better conditions, but their anxiety mounted on a daily basis; at a roll call at 4 pm every day, names would be read out of those who were to be sent on the next convoy. Once their names had been listed, they left within the hour. 'I admired the women as they were called from the ranks,' wrote Virginia in her journal. 'They rarely showed what they were really feeling. They walked straight, their heads held proudly erect. Sometimes, they smiled or turned to wave good-bye. Others would call out "*Au revoir, à bientôt! Vive la France!*" I always felt clutched by a deep emotion at those moments.'

No visits or letters were allowed at Romainville, but the women sometimes managed to get messages to their friends and families by giving hastily scribbled notes to those leaving to be deported; these were surreptitiously dropped from the windows of the buses that carried the prisoners out of the fort, on the off-chance that passers-by would pick them up and deliver them. Meanwhile, the women still held in Romainville could hear the sounds of approaching artillery fire, and prayed for deliverance by the advancing Allied forces. Progress had been slow in the weeks following D-Day; indeed, the losses sustained in gaining ground were heavier than during the Battle of the Somme in the First World War. But by the end of July, US troops had finally succeeded in taking Avranches in Normandy, opening the way to Paris. After ten days in Romainville, Virginia d'Albert-Lake was told by the camp commander that he believed she was more likely to be liberated by her countrymen than deported to Germany, and optimism spread among the women.

By this point, Christian Dior had discovered that Catherine was imprisoned in Romainville, and was desperate to save her from deportation. He contacted a childhood friend from Granville, Suzanne Luling, to ask her if she could seek the help of a well-connected acquaintance of hers, Raoul Nordling, the Swedish consul-general in Paris. In her memoir, Luling recalled the feverish atmosphere in the city at the time, and described Christian as 'dying of worry' about his sister. She duly got in touch with Nordling, who was doing his utmost to save all the political prisoners still held in and around Paris, including his own niece's husband (a resistant accused of sheltering Allied airmen). Even if they weren't deported before the Allies could liberate the city, Nordling feared that they would be massacred by the SS, as had already happened in Caen, where ninety French prisoners were executed on the day of the Allied landings, by order of the Gestapo.

Nordling was a businessman as well as a diplomat, and accustomed to dealing with opposing forces; he was on the board of a Swedish ball-bearing manufacturer which supplied the Germans as well as the British. On 10 August, he met with two men who he hoped would be able to help: a German Abwehr agent named Emil 'Bobby' Bender, who had extensive contacts within the military and diplomatic circles of Paris, and an Austrian officer, Erich Posch-Pastor von Camperfeld. Both were already working for British intelligence, and were prepared to do whatever they could behind the scenes to ensure that the political prisoners were transferred into the custody of the Red Cross. Nordling also hoped to ask the French politician Pierre Laval to intervene on behalf of the prisoners, but had not yet been granted an audience. The Swedish diplomat then telephoned Otto Abetz, the German ambassador, and mentioned the case of Georges Bruhat, the physics professor who had been arrested and tortured at Rue de la Pompe because he refused to name a student involved in the Resistance. Abetz responded angrily, declaring that Bruhat taught at 'a school of assassins', and that the Gestapo were 'too soft on such people'. When Nordling asked Abetz whether he condoned the murder of the political prisoners in Caen, the ambassador merely replied that shooting them was the only solution.

The eve of the Feast of the Assumption was on 14 August, and Yvonne Baratte, one of the resistants who had been so cruelly tortured at Rue de la Pompe, decorated a tiny makeshift altar at Romainville, placing wildflowers that she had gathered in the courtyard beneath a homemade wooden crucifix. She and the other women imprisoned in the fort were expecting the visit of a priest the following morning, to celebrate a mass commemorating the Virgin Mary. But that night, a German guard called Kratz told Yvonne and her companions, 'No mass, no mass . . . Everyone will go on the transport to Germany, all to die . . . all to die.' (This chilling encounter was reported in the memoir of another devout Catholic prisoner, Maisie Renault, who was part of a Resistance network founded by her brother Gilbert, the Confrérie Notre-Dame, which transmitted vital intelligence to the Free French in London.)

Yvonne remained resolute, as she had been at Rue de la Pompe the month before. Then, she had somehow managed to telephone her mother, and said to her simply, *'Maman, courage.'* Now, at Romainville, she wrote a last letter to her family: 'I am full of hope. They will not have time to take us from here . . . I love you all, and I'm sure we'll meet again soon.'

Just before dawn on 15 August, the Allies began their invasion of southern France, in Operation Dragoon, landing on the beaches of the Mediterranean coast after a ferocious air and naval bombardment of the German defences. With the Allies fighting on two fronts in France, the military situation seemed hopeful. But the Supreme Allied Commander, General Dwight D. Eisenhower (who was at this point based near Granville in Normandy), had already made the strategic decision to postpone the Liberation of Paris, and instead bypass and encircle the city. His reasoning was that the battle to take the capital was likely to require prolonged and heavy street fighting, and would divert precious resources, including fuel and food, from his overriding aim: to breach the Siegfried Line and cross the Rhine into Germany before winter set in.

At 8 am on the 15th, the women at Romainville were told to pack their belongings, as they were indeed being deported. Soon afterwards, an air-raid warning was sounded, and they were locked in underground caves dug into the ramparts surrounding the fort. There they were kept for much of the day, and with every hour that passed, their hopes mounted that the Allies would reach Paris in time to save them; or, at the very least, that the railway lines would have been destroyed by bombs. But at 4 pm, they heard the familiar sound of the requisitioned city buses pulling into the camp. Virginia d'Albert-Lake described what happened next: 'They stopped in front of the barred entrances of our caves and, out of them, swarmed armed SS – the kind with hard cruel faces and rapid brutal movements. We were ordered by them into the buses, and soon were so crowded and hot that we could hardly breathe.' She managed to bribe the French bus driver to pass on the messages that she and the other women needed to get to their families, telling them of their imminent deportation. He whispered to her that he'd been driving prisoners all day to the train station at Pantin, and that the Allies were rumoured to be at Rambouillet, thirty miles from Paris.

The prisoners had been divided up in alphabetical order, and Catherine Dior was on the same bus as Virginia. Like the other buses, it was so full that it couldn't make it up the hill outside the fortress; again, the women prayed for further delay. They were ordered off the bus and followed it on foot, before boarding it again once it had made it to the top. From there, they were driven through Paris, where many of the remaining Germans were packing up to leave.

Ernst Jünger had departed the day before, after bidding farewell to Florence Gould and his other close friends in Paris. In his diary on 8 August, he wrote: 'Stood outside the portal of Sacré-Cœur to cast a last glance over the great city. I watched the stones quiver in the hot sun, as if in expectation of new historical embraces. Cities are feminine and only smile on the victor.' Hitler, however, did not believe that Germany was vanquished; his psychotic faith in himself appeared to have been strengthened by the unsuccessful attempt on his life by Claus von Stauffenberg and others the previous month. In the aftermath of the failed assassination plot, Hitler declared that his survival was 'a divine moment in history'.

In her diary Virginia d'Albert-Lake described the bus journey through the crowded streets of Paris, where people stared at the women on board, some with a look of pity on their faces. News of the Allied landings along the southern coast had spread across the city, and she recalled her anguish that she would miss the day of Liberation: 'the day of which I have dreamed for nearly five years'. As it turned out, the German garrison in Paris surrendered just ten days later, on 25 August.

Eventually, the buses arrived at Gare de Pantin, delivering the human cargo to the '*quai aux bestiaux*' – the cattle platform. 'Most of the Paris stations had been destroyed by bombing, but this smaller suburban one was still untouched,' wrote Virginia. 'The yards were jammed with rolling stock, as this station served as one of the few remaining outlets from Paris for the Germans and everything they wanted to take with them. We stopped parallel with a track on which was waiting a line of box cars, so long that it appeared endless. From every car, as far as I could see, were anxious faces peering out of narrow rectangular ventilation openings and through cracks in the half closed doors. So this was the way we were to travel! I was so stunned I unconsciously hesitated to leave the bus, but suddenly received such a brutal shove from a female SS [guard] that I staggered unwittingly toward the gaping door of the nearest empty box car . . .'

To the shock of the women who had been interrogated at Rue de la Pompe, two of their torturers – Rachid Zulgadar and Théodore Leclercq – were waiting at Pantin to see them loaded onto the train, as if overseeing their animal stock being sent to the slaughterhouse. The double agent Emil Bender was also at the station, trying to bluff the SS commander in charge of the operation into delaying the departure.

Raoul Nordling was still making his own attempts to save the prisoners. The Swedish diplomat had finally arranged a meeting with Otto Abetz and Pierre Laval, to be held at 9.30 pm at Laval's official residence in Paris, the Hôtel Matignon on Rue de Varenne. The situation in Paris was changing rapidly: the French police had gone on strike during the day, and there was no electricity in the city. Laval's office was lit with a paraffin lamp, and Abetz arrived carrying a flashlight. Nordling begged the two men to show mercy to the prisoners who were locked in the overcrowded trains at Pantin; both refused, saying that they had more urgent matters to deal with.

And so just before midnight, the last convoy of deportees left Paris, with 2,100 men and four hundred women on board. Among them were 168 Allied airmen who had been arrested in France, classed as 'terrorists' rather than prisoners of war because they had been caught trying to escape from behind enemy lines. Virginia d'Albert-Lake recognised one of them as an American aviator whom she and her husband had sheltered for a time, while they were working for the Comet Escape Line (an organisation that helped Allied soldiers shot down in occupied territory). Two female SOE agents were also on board: Eileen Nearne, a twenty-three-year-old radio operator who had been arrested and tortured by the Gestapo in late July, and Alix d'Unienville, captured in Paris on D-Day. Five men, including Colonel André Rondenay, General de Gaulle's military representative in Paris, had been hauled off the train by the SS and then shot dead by a Gestapo squad in a forest just north of Paris. Six bodies of women who died in the heat of the padlocked railway carriages were discarded and dumped beside the tracks at Pantin. On board the train, there was no room to sit, let alone lie down, and many were already dangerously dehydrated; yet those who were able to, started singing *La Marseillaise* as they left the station.

The battle to save them was continuing on several fronts: Raoul Nordling had not ceased his negotiations, even meeting the recently appointed military governor of Paris, General von Choltitz, in the hope of persuading him to release the prisoners before the train crossed the French border. And a message had reached a Resistance cell to sabotage the railway line, in order to prevent the convoy of deportees reaching Germany. In the early hours of 16 August, the train was stopped in its tracks, when a group of resistants blew up sixty yards of the railway line just beyond the tunnel of Nanteuil-Saâcy, less than fifty miles from Paris. The SS guards on the train responded by ordering that it should be backed into the smoke-filled tunnel; inside the sealed carriages the prisoners were left gasping for air. Virginia d'Albert-Lake wrote in her memoir: 'Were we going to be deserted to suffer a slow death in that black cauldron? Already the heat and thirst were becoming almost unbearable . . .' But after three and a half hours, the engine came out of the tunnel, the doors were opened and the prisoners were forced to march four miles to another train. It was at this point that three women attempted to escape: one, Nicole de Witasse, darted into a farmyard and hid in a pile of straw beneath a hay-cart, but was spotted by the SS guards, dragged out and beaten. The two SOE agents also made a run for it: Alix d'Unienville managed to hide in the shadow of a doorway, and was then kept hidden by the local villagers until the Allies arrived two weeks later. Eileen Nearne was unluckier: after being swiftly recaptured, she was warned that if she or anyone else tried to escape again, everyone in her section of the train would be shot.

On the same day in Paris, Friedrich Berger and his gang were making their own plans to leave the city, but even at this late stage they continued to carry out operations against the Resistance, alongside the German SS officers Wenzel, Kleindienst and Kley. By nightfall, in a frenzied orgy of killing, they had shot forty-two young members of the Resistance: thirty-four were massacred in the Bois de Boulogne, not far from Avenue Foch; seven were shot dead at Rue de Leroux, and one of the leaders, a twenty-eight-year-old doctor named Henri Blanchet, was murdered by Berger himself at Avenue Victor Hugo. His body was dumped with those of the other resistants in woodland in the Bois de Boulogne; their mutilated corpses were discovered the following morning next to a waterfall. They had been killed with machine guns and grenades. Most were under twenty-five years old; the youngest, Jacques Delporte, was seventeen.

As was so often the case with Berger's activities, Dr Fernand Rousseau just happened to be present at one of the crime scenes: both he and his wife witnessed the shooting of Dr Blanchet. Afterwards, Mme Rousseau received a bundle of five-thousand-franc notes from Berger, though she later told the judicial inquiry that she didn't know how much it amounted to. But now the Rousseaus were scared: like a number of other fascist collaborators, they had been sent a pair of tiny coffins through the post, as a threat from those who knew about their behaviour during the Occupation. The couple therefore joined Berger and a motley crew of his men, their wives and mistresses, and assorted Gestapo officers, as they fled Paris on 17 August, in a convoy of vehicles carrying around fifty people and a vast quantity of cash.

This was the day when the bulk of the German forces were leaving the capital city. According to the journalist Jean Galtier-Boissière, a friend of Catherine's brother Raymond, it was 'the great flight of the Fritzes'. In his diary for the 17th, he observed: 'On every thoroughfare, scores, hundreds, of trucks, loaded cars, mounted artillery, ambulances full of wounded on stretchers, were in file or overtaking and crisscrossing one another . . . In the Rue Lafayette a flash of monocled generals sped past like shining torpedoes, accompanied by elegantly dressed blondes who seemed more on their way to some fashionable beach . . .'

That morning, Alois Brunner, the SS commander of the Drancy internment camp in the north-eastern suburbs of Paris, was also departing. His zeal for deporting Jews, which he had demonstrated throughout the war as Adolf Eichmann's assistant, had not diminished: on 31 July, a train containing 1,300 Jewish people, including 327 children, one of whom was a two-week-old baby boy, was dispatched to the gas chambers of Auschwitz. The first deportation from Drancy had taken place in March 1942, when the camp was still guarded by the French police; Brunner assumed command in June 1943. Altogether, by August 1944, nearly seventy thousand Jews had been sent by rail to the extermination camps. Brunner's final act as commandant was to

Suzanne Emmer-Besniée, *Voyage de Compiègne à Ravensbrück en wagon plombé*
('Journey from Compiègne to Ravensbrück in a sealed wagon').
Emmer-Besniée was deported to Ravensbrück in January 1944. This is the first of a series of
drawings she made on her return to France in 1945.

take fifty-one prisoners with him on his convoy to Germany: they were locked into a wagon with the words '*Juden terroristen*' ('Jewish terrorists') chalked on its side; the youngest was a twelve-year-old boy, who would die in Buchenwald.

It is estimated that between ten and twenty thousand French collaborators left Paris with the Germans, including Pierre Laval and his wife; while in Vichy, Marshal Pétain was driven off under armed guard, claiming that he was a prisoner. His destination, like that of Laval and other remnants of the Vichy regime, was the princely castle of Sigmaringen, high above the River Danube in southern Germany. They were joined there by Joseph Darnand, the leader of the Milice, and Louis-Ferdinand Céline, who subsequently published a novel about the episode: *D'un château l'autre*.

As the Germans streamed out of Paris, the families of the deportees on the train moving slowly eastwards across France had not yet given up hope. Marie-Hélène Lefaucheux, a member of the Resistance, had managed to follow its route, riding a bicycle for some of the way, from Pantin to Nanteuil-Saâcy. There she found her husband Pierre in the long line of prisoners being marched to the next train, further along the railway track. Continuing on her journey by car, Marie-Hélène pursued the convoy to Bar-le-Duc. Unbeknownst to her, this place had taken on a particular significance for Christian Dior: he had been told by Suzanne Luling that Raoul Nordling had negotiated an agreement whereby, if the train had not passed Bar-le-Duc by 2.45 pm on the 16th, Catherine would be released into Swedish hands. 'But it was too late,' wrote Luling in her memoir; the train had already gone through Bar-le-Duc by then, and the last chance of saving Catherine was lost.

On 17 August, Marie-Hélène Lefaucheux reached Nancy railway station, some fifty miles further on, still trailing her husband's tormented progress towards the German border. At least one man had already been shot as punishment for the previous escape attempts; several others were close to death from lack of air and water. Marie-Hélène stood in the corner of a platform, praying for a miracle; but none came. As the long train pulled out of the station, she heard some anguished cries, mingling with a faint chorus of *La Marseillaise*, and finally, silence.

The Abyss

When Catherine Dior arrived at Ravensbrück concentration camp, on 22 August 1944, she and her companions had been travelling for a week. Already exhausted, starving and tormented by thirst, they were met by a group of uniformed SS guards, shouting abuse and armed with batons, whips and snarling dogs. Ordered to climb out of the train and line up five abreast, the bewildered women found themselves on the goods platform at the railway station of Fürstenberg, a small town fifty miles north of Berlin. From there, they were made to march several miles to the camp; at first passing picturesque houses where adults and children stared at them out of the windows, and then entering a wooded landscape. If anyone stumbled, they were hit; if they slowed down, the dogs bared their teeth, and the guards shouted at them to go faster. '*Schnell, schnell!*' These were the first German words that everyone heard on arrival.

I follow the same route when I visit, although it would be easy to miss the inconspicuous sign on the outskirts of Fürstenberg that marks the turning to Ravensbrück. The narrow road to the camp is bordered by tall pine trees on one side, and on the other, the rippling waters of a lake, the Schwedtsee. The buildings that Catherine Dior would have seen as she approached the camp are still standing: the guards' barracks, which have been turned, somewhat eerily, into a youth hostel; beyond these, on a wooded slope, the senior officers' houses, looking like gingerbread cottages in a Brothers Grimm fairy tale; and the monolithic SS headquarters, from where the camp commandant ruled over his domain.

Women prisoners working as slave labourers at Ravensbrück.

The scenic view remains the same: across the shimmering lake, a church spire rises high above Fürstenberg.

The lake contains many secrets: when the end of the war was near, and Soviet troops were approaching, the SS guards burnt large numbers of written records and threw the ashes into the water, just as human ashes from the crematorium had been cast there before. But there are still some archives preserved at Ravensbrück, and permanent exhibitions of photographs, drawings and objects documenting its history as the only German concentration camp intended exclusively for women.

Before I went to Ravensbrück – I have visited twice, initially in the winter of 2018, and then the following summer – I had already begun researching the names of the women who travelled on the same railway convoy as Catherine Dior. (The men on the train were separated at Weimar and sent to Buchenwald concentration camp.) Every prisoner at Ravensbrück was assigned a number, according to alphabetical order and the time of their arrival; hence the first prisoners, who came in 1939, had the lowest numbers. The records show that Catherine was registered as number 57813, and her name appears close to some of the other resistants who had been tortured at Rue de la Pompe and then deported from Paris together: Yvonne Baratte, Jacqueline Bernard, Anne de Bauffremont, Madeleine Desbordes. In total, twenty-two women, including Catherine, who had fallen into the hands of the Rue de la Pompe gang were sent to Ravensbrück. Here, too, are other names familiar to me as having been on the train with Catherine: Elisabeth de Rothschild, arrested because she wouldn't sit next to the wife of the German ambassador at the Schiaparelli show; Nicole de Witasse, who was beaten when she tried to escape during the journey; Virginia d'Albert-Lake, the American resistant who kept an insightful diary; Eileen Nearne, the twenty-three-year-old SOE agent; Maisie Renault and her younger sister Isabelle, who were both at Romainville with Catherine.

Aside from the journals written by Virginia d'Albert-Lake and Maisie Renault, I have also read the accounts of several other French resistants who survived Ravensbrück: Germaine Tillion, who was deported to the camp in October 1943 and kept secret notes of her time there; Denise Dufournier, who arrived early in 1944 and wrote a memoir the following year; and Jacqueline d'Alincourt and Geneviève de Gaulle (the twenty-three-year-old niece of General de Gaulle). All describe the shock of their arrival, passing through the immense iron gates into a hell on earth. 'When I was in Fresnes prison there would sometimes be a gleam of light,' wrote Geneviève de Gaulle, 'even during the terrible journey to Ravensbrück. But as we went into the camp, it was as if God had remained outside . . .'

During the six years of Ravensbrück's existence, about 130,000 women entered these gates. No one knows exactly how many died here: estimates have been made between thirty thousand and ninety thousand. As a memorial site, it has never drawn the same attention as Auschwitz; and unlike Dachau, Buchenwald and Bergen-Belsen, where British and US troops documented the carnage they discovered – recording official films of vast piles of corpses, mass graves filled with mutilated bodies, and haunting images of emaciated survivors – at Ravensbrück, the Soviets who arrived at the end of April 1945 took fewer photographs. The air of secrecy surrounding Ravensbrück extends to its liberation; unsurprising, perhaps, given that some of the frontline Red Army soldiers, who were already engaging in the systematic rape of German women, also raped a number of the prisoners.

After the war, when this district fell within East Germany, the Soviet Army continued to occupy part of the camp, which remained out of bounds to visitors. However, a small area of the camp was opened as the Ravensbrück National Memorial in 1959, and several sculptures symbolising the suffering of the female prisoners, created by the German artist Will Lammert, were erected beside the lake and the crematorium. In the wake of the reunification of Germany, additional sections of the site were made accessible to visitors in 1993.

The crematorium still stands today, the doors to its ovens that used to burn night and day now open. Nearby a long dark passage known as 'the shooting alley' leads to the prison building, with seventy-eight cells, where women would be beaten and subjected to solitary confinement. The gas chamber beside the crematorium has gone, but its position is marked with a commemorative stone. The accommodation huts, or blocks, have also been destroyed, but if you walk through the gates into the main compound, their outlines can be seen on the ground, in the form of shallow depressions. A map shows the location of various other blocks, including the one where the women were processed after their arrival: here, their clothes and possessions were taken from them, their heads were shaved, and they were made to stand naked, sometimes for hours on end. During this process, they were subjected to degrading gynaecological examinations, often while being watched and mocked by the SS guards.

At the far end of the vast compound are the textile workshops, now empty of their machinery, but containing a gallery of photographs that show the prisoners at work, heads bowed, sewing SS uniforms and the striped dresses worn by the camp inmates. By the time Catherine Dior reached Ravensbrück in August 1944, the prison stripes were in short supply; instead she and her companions were assigned a ragged assortment of outfits from the vast store of clothes that had been seized from previous arrivals and marked with a painted cross. Each woman had to sew a felt triangle onto the top of her sleeve, with her camp number on it; the colour of the fabric showed the category she had been placed in. The Frenchwomen wore red triangles, to denote that they were political prisoners; black triangles were for 'asocials' (a classification which grouped Roma and Sinti people together with lesbians and prostitutes); green indicated criminals; lilac was for Jehovah's Witnesses; yellow for Jews. Such was the mania for detail that the Jewish women who had been arrested for political crimes were made to sew their yellow triangle onto a red background.

The leader of the SS, Heinrich Himmler, took a particularly keen interest in Ravensbrück; he had personally approved the choice of the location before construction of the camp began in November 1938. The rail connections were good; it was hidden from view; and it was conveniently placed for Himmler to be able to visit two of his friends: Oswald Pohl, the head of the SS economic office, who had a nearby country estate, and Karl Gebhardt, his personal physician. Gebhardt ran the SS medical clinic at Hohenlychen, from where doctors could visit Ravensbrück to perform operations. By January 1941, Himmler had acquired his own estate, Brückentin, just five miles from Ravensbrück, where he discreetly installed his mistress, Hedwig Potthast. Himmler was already married with one daughter – Gudrun, born in August 1929 – but in 1939 he began a secret relationship with Hedwig, his private secretary at the time, whom he fondly referred to as 'Häschen' ('Bunny'). When she became pregnant, Himmler asked Gebhardt – whom he had known since childhood – to deliver the baby at Hohenlychen; their son was born at the clinic on 15 February 1942, and Gebhardt became the boy's godfather. A second child, a daughter, was born on 20 July 1944. Hedwig's parents disapproved of this extramarital relationship, and although Himmler's wife Margarete was aware of the affair, she did not know that her husband fathered two children with his lover. Naturally, the true nature of Himmler's complex personal life was also concealed from public view; for although his views on the sanctity of marriage shifted over the years, depending on his own circumstances, he always maintained a facade of virtue and self-control.

Such dissembling might have come easily to the man in whose vast empire of concentration camps the ambiguous use of language was common practice. At Ravensbrück, as elsewhere, many of the activities were disguised in euphemistic terms. '*Sonderbehandlung*' ('special treatment'), for example, referred to the murder of prisoners, while 'protective custody' was a cover for indefinite detention without trial. Unlike the extermination camps – including Belzec, Sobibor and Treblinka – where millions of Jews were gassed within hours of arrival, Ravensbrück exploited its inmates as slave labour. Yet Himmler's original conception of Ravensbrück – much like the earlier concentration camps, such as Dachau, that he had established several years before the war – was that the punishing regime would reform some of those 'deviants' and 'degenerates' incarcerated there. That the vast majority of prisoners were destined to be killed in one way or another did not prevent Himmler, the son of a Catholic schoolmaster, from emphasising that the camps had educative purposes. During a speech on German radio on 29 January 1939, he made a rare public reference to the SS camps, describing them as 'strict but fair'. He went on: 'The slogan that stands above these camps is: "There is a path to freedom." Its milestones are: obedience, diligence, honesty, orderliness, cleanliness, sobriety, truthfulness, readiness to make sacrifices, and love of the fatherland.' A similar motto had been used before: since 1936, the iron gates leading into Dachau bore the words: '*Arbeit Macht Frei*' ('work sets you free'), a slogan that was subsequently added to the camp gates at Sachsenhausen, Flossenbürg and, perhaps most famously, Auschwitz.

In reality, work was used as a form of systemised killing, known as 'extermination through labour', whereby prisoners died from exhaustion, sickness and starvation, if they had not already been beaten to death, shot, savaged by guard dogs or sent to the gas chambers. 'Cleanliness' was impossible at Ravensbrück: the water was polluted with sewage, the latrines were blocked and overflowing, and the three-tier bunk beds were crawling with fleas and lice. 'Orderliness' was distorted into a series of baffling, incomprehensibly cruel rules. Virginia d'Albert-Lake wrote of her shock at her first experience of *Appell* – daily roll calls that would go on for hours, while the prisoners were forced to stand to attention. 'At 3.30 in the morning, we heard the wail of the camp siren and lights flashed on in the buildings. At 4.15 we heard them again, and immediately, women started swarming out of the "blocs", hundreds, thousands of them.' There they stayed, being counted and recounted by the guards, until 6 am, when work began.

Himmler's belief was that the concentration camps should be profitable – combining mass murder with mass production – and in January 1942 he appointed his friend Oswald Pohl as overall head of the system

Heinrich Himmler inspecting the female guards on a visit to Ravensbrück in 1941.

Female guards at Ravensbrück.

with this aim in mind. When Pohl summoned the top SS camp officials to a major conference in April 1942, he announced that the immediate goal was to increase profits and step up armaments production. The way to do this, he declared, was to extend the prisoners' working hours: 'To attain the utmost performance, this action must literally be exhausting.' At Ravensbrück, some prisoners were worked to death in the textile workshops, others shovelling sand, or dragging a giant iron roller to level the ground, or in the adjacent Siemens factory, manufacturing components for the armaments industry. Founded in the nineteenth century as Siemens & Halske, it had grown to become Germany's biggest electrical engineering company by the 1930s. During the war, it secured lucrative arms contracts and an apparently limitless supply of slave labour, and its chairman, Rudolf Bingel, was a generous member of the 'Friends of the Reichsführer-SS'.

Little remains of the Siemens section of the camp, and on my first visit, on a bitterly cold winter's day, twilight descended so early that I lost my way trying to find it. Six months later, when I return in midsummer, it still feels disorientating, as I walk along overgrown footpaths, past derelict buildings; I think I can hear a knocking from inside one of them, then realise it is the sound of my own pounding heart. A cuckoo's call is echoing in the wasteland, as I stumble through the long dry grass. The path has disappeared, and then I trip over a narrow-gauge railway track that leads to a crumbling stone ramp. This entire area looks utterly abandoned – and even in the warm sunlight of a June afternoon, there is a sense that something wicked might be hiding here. It is only later that I see one of the few surviving photographs taken by the Soviet doctors who arrived at the liberated camp on 2 May 1945: innumerable corpses were strewn on the ground beside a Siemens plant. Despite the best efforts of the Soviet medical team, hundreds more desperately sick prisoners died soon afterwards.

★

Even in its empty spaces, Ravensbrück is disturbing, as if the air is filled with the dust of the dead; and the memory of all those who suffered here hangs heavily, as do my own childhood fears. For when I was growing up, a nameless concentration camp was the familiar yet dreaded landscape of my nightmares: surrounded by electrified barbed wire, searchlights, men wielding machine guns and unleashing ferocious dogs. Escape was impossible, yet night after night I tried to flee, carrying my younger sister, or sometimes pulling her by the hand. But we could not run fast enough, or we seemed to be moving in slow motion, and the nightmares always ended in death, as we were stabbed or shot or gassed. I would wake up shaking, choking, drenched in sweat. There were nights when I was too frightened to go to sleep at all, though insomnia brought its own horrors: what was that shape in the dark corner of the room? Whose were the footsteps on the stairs?

Even in daylight, the camp did not vanish; for my father, who was born to Jewish parents in 1936, often talked about it, during his angry, anguished monologues on the Holocaust and the continuing threats of anti-Semitism. My sister Ruth and I did not have a religious upbringing, yet we were shaped, in part, by the fear engendered in us by our father, who was possessed by a deep and consuming rage about the fate of the six million Jews murdered by the Nazis. Now that I am older, I can better understand what motivated his fury. His parents never talked about the war – as was the case with so many Jewish survivors of that era; a corrosive silence that was in itself another manifestation of pain and grief. But my father eventually found out that a number of their relatives, who had stayed in Europe, including some in France, were killed at Auschwitz and other extermination camps.

The worst abuse that my father could throw at anyone was that they were a fascist – and there were occasions, when he was in the grip of the manic-depressive episodes that dominated our lives, that he called me a Nazi, and reminded me that I wasn't Jewish, because I didn't have a Jewish mother. My relationship with my father has always been awkward;

but I think of him, and our unknown ancestors, on my journey to Ravensbrück. I am accompanied, too, by the memory of my sister, my anchor within our fragmented family, who died of breast cancer at the age of thirty-three. My identity has been defined by this sisterhood, and by my love for Ruth, and hers for me; her death has not extinguished this love. Yet when I write about the women who died at Ravensbrück, I am assailed by the agonising memories of Ruth's death. 'I love you,' she whispers . . . as a child, a teenage girl, a young bride, a mother of new-born twins, in her dying moments. 'I love you too,' I whisper to my sister, into the darkness, into the light. 'I will always love you . . .'

These are the ghosts that walk with me through Ravensbrück; this is the unwieldy baggage that I have dragged here with me. But isn't it the case for everyone who comes to Holocaust memorials? In the context of the immensity of human suffering wrought by the Nazi regime, the losses of my own fractured family seem so infinitesimal as to make me feel guilty for even mentioning them. And yet, in witnessing the death of my beloved sister, I know that every death is meaningful; none should be forgotten. Each contains its own story that deserves to be told.

★

There are many places in Ravensbrück where the sense of evil is palpable, but nowhere more so than the commandant's house: the largest of the four *Führerhäuser* on the hillside, reached by a neat pathway from the SS headquarters. From the outside, it almost has the look of a pleasant holiday home, set amidst the pine trees, with green-painted shutters, sturdy wooden cladding and a handsome gabled roof. But when I went inside for the first time, as dusk gathered around Ravensbrück, the electric lighting flickered, as though someone was switching it on and off; then it stayed dark, and whatever was watching from the shadows drove me out of the house. On my return visit, in daylight, I force myself to sit down and write notes. The layout of the rooms has been preserved, and much of the early decoration: the paint scraped away to reveal patterned wallpaper. Scrubbed white porcelain tiles remain on the kitchen floor. The bathroom still has its original porcelain fittings, where the lavatory looks oddly obscene. Why this in particular, given all the horrors elsewhere in the camp? Perhaps because I've just read about what was termed 'excremental assault': the misery endured by prisoners who were denied access to latrines and sanitation.

At the front of the house, the windows and verandah have a view of the SS headquarters, the lake and part of the camp. At the back, there is leafy woodland. A fly bangs into the locked windows; I can see swallows outside, swooping between the trees, but there is little sound of birdsong, aside from the pigeons cooing on the roof. My head is throbbing, my eyes ache. I don't want to be alone in here, with the dead men in the photographs that hang on the walls. For these are the men who lived in this house, who dined heartily and warmed themselves beside the big fireplace; the men who climbed the circular wooden stairs to the first floor, to wash away their daily work in the well-appointed bathroom, before going to sleep in the master bedroom at night. The first commandant, Max Koegel, looks stern in his portrait, his mouth downturned in apparent disapproval as he stares out at me. The second, Fritz Suhren, wears a jovial smile on his face; his SS peaked cap, with its Death's Head insignia, is slightly tilted on his head, as if to appear more jaunty.

Max Koegel had been actively involved in the planning of the Ravensbrück camp, and became its acting commander when it opened in May 1939; he was formally appointed commandant in January 1940. His second wife Anna, whom he had married in 1934 when he was adjutant of the SS guard squad at Dachau, came with him to Ravensbrück. Here the couple enjoyed a comfortable way of life, with servants from the camp to do the housework and gardening, while she made regular excursions to the shops at Fürstenberg. A photograph of Anna Koegel hangs in another room in the house; she is wearing a fashionable satin blouse with a pussy-bow tied at her neck, her dark

The camp commandant's house at Ravensbrück.

hair smooth and coiffed. A note below this picture states that a prisoner who worked at the SS hair salon remembered Frau Koegel's anger when a Polish woman, whose hands were stained with hair dye, was assigned to wash her hair: 'she said she mustn't be touched with hands like that and it was a disgrace.'

An early recruit to the SS unit at Dachau, Max Koegel was particularly enthusiastic about punishing prisoners: so much so that he took the initiative in suggesting to Himmler that the most brutal forms of corporal punishment should be used against the female inmates. Koegel also organised the building of the prison block, where women could be kept in total darkness and constant isolation. Odette Sansom, the famed SOE agent, was held in one of these cells for several months, as was Geneviève de Gaulle, who described her incarceration in her memoir: 'there's no blanket, no mattress, bread is given out every three days, soup every five.'

In August 1942, Koegel was transferred to another concentration camp, Majdanek in Poland, where gas chambers were built shortly after he became commandant. His replacement was Fritz Suhren, who moved into this house with his wife and family. Born in 1908, Suhren had previously worked for his family's textile business; he joined the Nazi party in 1928 and volunteered for the SS in 1931. Suhren was just thirty-four when he took over at Ravensbrück, but had already risen to the position of deputy commandant at Sachsenhausen, where he oversaw the mass murder of twelve thousand Soviet prisoners of war. At Ravensbrück, he was tasked with increasing the deployment of prisoners as slave labourers for the German armaments industry, and sending them in large numbers to satellite camps around the country.

Suhren's wife, Elfriede Bruns, had trained as a seamstress, but gave up work when she married him in 1936, by which time he was already a well-established SS officer. As her husband's career progressed, Elfriede followed him from one posting to another, eventually settling at Ravensbrück with their four children, until the fall of the Third Reich.

When I look out of the windows at the front of the house, I try to imagine how it might have felt, as a mother, to bring up a young family in the shadow of Ravensbrück. It is close enough to have seen the pitiful processions of skeletal women coming in and out of the camp; near enough to have heard the sound of the dogs barking, the guards shouting, the prisoners screaming, and to smell the ceaseless burning in the crematorium. Did the ash from the furnaces fall like grey snow on their garden? Could the commandant's children hear the cries of other children, from inside the camp?

'Words fail me,' I write in my notebook. The failure of language is, perhaps, an inevitable consequence of any attempt to write about the unspeakable hell of the camps. Yet the commandant's house survives as a reminder of Himmler's ideology that underpinned the SS and extended to their family life. In a speech that he delivered to SS officers in 1937, Himmler declared: 'The SS is a National Socialist order of soldiers of the Nordic race and a community of their clan bound together by oath . . . Fiancées and wives, as well as their husbands, also belong, according to our laws, to this community, this order.' Prospective brides had to be approved by the 'Race and Settlement Office' of the SS – a protracted process that involved checking a woman was 'racially suitable' and had 'reproductive capability' – to ensure that 'good blood' would flow through the veins of SS families.

In this way, Himmler – whose own physical attributes were curiously unprepossessing, with his pudgy body and receding chin – saw himself as establishing 'a new ruling class destined to last for centuries and the product of repeated selection, a new aristocracy continuously renewed from the best of the sons and daughters of our nation, a nobility that never ages . . . representing eternal youth for our nation'. In 1943 Himmler went further, and explained that after one year of marriage, wives would 'become members of the SS and after ten years their children also become members, and they enjoy all the protection and care that we offer our clan'.

Thus the commandant's hillside villa in Ravensbrück was a utopian home built for a family of good Nazis. It reminds me of a child's doll's house I saw in the German History Museum in Berlin: designed in the 1930s in accordance with National Socialist principles, every room is perfectly decorated, with miniature parquet floors, patterned wallpaper and chintz curtains; pictures of Hitler adorn the downstairs rooms, and upstairs in the diminutive bedroom the furnishings are pink and lace-trimmed. As for the life-size commandant's house at Ravensbrück, two details lodge in my mind, from the testimony of a Frenchwoman who ventured inside soon after the liberation of the camp: firstly, there was a piano in the living room, where she sat and played for a while; secondly, a pink eiderdown on a big bed, beneath which one of her fellow former prisoners was curled up and sleeping.

The fact that an idealised family home could exist alongside a horrific concentration camp did not pose a problem for Himmler, nor the men he commanded. In the course of a long speech he made in October 1943, to an audience of senior SS officers, Himmler praised the 'decency' with which they had undertaken the extermination of Jews. 'Most of you will know what it is like to see one hundred corpses lying side by side or five hundred or one thousand of them,' he said, and then added, encouragingly, that it was a great achievement for the SS 'to have coped with this and – except for cases of human weakness – remained decent'. In the same speech, Himmler emphasised that the absolute rule for the SS was to be 'honest, decent, loyal and comradely to those of our own blood and to no one else. How the Russians or the Czechs fare is a matter of complete indifference to me . . . Whether or not ten thousand Russian women collapse with exhaustion while digging an anti-tank ditch concerns me only insofar as the anti-tank ditch is being dug for Germany . . . We Germans, who alone on this earth have a decent attitude to animals, will of course adopt a decent attitude to these human animals, but it is a crime against our own blood to worry about them and to apply ideals to them so that our sons and grandsons have an even harder time with them. If anyone comes to me and says: "I can't make the anti-tank ditch with women and children. It's inhuman because they'll die," then I am forced to say: "You are murdering your own blood, for if the ditch is not made then German soldiers will die and these are the sons of German mothers . . ."'

Himmler's bizarre concept of 'decency' – a theme that often appears in his speeches – was of course perverse; in the words of his biographer Peter Longerich, 'it was decent not to treat one's enemies decently'. As a consequence, for all the much-vaunted SS values of orderliness and efficiency, by the time Catherine Dior arrived at Ravensbrück, the camp was in a state of indecent chaos. More than forty thousand prisoners were now crammed into rat-infested accommodation that had first been designed to hold three thousand, and the numbers were increasing every day. Hitler had ordered that no prisoner of the Reich should be set free, even though the Allied forces were advancing towards Germany. Just as women were being sent to Ravensbrück from Paris in the final days before the Liberation, so too they were arriving from the eastern territories, principally Poland. A huge influx of prisoners came from Warsaw, which had been destroyed by German forces after the failed uprising of the Polish Resistance in early August 1944. In the weeks that followed, an estimated twelve thousand Poles – including pregnant women, children and babies – had arrived at Ravensbrück, where countless numbers died, having been given no access to running water or latrines.

Maisie Renault, who had shared the same train journey from Paris as Catherine Dior, described in her memoir the squalor and overcrowded conditions that they encountered in the camp: 'three persons must occupy a single bed. It's impossible to sleep flat or turn over . . . Many of our companions are suffering with purulent wounds . . . Dysentery begins to spread . . . a nauseating odour prevails in the dormitory.' Even more horrific was the sight of dead bodies lying in the filthy washroom. 'In this room,' she observed, 'where a crowd of naked, emaciated bodies, marked with lice bites and wounds from vitamin deficiencies, jostles each other . . . lie the dead of the block, continually splashed with dirty water while waiting transport to the morgue.' Further traumas awaited them outside on the *Appellplatz*; after roll call, they watched with bewilderment as a fat SS officer on a bicycle rode around the lines of prisoners, lashing out at them with a whip or his fists. This, they learned, was the director of the work office, Hans Pflaum, who made the selections for slave labour during yet another humiliating process, which involved the women standing in the courtyard, stripped naked, waiting to have their hands, teeth and bodies examined. According to Germaine Tillion, Pflaum was known as 'the cattle merchant': a vicious thug 'who mercilessly abused every woman who came within reach'.

By early September, Catherine and her companions were struggling with the combined effects of backbreaking work and meagre rations limited to thin, watery soup that made most of them sick. Maisie Renault wrote that as a group, they were ordered to shovel sand in marshy terrain from dawn onwards. 'Dressed in our little summer dresses with short sleeves, we shiver in the thick fog, which rises from the lake and covers the marshes. The sand is wet and cold and our freezing hands have difficulty holding the shovels . . .'

Astonishingly, despite the constant danger of being attacked by the guards and their dogs for any perceived transgression (real or otherwise), the women found ways to subvert the regime. Indeed, having been stripped of their identities, they feared becoming as desperate as the prisoners known in the language of the camp as '*Schmuckstücke*' (the direct translation is a trinket or piece of jewellery; the guards also referred to prisoners simply as '*Stücke*' – or 'pieces'). These women were in the final stage of malnutrition and exhaustion, and seemed to have become the living dead. Germaine Tillion, an ethnologist and anthropologist by training, wrote with horror about seeing 'an apparently human creature' who would 'throw herself face-down in the mud to lick up the remains from an overturned soup bowl; without friends, hope, or dignity . . . transformed by fear and hunger, and finally destined to be gassed like rodents . . .'

For Catherine Dior – who would rarely speak about what she had endured at Ravensbrück – it was therefore imperative not to lose her self-respect. When I talked to her godson, Nicolas Crespelle, he said that Catherine told him only one story from that time: that she would never fall to the ground to pick up a piece of food that an SS guard had thrown there. 'She said that if you did that, then your life was over . . .'

According to Germaine Tillion, whose secret notes subsequently formed the basis for her painfully detailed eyewitness account of the camp: 'The fact that I survived Ravensbrück I owe first – and most definitely – to chance, then to anger and the motivation to reveal the crimes I had witnessed, and finally to a union of friendship, since I had lost the instinctive and physical desire to live. This tenuous web of friendship was, in a way, almost submerged by the stark brutality of selfishness and the struggle for survival, but somehow everyone in the camp was invisibly woven into it.' For the Frenchwomen, this involved banding together, as if in a surrogate extended family.

Jacqueline d'Alincourt, a twenty-four-year-old resistant who had arrived at Ravensbrück in April 1944, just a few months before Catherine, wrote in her own memoir: 'What mattered was hanging on, despite the exhaustion, not being intimidated, not yielding to despair. The possibilities of resistance were minimal, but vital . . . Imagination, tenacity, even fury were our only weapons with which to battle despair . . .' Jacqueline had been assigned to one of the textile workshops, where the hours were long and the supervisors were as brutal as everywhere else in the camp, hurling scissors at the women if they weren't working fast enough, or smashing their faces into the sewing machines; even kicking them to death. So for her to succeed in secretly making mittens for her French companions in the camp was an act of valour. 'One risked one's life in doing so; one could not afford to be caught. The strategy consisted of breaking down each step of the work into a series of quick and fleeting movements . . . This could last all night – or all day.' Once the mittens were finished, they had to be smuggled out of the workshop, and then 'furtively passed to some comrade in our bloc whom they kept warm . . . The inexpressible joy of defying our tormentors in this way!'

The clandestine objects that were created by the prisoners – whose most personal possessions, including their wedding rings, had been taken from them – were intensely powerful symbols of solidarity and resistance. A remarkable collection of these is displayed in the former SS headquarters; some were donated by survivors to the first Ravensbrück museum when it opened in 1959. Since then, the collection has been expanded, with additional drawings and found objects, including a lipstick case decorated with an engraving of the Eiffel Tower and a porcelain miniature of the Virgin Mary, unearthed by Soviet soldiers when they were stationed at the camp. Together, they form an extraordinary tapestry of memory and humanity.

The assembled objects also act as a vivid counterbalance to the impersonal lists of numbers in the archives, and to the images from SS photograph albums on display, depicting the camp staff in polished boots and Nazi uniforms, complete with the macabre skull and crossbones badge. One of these is particularly arresting: it shows the female guards standing to attention to greet Heinrich Himmler when he visited Ravensbrück in January 1941. Many were recruited locally, attracted by the salaries (about twice that of a factory worker at the time) and the comfortable, newly built living quarters. They became a familiar sight in Fürstenberg, wearing their smart grey jackets and skirts, and caps bearing the imperial eagle symbol to show that they were employees of the Reich. In 1939, there were about fifty-five women guards, but their numbers increased over the years, and they were every bit as brutal as their male colleagues. Another individual portrait is of Dorothea Binz, a local girl who started working at Ravensbrück in August 1939, when she was just nineteen; she swiftly rose to become supervisor of the prison block, and was noted for her unyielding sadism. According to the French resistant Denise Dufournier, 'She was a petite blonde with rather an ingenuous face, quite pretty, but whenever she appeared, silence fell. She had a big

A doll with a shaved head, made by a prisoner at Ravensbrück.

An embroidered heart; and a carved basket made from a cherry stone,
given as a birthday present to a prisoner in March 1944. Both are part of the collection
of miniature objects at the Ravensbrück Memorial Museum.

dog and always carried a riding crop . . . She lived in a little house outside the camp with one of the male guards, so she must have had some kind of human existence, but in the camp, well, she'd kick a woman to death as soon as look at her.'

There are 1,500 handmade objects in the Ravensbrück collection, ranging from Catholic rosaries and crucifixes to a Communist badge with a Soviet hammer and sickle; tiny carved animals (a hare, a horse, a dog); hand-painted card games and greeting cards, decorated with tender hearts and flowers; lovingly crafted rag dolls and exquisitely embroidered bags. They reveal the extraordinary number of different nationalities – more than thirty – of the prisoners, and their varied political and religious beliefs. Above all, they show how hard it is to generalise about the women in the camp. A small minority became functionaries for the SS: *Blockovas*, for example, who were in charge of a dormitory block, assisted by *Stubovas*; in return, they enjoyed better living conditions and proved themselves capable of great cruelty. Among the most notoriously ruthless *Blockovas* was Carmen Mory, a Swiss-born journalist who had worked for the Gestapo and was then arrested on suspicion of being a double agent. At Ravensbrück, she was in charge of Block 10, a so-called 'hospital' block, where she was more likely to kill her patients than offer them any care. As a consequence, Mory was feared throughout the camp, and nicknamed the Black Angel or the Witch. When a young resistant named Anne Spoerry was deported from Paris to Ravensbrück in January 1944, her medical training ensured that she ended up working for Mory in Block 10. There she survived by becoming Mory's lover and obeying her orders: dispensing lethal injections to the 'lunatics' – women who had been driven mad by the relentless horror of the camp.

Some prisoners were sustained by their religious faith or political convictions, or both, as in the case of Geneviève de Gaulle. An early and committed member of the French Resistance, she had been deported to Ravensbrück in February 1944, and her profoundly moving memoir describes how she fought to maintain her faith, even when overcome by despair. 'I was obsessed by the certainty that much worse than death was the destruction of our souls, which was the agenda of the concentration camp world . . . at all costs I wished not to isolate myself in my prayers from the most wretched among the women – those who stole bread, fought us for soup when it was given out, or worse, lay in a corner amid their lice and filth. They were a reflection of what we ourselves could so easily become, and I ought to share their humiliation, as I did the comradeship and bread . . .'

For Denise Dufournier, the chance to look up at the skies during the long hours of roll call gave her a glimmer of hope. 'The sun was now etching delicately tinted wisps of cloud on the sky. The rising and the setting of the sun were the only things of beauty in this desolate country, the only token of friendship offered to us by that other world from which we were banished.' Some of her comrades discovered inner creative resources, such as Jeannette L'Herminier, a French resistant who was deported to Ravensbrück in January 1944, and drew a series of remarkable portraits of her friends in the camp: all of them faceless, yet filled with the spirit of humanity.

Courage and creativity, however, were by no means enough to save everyone, as epidemics of typhus, tuberculosis and typhoid fever raged throughout the camp, killing prisoners who were already starving and weakened by the relentless demands of forced labour. Jacqueline d'Alincourt described sharing a precious prayer book with her friend Anne de Bauffremont. 'She had been shorn and her face was deeply drawn, the sign we had come to recognise: her end was near, inescapable.' The two young women prayed together, but Jacqueline knew that Anne was close to death, and that neither faith nor friendship would keep her alive. Anne died at Ravensbrück on 15 February 1945; she was twenty-five years old. Germaine Tillion's mother Emilie, who had also been deported to Ravensbrück for supporting the Resistance, was murdered in the gas chamber there on 2 March 1945, just a few days after her sixty-ninth birthday. Then came the death of Yvonne Baratte, who

Drawings made in secret by Jeannette L'Herminier.
Top: Two unnamed Frenchwomen. Above: Mathilde ('Tilly') Fritz and Eliane Jeannin,
former students of the University of Strasbourg and the Ecole des Beaux-Arts in Paris.

had made an altar the night before her deportation from Paris, and whose final letter to her family, written at Romainville, spoke of hope. Yvonne died on 25 March, at the age of thirty-four. Five days later, the dwindling number of French prisoners mourned the loss of Nicole de Witasse, the spirited girl who had attempted to escape from the convoy of deportees.

Violette Lecoq, another member of the French Resistance who had been a Red Cross nurse at the outbreak of the war, was assigned to work for Carmen Mory at the 'hospital' block, and although she tried to help the patients, she also saw how many were simply left to die, or murdered, or dispatched to the gas chambers. Her drawings – made in secret on stolen black carbon paper – survive as graphic testimony to the horrifying scenes that she witnessed. Her friend, a French doctor named Louise Le Porz, who had been sent to Ravensbrück in June 1944, also worked in the same block. Many years later, when Dr Le Porz was interviewed by the British writer Sarah Helm, she described what she and Violette once saw together: 'It was night and the electric light suddenly came on. We were by the big gates . . . I said to Violette: "If one day someone makes a film they must film this scene. This night. This moment." Because there we were – a little nurse from Paris and a young doctor all the way from Bordeaux. There was a lorry that suddenly arrives and it turns around and reverses towards us. And it lifts up and it tips out a whole pile of corpses. We were there because we'd just taken one of our dead to the mortuary. And suddenly we were in front of a mountain of bodies. And if we recount that one day, we said to each other, nobody would believe us. And they didn't. When we came back, nobody wanted to know.'

Nobody wanted to know . . . Her words echo through my mind. So many terrible episodes occurred at Ravensbrück – scenes that you don't want to have in your head, but once you know about them, you will never be able to forget them. According to Germaine Tillion, some of her companions in the camp could not bear to be told 'when some new horror was revealed: "Even if it's true, I don't want to know about it," was the reply of quite a few comrades I tried to enlighten.' But for Germaine, it seemed vital to record the crimes that took place at Ravensbrück: the enforced sterilisation of Roma and Sinti prisoners, including girls as young as eight years old; the late-term abortions on pregnant women, whose babies would be drowned or smothered if born alive; the *Kinder-zimmer*, or 'children's room', where infants were left alone to slowly starve to death. She estimated that 850 babies died under these circumstances in six months alone, from October 1944 to March 1945.

Germaine Tillion was also determined to gather evidence about the experimental operations that were conducted on women at Ravensbrück. These and other atrocities, she discovered, had taken place in the aftermath of the death of Reinhard Heydrich, the director of the Reich Security Main Office (the overarching organisation set up by Himmler to control all intelligence and security matters in the Reich). On 27 May 1942, Czech resistance fighters had attempted to assassinate Heydrich, as he was being driven to Prague Castle. Himmler's trusted friend and the Nazis' leading surgeon, Karl Gebhardt, was flown out to Prague but arrived too late to operate. Emergency surgery had already been carried out by local doctors, infection set in, and Gebhardt failed to prevent the spread of gangrene. Heydrich died of his injuries a week later, and in retaliation, the nearby villages of Lidice and Ležáky were destroyed; all the men and boys over the age of fifteen were shot, and the women and children were sent to concentration camps, including 184 women deported to Ravensbrück, where they were met with the utmost cruelty.

As a consequence of Heydrich's death, Gebhardt faced questions as to why he had not treated the patient's gangrenous wounds with new antibacterial drugs, known as sulphonamides. Partly to help Gebhardt clear his name, Himmler suggested that he should test the drugs on suitable human subjects at Ravensbrück. The experiments duly went

Overleaf: Drawings by Violette Lecoq of the scenes she witnessed at Ravensbrück.

1. — Welcome...

2. — Deux heures après...

5. — Douceur du rêve...

6. — Détournement...

9. — La loi du plus fort...

10. — Travaux...

12. — Rien n'était dédié...

14. — Après l'appel...

17. — Inspection...

18. — Après juin...

3. — Listag venez...

4. — Veretes...

5. — Travail...

6. — Gotironnerie...

VI. — L'antre...

12. — Les pires prend les pires / Les N. N...

13. — Les valides...

16. — Amitié...

19. — Nouvellaux berceins...

20. — Hygiène...

ahead on seventy-four healthy Polish girls, the youngest of whom was fourteen. They had severe wounds inflicted on their legs, which were deliberately infected with bacteria and foreign objects, such as pieces of wood and glass. They were then either treated with sulphonamides, or different drugs, or nothing at all. Predictably, the results of Gebhardt's experiments proved inconclusive; it was not in his interest to show that sulphonamides were effective.

Dr Gebhardt, who was president of the German Red Cross at this time, soon lost interest in his human guinea pigs; those who survived were mutilated and disabled, and became known throughout the camp as 'the rabbits'. Towards the end of 1942, Himmler gave his approval for the medical experiments at Ravensbrück to be continued. These were undertaken by one of Gebhardt's SS colleagues at the Hohenlychen clinic, Dr Ludwig Stumpfegger, who broke the bones of yet more young women and teenagers. It is a testament to Germaine Tillion's extraordinary resolve that she was able to gather vital evidence that would be used in the post-war trials against the Nazi doctors and nurses who had participated in these and other operations in the camp, torturing women and children, killing babies, and destroying countless lives. Yet so widespread were the crimes that there is no way of knowing exactly how many victims died as a result of them.

★

When I visited Ravensbrück in early June, there were pleasure boats on the lake, just as there had been before the war. Fürstenberg is a neat, well-kept, respectable-looking town – and people still come to enjoy themselves here. At the camp's memorial site, however, I found myself almost entirely alone. I stood at the edge of the lake, and I could see canoes and cruise vessels in the distance, but no one came close to this side of the shoreline. Iridescent dragonflies skimmed across the water lilies, a pair of herons took flight, and the cuckoo's call still echoed from the woodland. Blue tits were nesting in the high stone boundary wall that is now part of the memorial; I could hear their baby chicks as I walked along the wall, reading the names of the dead who are remembered here. At the foot of the wall, previous visitors have left their own offerings: shells, pebbles, flowers, poems and drawings. Some have written messages, praying that the dead may rest in peace. I do not feel peaceful in their presence; but there is a sense of quiet acknowledgement. I look up, above the high wall, up to the sky . . . and I think of the prisoners who gazed at the same skies, and of the smoke of their dead sisters that rose from the crematorium chimney, billowing into the air, escaping at last, mingling with the stardust.

Beside the wall is the mass grave, containing ashes from the crematorium, and it is covered with hundreds of rose bushes. The first were planted in April 1958 by former prisoners from Lidice, who brought cuttings from the rose garden they had already established on the site of their destroyed village.

A number of the keepsakes in the museum collection are decorated with a rose motif: drawn on birthday cards, or embroidered onto tiny pieces of fabric, and given as a token of friendship and an emblem of freedom. So the rose already had a special meaning for the women of Ravensbrück, and in the year following the planting of the first roses on the mass grave, more were donated by former prisoners' associations from around Europe, in preparation for the inauguration of the camp memorial on 12 September 1959.

The winters in this part of Germany are particularly harsh, and not all of the roses survived, so in 1973, Marcelle Dudach-Roset, a French resistant and communist who had been deported to the camp, arranged for a new, hardier rose to be bred for Ravensbrück, named 'Résurrection'. These were first planted on the thirtieth anniversary of the liberation of the camp, 26 April 1974. Since then, 'Résurrection' roses have been planted as a living memorial in more than six hundred locations around France, the Czech Republic, Norway and Germany, and they continue to grow

A handmade card decorated with roses, given by Czech prisoners to
Vera Žahourková on her twentieth birthday in March 1945.

at Ravensbrück, alongside several other varieties. There is also a plaque etched with a poem written by Dudach-Roset, to celebrate the rose:

Je suis 'Résurrection'
Et tout au long des ans
Tout au long des saisons
Je resterai le témoin de vie
Qui protégera de la barbarie
Tous les enfants du monde
Même lorsque je serai devenu eglantine
Illuminant tous les chemins . . .

I am 'Résurrection'
And year after year
Season after season
I will bear witness to life
Protecting from barbarism
All the children of the world
Even as I become a wild rose
Illuminating every path . . .

I knew nothing of this story until I visited Ravensbrück; and as I write about it now, I am transported there again, as if in a waking dream, to a lakeside rose garden that has grown out of the ashes of the past, commemorating the dead, while also representing an act of hope for the future.

In early summer, when white swans glide across the lake, the rosebuds are still furled, like tiny clenched fists. Yet in late November, as I stand beside the mass grave, the flowers are miraculously in bloom, their fragile petals open beneath the dark winter sky, even as an icy wind sweeps in from the north.

Women at Ravensbrück. The white crosses were painted on their clothes
to mark them out as prisoners.

The Underworld

In a fast car driven by my husband, the journey from Ravensbrück to Torgau takes less than three hours; but for Catherine Dior, locked in a cattle wagon yet again, it took three days by rail. She was part of a contingent of five hundred women who were selected in the second week of September 1944 to be sent south to Torgau: one of dozens of slave labour sites that came under the administration of Buchenwald concentration camp.

Although I have read Virginia d'Albert-Lake's account of their eventual arrival at Torgau, which is about a hundred miles south of Berlin, I can find no record on a map of where the sub-camp was situated. Virginia wrote that they marched for half an hour from the railway station, and on the way they passed 'hundreds of French prisoners of war' (who would have been held in the Stalag IV-D POW camp at Torgau). In search of information, I go first to Schloss Hartenfels, a forbidding medieval castle that dominates the town, overlooking the bridge across the River Elbe where Soviet and American troops met on 25 April 1945. The castle is now a museum, containing an archive that covers its history as a prison during the Second World War and in the Soviet era. There is an extensive exhibition that covers this grim heritage, but no mention of the sub-camp; fortunately, a helpful guide offers to introduce me to the museum archivist, who turns out to know its precise location. So we set off again, my patient husband accompanying me on this strange quest.

Nothing remains as a memorial to the camp, despite the many who died here. It is a bleak no man's land, where scrubby fields are interspersed with a few derelict-looking industrial buildings. A winter wind whips up the gritty dust on the road where my husband has parked; he stays in the car, while I get out to look for any clues. All trace of the wartime past seems to have vanished; but then I see a disused narrow-gauge railway track, similar to the one at the Siemens site at Ravensbrück. I follow it, walking through dead grass, until I am entirely alone, in the middle of nowhere. I look back at the direction I came from. The car has disappeared from view, and the vast grey November sky is darkening. The train track terminates; I am at the end of the line, yet still searching for answers.

In her journal, Virginia d'Albert-Lake describes the moment when the women realised that they had been sent to work at a munitions factory, as they filed past the guards and entered the camp for the first time. 'We crossed a railway siding on which were several box cars. As we passed beside them we could read, stamped on their sides the word: "Ammunition." . . . A hot sick feeling swept over me . . . It looked as though we were going to live in the very centre of the factory . . .'

The group dispatched to Torgau included Jeannie Rousseau, a twenty-four-year-old resistant who had arrived at Ravensbrück the week before Catherine Dior. Fluent in German, Jeannie had previously worked as an interpreter for Wehrmacht officers and French industrialists in Paris, passing on vital intelligence to the British about the development of Hitler's V-2 rockets, the long-range missiles that were designed to hit Allied targets, including London. Soon after arriving at Torgau, she called a meeting of the women and declared that they should stand up for their rights under the Geneva Convention, which prohibited prisoners of war being forced to make weapons.

According to Virginia: 'We decided that we were belligerents and that no one, not even the Nazis, had the right to make us work in the munitions factory. Perhaps the women who instigated this "Bill of Rights" and those who voted for it should be admired for their courage, but when they announced their decision that Sunday morning to the alcoholic adjutant under whose direct command we had been placed, they did not realise that they had put a match to a fuse of dynamite . . . "Of course it can be arranged," he said. "Those of you who refuse to work in the factory will simply be sent back to Ravensbrück."'

The prospect of returning to the hellish conditions at Ravensbrück created understandable uncertainty within the group. 'Many of the women changed their decision at this threat, while those who were willing to take the risk were scornful of their comrades' cowardice,' wrote Virginia. Lists were drawn up of those who were prepared to stay or go, but the arguments continued. Some pointed out that the war was nearly over, and the munitions they made might never be used; others said that Ravensbrück would ensure their 'slow death', and they should avoid going back there 'at any price'. In her diary, Virginia recalled the words of one of the women who spoke in favour of remaining at Torgau: 'We have parents and husbands and children in France who need us; the future France needs us. Our work isn't done yet. We have grave responsibilities for the future.' Virginia was as conflicted as everyone else: 'I didn't want to be a coward. Half-heartedly I signed up for Ravensbrück, but an hour later someone convinced me that it was lunacy, and I took my name off the list . . . We all suffered that day . . . We were torn between courage and fear, idealism and realism, pride and shame. All the while the Germans were laughing at us, teasing us, torturing us, and in the end they did exactly as they pleased.'

Jeannie Rousseau was punished by being locked in a prison cell for three weeks, where she was doused with cold water every morning and beaten, while the majority of the other women, including Catherine Dior, were set to work in the factory, dipping copper shell cases into deep trays of acid. The twelve-hour shifts were exhausting, and the sulphuric fumes damaged their lungs and skin. Yet even there, they were able to engage in covert acts of resistance, sabotaging the machinery, so that every so often it broke down.

Virginia d'Albert-Lake was relatively fortunate to be assigned to the camp kitchen, peeling vegetables, and then out in the fields, digging potatoes. 'It was already the first of October and heavy frosts were imminent,' she observed. The potato patches were scattered around the camp, and as she walked between them, she gained a sense of the scale of the industrial operation. Stores of munitions were kept out of sight in huge underground caves. Small ventilator shafts were the only sign of these subterranean areas, and they were well hidden by a carpet of wild grasses and small fir trees. Rail tracks branched out in several directions, but Virginia saw no signs of houses or civilians. 'The whole place seemed shrouded in mystery and secrecy.'

The Torgau contingent was designated as 'French', but also contained five agents from the British Special Operations Executive (SOE): Lilian Rolfe, Violette Szabo, Denise Bloch, Eileen Nearne and Yvonne Rudellat. Dubbed 'Churchill's Secret Army', SOE had been created in London in July 1940 to conduct espionage, sabotage and reconnaissance in Occupied Europe, as well as supporting local resistance networks. Its 'F section' operated in France, and forty-one female agents served there, of whom only twenty-five survived the war. All of the SOE agents at Torgau were still using their aliases, although their friends in the group knew them as 'the English girls' or 'the little paratroopers'. Yvonne Rudellat was the oldest of the five: born in France in 1897, she had lived in London for more than two decades by the time she was recruited. She was the first agent to arrive in France (on 30 July 1942), and proved to be a highly capable member of SOE's largest resistance network, the Prosper Circuit. But she was eventually captured in June 1943, sustaining a serious gunshot wound to the head at the time of her arrest.

Yvonne was clearly unwell by the time she arrived at Ravensbrück in August 1944: she had already spent a year in prison at Fresnes, and had never fully recovered from the head wound; her hair had turned white, and at forty-seven, she was more at risk than the younger women. Anyone deemed too old for forced labour was liable to be killed; according to Himmler, this was a 'practical necessity' to ensure maximum efficiency in the camps. When it became apparent that she was too sick to work at Torgau, she was sent back to Ravensbrück, and then transferred to Bergen-Belsen in March 1945. Starving and suffering from typhus and dysentery, Yvonne was barely alive when the British army arrived at the camp on 15 April 1945, and she died a week later. Between January 1945 and the Liberation, an estimated thirty-five thousand prisoners perished as a result of disease and starvation at Bergen-Belsen, which was piled high with unburied corpses; a further fourteen thousand died in the following two months.

Lilian Rolfe was also looking noticeably frail at Torgau – she had to be helped to walk from the railway station to the camp by Jacqueline Bernard, the French journalist and resistant who had been tortured at Rue de la Pompe soon after Catherine Dior. In common with all the women recruited as F-section SOE agents, Lilian's key qualification was her fluency in French, having spent the first sixteen years of her life in Paris. As a member of the Women's Auxiliary Air Force (WAAF), she came to the attention of SOE towards the end of 1943; on 5 April 1944 she was parachuted into France, and worked as a wireless operator until her arrest in late July. Lilian was repeatedly interrogated and tortured in Fresnes prison, and then transported by train to Germany on 8 August, shackled in chains with Denise Bloch and Violette Szabo. By the time she was put to work at Ravensbrück, Lilian was so weak that she could barely hold her spade while shovelling sand. At Torgau, Virginia d'Albert-Lake noted in her diary that Lilian was 'very quiet and sensitive . . . She appeared doomed from the start.'

The remaining three SOE agents seemed stronger. Denise Bloch, who was born into a Jewish family in Paris in 1916, had been trained in London as a wireless operator and parachuted into France in March 1944. Virginia described her as 'a tall, good-looking girl, who was very much in love with a well-known French automobile racing champion'. This was Denise's fellow agent Robert Benoist, a daring Grand Prix driver and First World War pilot who had been commissioned into the British Army as a captain. He was arrested with Denise in June 1944 and

The SOE agents who were in the same group as Catherine Dior, dispatched from Ravensbrück to Torgau as slave labour. This page, top left: Eileen Nearne; top right: Denise Bloch; below: Yvonne Rudellat with her daughter, and in a later photograph. Opposite page, top left: Violette Szabo; top right: Lilian Rolfe; below: Violette Szabo on her wedding day in August 1940 and as a girl.

deported on the same train. When it reached Germany, Benoist was sent to Buchenwald, where he was executed in early September.

Eileen Nearne and Violette Szabo were the two youngest SOE agents at Torgau – both just twenty-three. Violette, the daughter of an English taxi driver and a French dressmaker, had grown up in London, completely bilingual. After a whirlwind romance in the summer of 1940, she married Etienne Szabo, an officer in the French Foreign Legion, who was killed in action in North Africa in 1942, having never seen their newborn daughter. Despite being a young widow with a baby, Violette was recruited by SOE the following year, and in early April 1944 she parachuted into northern France to undertake her first reconnaissance mission. Once this was successfully completed, she went shopping in Paris and bought three dresses for herself from the Molyneux couture salon on Rue Royale, and an outfit for her daughter, before returning safely to England.

For her next mission, Violette was dropped into France in the early hours of 8 June 1944, aiming to liaise with the Resistance in its efforts to sabotage German communications after D-Day. She was arrested at a roadblock just two days later and interrogated by the Gestapo at Avenue Foch, then transferred to Fresnes prison, and deported to Ravensbrück along with Denise Bloch and Lilian Rolfe.

At Torgau, Virginia d'Albert-Lake recalled Violette Szabo as 'young, charming and attractive. She used to stretch her limbs like a cat as she lay on her bunk not far from mine; to me, that stretch expressed a love of life and the desire to be back in the world of dancing and danger. Violet [*sic*] was always planning to escape and, night after night, her plan was to be culminated. Somehow, it never worked and although she spent hours waiting for her chance, it never came.'

Eileen Nearne maintained a lower profile, but was equally keen to escape from Torgau. Born in London in March 1921 to an English father and French mother, Eileen (known as Didi to her friends and family) had spent much of her childhood in France. Both she and her elder sister Jacqueline were recruited as SOE agents, as was her brother Francis. Trained as a wireless operator, Eileen had arrived in France in March 1944, and operated in Paris until her arrest on 21 July. After the ruthless standardised sequence of interrogation and torture by the Gestapo and imprisonment at Fresnes, she was deported on the same train as Catherine Dior in August.

★

At the end of the first week of October, the women at Torgau were divided into two: half, including Catherine Dior and Eileen Nearne, were told they were being sent to another munitions factory; the other half, including Virginia, Violette, Denise and Lilian, were sent back to Ravensbrück. 'This breaking up of our group was painful,' wrote Virginia in her diary. 'We had left Paris together and we had been together ever since. Already a strong attachment, born of the same ideas, the same suffering, the same hopes, had made us one . . . We wanted to stay together. There were many tearful faces and forced smiles that morning . . .' Virginia and her companions did not spend long at Ravensbrück; on 16 October they were dispatched as slave labour to a different sub-camp in Königsberg. There Lilian grew weaker and Denise suffered from a septic wound on her foot, but Violette remained remarkably hopeful, talking often about being reunited with her little daughter, and singing 'God Save the King' on Christmas Day. In mid-January, the three SOE agents were told that they were returning to Ravensbrück; Violette remained confident that they would be liberated from there, and told a French friend, 'It is King George who has asked for us. I will go and see him when I get back and demand a plane. I'll come and rescue you myself.'

In fact, a brutal death awaited them at Ravensbrück; they were taken first to the prison block, where they remained for a few days, and were then executed beside the crematorium. Lilian Rolfe and Denise Bloch were by now desperately ill, and too weak to walk, so were dragged to their execution. The camp commandant, Fritz Suhren, watched as all three women were shot, one by one, in the back of the neck.

★

On 9 October 1944, Catherine Dior was in the group of 250 French-women who left Torgau – travelling by railway, again in cattle trucks – on the journey west to another Buchenwald sub-camp, named Abteroda. This was situated two hundred miles away, in Thuringia, and as I embark on my own journey to find the site, it seems even more remote than Torgau. Its sense of isolation may have been heightened during the Cold War, as it was in an area of East Germany so close to the border with the West that access was severely restricted. By the time we turn into the lane that leads to the former camp, the weak afternoon light is already fading. There is no signpost, no memorial; I'm in the middle of rural farmland, and can hear the lowing of cows in nearby barns. The archivist at Torgau has given me a detailed map reference, but there seems to be nothing but a desolate field of mud and stinging nettles. And then I see the evidence I'm searching for: a small, brick-built entrance to a concealed mine shaft. Stone steps lead downwards into the pitch darkness; a sinister, narrow hole in the ground.

Everything else has been obliterated, yet when Catherine arrived here, BMW was manufacturing aircraft engines in a former potash mine. The disused mining tunnels had originally been taken over by the Wehrmacht just before the war, and used as a munitions depot. By the summer of 1944, Allied bombing raids were disrupting the production of military jet engines at the BMW plant in the town of Eisenach, twenty or so miles away, and the decision was made to move to Abteroda's hidden underground tunnels. At first, BMW relied on male slave labour from the main concentration camp at Buchenwald, but then added to their workforce with the 250 Frenchwomen from Torgau. The exploitation of forced labour by the Munich-based BMW had begun as early as March

1942, when it used inmates from Dachau at a newly built factory nearby. (On the occasion of its centenary celebrations in 2016, the company expressed 'the most profound regret' for its role in supporting the Nazi regime.)

Conditions at Abteroda were dire: the women were expected to sleep on a cold cement floor, in the same building as a factory workshop. There were no latrines; rations were minimal (nothing more than watery soup and the occasional piece of dry bread); their shifts were at least twelve hours long, and they were beaten by SS guards if they worked too slowly. They were also warned that anyone who refused to work would immediately be shot. Yet the Frenchwomen were still determined to resist the Germans, and wherever possible they would tamper with the tiny sub-components of the BMW engines. Their aim was to ensure that no faults would be picked up in the quality-control inspections, but that the sabotage would eventually cause the aircraft engines to fail.

Jacqueline Marié, who joined the Resistance as a teenager, had been deported to Ravensbrück with her mother Marceline on the same train as Catherine Dior. They, too, were sent to Torgau, and onwards to Abteroda, where they endured sub-zero temperatures. In her memoir, Jacqueline recalled a night when they were forced to walk for a mile through the snow and ice to a nearby prisoner-of-war camp, in order to have a shower. There they stood naked and freezing for several hours after washing, before their filthy clothes were returned to them.

Despite these wretched circumstances, on Christmas Eve they found a way of marking the occasion. Jacqueline described how some of her French companions, including a young milliner, 'managed to put together a nativity scene with pieces of fabric, bits of straw, paper and cardboard brought from the factory (which was completely forbidden and punishable). From the fingers of our friends came the most moving of all nativity scenes . . . Holding each other tightly, believers and non-believers, we spoke the words of Mass . . .' On New Year's Day 1945, she continued, 'the factory machinery wouldn't start, and we were

Hungarian Jewish women selected for forced labour at Auschwitz, after their heads had been shaved. This group was sent to the sub-camp at Markkleeberg, where they worked alongside the French contingent including Catherine Dior.

plunged into darkness. We were so cold: it was minus 20 degrees outside; the snow covered everything around us.' Jacqueline, who had turned twenty-one the previous month, was increasingly alarmed by the sight of her mother's emaciation. Although there were no mirrors, each of the women could recognise their own physical deterioration reflected in the gaunt faces and skeletal bodies of their friends.

As the war progressed and the Allies intensified their bombing campaign against Germany, the Frenchwomen were transferred in two groups to another satellite camp, this one in Markkleeberg, near Leipzig. Once again, they made the slow journey over several days by rail, without any food or water. Records show that Catherine Dior travelled in the second group, arriving at her new destination in the last week of February 1945.

★

I am on the verge of arguing with my husband about the shortcomings of his satnav system, as we struggle to locate the site of the camp in the small town of Markkleeberg, when we see three young girls on their bicycles. They smile at us, and my husband, who speaks German, asks if they know where the camp might be. Two of them shake their heads, but one – whose name is Anastasia – says that she does, because her teacher told her about it at school. She leads us down a quiet residential street to a modern industrial estate, next to a railway line. There Anastasia points to an inconspicuous memorial plaque, set on a brick wall, with a rose bush planted beneath it.

The text on the stone is in German, and my husband translates it for me: 'From 31 August 1944 until 13 April 1945, here at Wolfswinkel was a sub-camp of the Buchenwald concentration camp, in which more than one thousand Hungarian Jewish women and 250 captured women of the French Resistance were imprisoned. These inmates were obliged to do forced labour, under inhuman conditions, and began their Death March from here. We honour the memory of these women who are victims of

Nazism.' Two wilted yellow roses lie on the ground in front of the stone, crossed over, as if in a mark of respect. Their petals are frozen, and I shiver as I reach out to touch them, in the wintery rain.

Before coming to Markkleeberg, I had learnt something of the camp's history, thanks to one of its former prisoners: Zahava Szász Stessel, who worked there as a slave at the age of fourteen, along with her thirteen-year-old sister Erzsike. The two girls were the only survivors of a Hungarian Jewish family; their parents and grandparents were gassed at Auschwitz in May 1944. But the sisters had been pulled out of the line for the gas chambers by the notorious Dr Mengele, who believed they were twins, and therefore potentially suitable for his medical experiments. Astonishingly, they survived Auschwitz, then Bergen-Belsen, and were transferred to Markkleeberg in December 1944 to work in the Junkers aircraft-engine factory. After the war, Zahava married another Holocaust survivor, emigrated with her husband to America, raised a family, trained as a librarian and completed a doctorate. After retiring from her job at the New York Public Library, she researched the previously unknown history of the Markkleeberg camp, and published an impressive book about it called *Snow Flowers*. I'd read the book, and contacted her; we talked for a long time on the phone, and then I went to meet her at her home in New York in September 2018.

Zahava has lived alone ever since the death of her husband in 2015; pictures of the two of them, and their children and grandchildren, decorate the house, alongside an abundance of potted plants and vases of flowers. We sit in the kitchen together, and she urges me to eat the generous array of biscuits that she has laid out on the table. Now in her eighties, she is still very elegant: graceful in a tailored dress, and perfectly groomed, her nails polished, her silver hair waved in a smooth coif. Her voice is gentle, her gaze steady, her memories vivid. She tells me about the surprise she felt at seeing the Frenchwomen in the camp, particularly when she discovered that some would choose to apply a precious ration of margarine to their faces, rather than eat it. 'They wanted to be pretty;

they rubbed the margarine on their face – it was so important to them to be pretty. We were amazed . . .' It is possible that their motives for doing so were those of self-defence, for if they looked healthy, they were less likely to be selected for extermination. Yet Zahava also remembers that the French group somehow managed to appear chic, even in their prison uniforms: 'To cover their shaved heads, they unravelled part of their mattresses and, from the threads, they knitted turbans.' At night, she and her sister would hear them singing *La Marseillaise*, and during the day 'they showed us the V sign for victory.' She was well aware of the risks that the French prisoners were running in their continuing attempts to sabotage the components of the aircraft engines they were supposed to be manufacturing. And when we talk about Catherine Dior, Zahava says: 'She didn't want to be pitied. She was the captain of her own soul . . .'

Despite the impression of strength and style that the Frenchwomen gave to Zahava, their own accounts suggest that they were beset with growing despair. Aside from the long hours in the factory, some of them were assigned to work outdoors. Jacqueline Marié recalled the gruelling shifts she spent in a quarry, extracting stones from the frozen ground, or being hitched to a huge roller, pulling it along roads, or unloading coal from wagons. 'At the camp, various chores awaited us, the worst being emptying the cesspits by bailing them out with buckets. We were mere ghosts of women, and so ugly. In the evening, after roll call, we collapsed onto our mattresses without undressing. In the early morning, everything started again . . .'

As at Ravensbrück, malnutrition and disease were endemic: typhus, typhoid, dysentery and tuberculosis were commonplace, and the women were also at risk of diphtheria, pneumonia and meningitis. Eileen Nearne's memories of Markkleeberg, shared with her biographer Susan Ottaway, were of 'wandering around as if drugged'. By this point, Eileen was suffering from dysentery and a severe chest infection, and yet she retained a faith in God and a determination to stay alive. 'The most important thing was the will to carry on . . .'

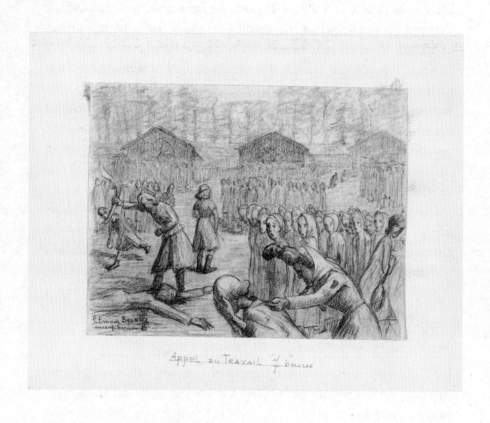

Suzanne Emmer-Besniée, *L'Appel du travail* ('The call to work').

Corvée de réfection des chaussées

Suzanne Emmer-Besniée, *Corvée de réfection des chaussées* ('Road repair work').

For Catherine Dior, her focus was on a single fierce desire: to return to the family home she had left in Provence, and see the sunrise and sunset in her own beloved country again. This, she subsequently told a friend, on one of the rare occasions she referred to her imprisonment, was what sustained her through those terrible days at the camp. And as the skies above Leipzig were filled with the fires and smoke of Allied bombing raids, Catherine and her comrades clung to the belief that the war was finally coming to an end.

★

On 11 April 1945, the US army entered Buchenwald, and Allied forces were approaching Leipzig. Yet it was not until the morning of Friday 13th that the SS officers at Markkleeberg received orders to evacuate the prisoners; although in the words of Zahava Szász Stessel, 'Evacuation turned out to be a euphemism for the death march.'

For by now, the SS were forcing hundreds of thousands of concentration camp prisoners through what was left of Nazi-controlled territory, with a view to exploiting them in a last desperate effort to produce armaments, or to clear rubble in the bombed cities. Some of these journeys went on for hundreds of miles, and the death toll was immense; as always, the SS were following the orders of Heinrich Himmler, who had issued a directive that 'No prisoner must fall alive into enemy hands.' The reasoning for these chaotic evacuations was as perverse as Himmler's earlier justifications for the concentration camp system. As Professor Mary Fulbrook observes in *Reckonings*, her magisterial account of the Holocaust: 'The death marches – during which around one-third of the prisoners died, perhaps 200,000 to 250,000 – illustrate the absurdity of trying to keep alive those last few prisoners who might still be economically useful while killing those who tried to escape or dropped with fatigue. Even the character of the marches was itself just another form of extermination.' The difference with these killings was that they took place in plain sight, right across Germany, at roadsides, in villages and towns, rather than in the hidden death camps of the east.

The women and girls leaving Markkleeberg were ordered to march five abreast, and were kept in line by armed SS guards and snarling dogs. Those who were too sick to walk were carried by their friends, or pulled by them on small carts; some of the prisoners were also harnessed to a large carriage loaded with the possessions of the camp commandant and his SS subordinates. Such was the desperate exhaustion, thirst and hunger of the women that the journey took on a hallucinatory quality. Jacqueline Marié described the sense of nightmarish delirium, as they walked through the night as if in a trance, struggling not to fall unconscious to the ground. 'We were like zombies, threatened with machine-guns, guarded by ferocious SS men who were ready to fire, which they did . . .' The route was circuitous because of Allied bombing; Jacqueline remembered 'moving forward, then retreating, crossing the Elbe River several times'.

Soon their feet were bloodied from marching in badly fitting wooden clogs; yet still the beatings and shootings continued, if anyone slipped behind. On several occasions, they found themselves in the midst of Allied air raids. Zahava recalls seeing dozens of her companions wounded, and some killed, as a consequence of these attacks. 'Allied bombing that never came to destroy the railroads leading into Auschwitz reached us during the death march,' she says. 'Low-flying planes continually machine-gunned the escape route.'

Zahava and her sister were too frightened to try to escape, fearing that they would be shot by the guards, but eventually they found themselves left behind, having jumped into a ditch beside the road during an air raid. 'We were so terribly tired and weak at that point that soon we both fell asleep. When we woke up and climbed out of the ditch, we discovered that the rest of the marchers had already gone. Maybe they thought we were dead . . .' They took refuge in a small cabin in a forest, and remained there until they discovered that the war was over. The sisters were among the very few Jewish survivors who returned to their hometown in Hungary, and they waited at the local train station for weeks on end, hoping that their parents or grandparents might arrive. Finally, and reluctantly, they gave up the long vigil; and so began another arduous journey: this time to Palestine, where they found sanctuary at last.

Meanwhile, Catherine Dior, Eileen Nearne, Jacqueline Marié and her mother were among those who managed to escape from the death march. Eileen was the first to make a break for it, despite her weak and confused state, slipping away into thick woodlands beyond Markkleeberg. There, hiding in the trees, she found two young Frenchwomen whom she knew from the camp, and together they sheltered in a bombed-out house. Somehow the trio made it to a village on the outskirts of Leipzig, where they were given refuge by a Catholic priest who kept them hidden until Allied troops arrived in the area. Even then, Eileen's ordeal was not over, as the American intelligence officer who questioned her in Leipzig found her account so muddled that she was treated as a potential enemy agent. It was not until SOE was alerted to her detention by a memo forwarded from US army headquarters that she was eventually freed, and flew back to England on 23 May.

Eileen Nearne never fully recovered from the trauma of her imprisonment, and when she died alone in 2010, in her tiny flat in the seaside town of Torquay, her body lay undiscovered for some days. Her wartime past, and her various medals, came as a complete surprise to her neighbours. She had received the Croix de Guerre from the French government and the award of an MBE from the British, for which the citation referred to 'her steady courage and unfailing devotion to duty'.

Jacqueline Marié and her mother fared better, perhaps because they had shared such suffering together. They escaped from the death march with two friends and hid in a small shed in a quarry, where they were fortunate to be discovered by French prisoners of war, who helped them reach safety. Tellingly, though, when they returned home to France in early June 1945, Jacqueline sensed that the horror of the camps was 'a world incomprehensible to others . . . Like so many other deportees, we felt that we had been forgotten and that some would have preferred never to see us again.'

As for Catherine Dior, she always avoided talking to her friends and family in any detail about her time in the camps, or her final days in Germany. All they knew was that she had been liberated by Soviet troops. Her records show that she escaped from the death march on 21 April 1945 in Dresden.

Liberation by the Soviet army did not always represent the end of a prisoner's ordeal. The evidence is clear that any woman or girl who encountered the Red Army at this point ran the risk of being raped – even if she were a concentration camp survivor, and whatever her age or nationality. Historians have estimated that up to two million women were raped in Germany, although these numbers are still a matter of debate; such was the taboo on discussing the subject openly that the true figures may never be known. Jacqueline Marié spoke of her experience at the Czech border in early May, where 'some of our comrades were raped', as did Micheline Maurel, a French resistant who had survived Ravensbrück, only to witness her friends being violated by Soviet soldiers. In her memoir, Micheline wrote of how the rapes began even before liberation: she had been sleeping in a barn with three friends, and woke up to discover one of them had already been raped by a Soviet soldier, 'a big bully fellow . . . who left immediately, running across country as machine-gun bullets clipped the branches all around him.' Some of the Polish survivors known as the Ravensbrück 'rabbits', whose legs had been mutilated in medical experiments at the camp, then fell prey to Soviet rapists, while Zahava Szász Stessel knew of several Hungarian Jewish victims who did not survive the sexual assaults they had experienced. In her book she writes simply: 'Most Markkleeberg survivors will tell stories of their comrades' suffering at the hands of the Russians, but they are reluctant to talk about their own possible sexual abuse by Russian soldiers.' Thus the unimaginable horrors of the Nazi camps gave way to the death throes of the Reich, and a pitiless alternative dystopia.

When Catherine escaped into Dresden, the once beautiful city was in ruins, having been razed by Allied bombing. The main aerial raids had taken place in mid-February 1945, creating a gigantic firestorm that killed an estimated twenty-five thousand people; these were followed by smaller raids in March and April. Zahava remembers it as a scene out of hell: 'It was impossible to see where a house had been, what a street was. There were only piles of stone . . . It became impossible to walk, and we had to climb or crawl . . . Bodies were not visible, but the smell of decaying flesh filled the air.'

Dresden had turned into an ashen land of the dying and the dead; freedom brought with it the fear of violation; liberators could be abusers too. These were the dark shadows out of which Catherine Dior emerged. This was the truly terrible place that marked an ending, as well as the beginning of a new life in the aftermath of the war.

View of Dresden from the City Hall Tower, after Allied bombing raids destroyed much of the city in 1945. Photograph by Richard Peter

Catherine Dior in 1945, wearing the uniform of the
Forces Françaises Combattantes.

The Homecoming

When Catherine Dior vanished into Germany in August 1944, her family endured the agony of not knowing where she was, or whether she would ever return. And as reports about the devastating conditions in concentration camps began to surface in the early months of 1945, Hervé des Charbonneries was forced to contemplate the possibility that she had not survived. His son Hubert told a Dior archivist, 'We thought she would never come back. My father was in Paris during the Liberation, and then returned to Cannes. We still had no news of Catherine . . . The family heard nothing from her for nine months.'

Christian, meanwhile, continued to work as a designer in Paris for Lucien Lelong. When he reflected on this period in his memoir, he wrote: 'I sometimes wonder how I managed to carry on at all . . . for my sister, with whom I had shared the cares and joys of the garden at Callian, had been arrested and then deported . . . I exhausted myself in vain in trying to trace her. Work – exigent, all-absorbing work – was the only drug which enabled me to forget her . . .'

And yet Christian did not forget Catherine; nor did he give up on her, but instead came to rely on a clairvoyant in Paris named Mme Delahaye, who told him that his sister would return. Indeed, in the opening pages of his memoir, Catherine and clairvoyance are linked, when Christian acknowledges the 'good luck' that was such an important feature of his life 'and the fortune tellers who have predicted it', placing particular emphasis on the clairvoyant who 'obstinately predicted' Catherine's safe homecoming, 'even at the worst moments of our despair'.

19 avril

mon petit père,

il faut être courageux et patient. —
Combien de temps nous
faudra-t-il encore pour revoir
notre chérie. —

C'est Alix Audoynean (de Joost)
qui, sans m'en prévenir, est allée
en voiture jusqu'à Weimar pour
ramener Catherine et d'autres amis
à elle. — Elle est arrivée le
lendemain de la libération du
camp. —

De toutes les personnes qu'elle

Christian Dior's letter to his father, written on 19 April 1945, with the first news
of Catherine since her deportation to Germany.

recherchait, ce n'est que de notre chérie qu'elle a pu retrouver la trace. — Nous avons donc, relativement! de la chance.

Deux ou trois jours avant la libération du camp la moitié des déportés dont presque toutes les femmes a été expédiée vers la tchécoslovaquie. — Alice a donné le nom de Catherine sur la liste qui, par chance, en est restée au camp de Weimar.

La guerre va vite. Espérons donc que sa délivrance arrivera avant qu'elle ne soit épuisée. —

Je vous embrasse tous les deux bien bien tendrement, malgré notre espoir si déçu, il faut garder confiance. —

Vous avez dû recevoir mandat télégraphique pour mensuelle et ce que je demandais à Na pour huile charbon.

But the first real information about Catherine did not emerge until the middle of April 1945, thanks to a well-connected acquaintance named Alix Auboyneau, whose brother-in-law led the Free French naval forces, and whose husband was appointed as a diplomat by General de Gaulle. On 19 April, Christian sent a letter to his father, from his Rue Royale apartment. Maurice Dior was seventy-three years old and still living in the farmhouse in Callian, cared for by Catherine's former governess, the faithful Marthe Lefebvre. '*Mon petit papa*,' wrote Christian, 'you must be strong. How much longer must we wait until we see our darling [Catherine] again?' He goes on to explain that Alix had driven by car to Weimar, in central Germany, in search of Catherine and other friends of hers: 'She arrived the day after the liberation of the camp.' The timing and location suggests that the camp in question was Buchenwald, which was six miles to the north-west of Weimar, and liberated by US forces on 11 April. At this point Catherine was still being held eighty miles to the east, in the Buchenwald sub-camp of Markkleeberg.

Christian's letter continues: 'Of all the people that she was searching for, she could only find a trace of our darling [Catherine]. So we have – relatively – a chance. Two or three days before the liberation of the camp, the majority of the deportees, nearly all of the women, had been dispatched towards Czechoslovakia. Alix found Catherine's name on a list that, by chance, remained at the camp in Weimar.

'The war is moving fast. Let us hope that her release will come before she gives up. I send my love to both of you, and despite our dashed hopes, we must have faith . . .'

On the same day that Christian wrote to his father, and Catherine was in the final stages of the death march, Janet Flanner composed her 'Letter from Paris' for the *New Yorker*. In it, she reported the sorrow that the French felt at learning of President Roosevelt's recent death, following a brain haemorrhage at the age of sixty-three. 'The increasing malaise, now that Roosevelt must be absent from the peace, and the unexpected return last Saturday of thousands of French prisoners liberated from Germany, juxtaposed fear and happiness in a melange that Parisians will probably always remember in recalling that historic weekend . . .'

The first contingent of prisoners of war flew back in American transport planes: eight thousand men landed in Paris on 14 April. Flanner described them as looking thin and weary; but it was the appearance of three hundred women the next day that truly shocked her. They came from Ravensbrück (which had not yet been liberated, but the Swedish Red Cross had succeeded in negotiating their early release in exchange for Germans held in France). Their stricken faces and broken bodies were the visceral proof of the atrocities they had endured. 'They arrived at the Gare de Lyon at eleven in the morning and were met by a nearly speechless crowd ready with welcoming bouquets of lilacs and other spring flowers, and by General de Gaulle, who wept . . . There was a general, anguished babble of search, of finding or not finding. There was almost no joy; the emotion penetrated beyond that, to something nearer pain. Too much suffering lay behind this homecoming . . .'

Of this group of three hundred women, eleven had died on the journey back to France. One of the survivors, wrote Flanner, 'six years ago renowned in Paris for her elegance, had become a bent, dazed, shabby old woman. When her smartly attired brother, who met her, said, like an automaton, "Where is your luggage?", she silently handed him what looked like a dirty black sweater fastened with safety pins around whatever small belongings were rolled inside. In a way, all the women looked alike: their faces were gray-green, with reddish-brown circles around their eyes, which seemed to see but not to take in. They were dressed like scarecrows, in what had been given them at camp, clothes taken from the dead of all nationalities. As the lilacs fell from inert hands, the flowers made a purple carpet on the platform and the perfume of the trampled flowers mixed with the stench of illness and dirt.'

In the following weeks, more women returned from Germany, all of them bearing physical scars and psychological wounds. Catherine Dior was among those who arrived in Paris at the end of May 1945; her brother

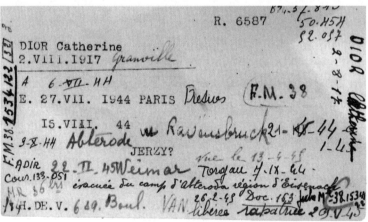

Top: General de Gaulle welcoming the first group of Ravensbrück survivors,
who returned by train to Paris in April 1945.
Above: Catherine Dior's official record of imprisonment and deportation.

Christian met her at the train station, but such was her emaciation that he did not recognise her at first. He took her back to his apartment at Rue Royale, where he had lovingly prepared a celebratory dinner for her, but she was too sick to eat it. On 29 May, their father and Marthe Lefebvre both wrote to Catherine from Callian, rejoicing at her safe return. The two letters survive in the Dior archives as memorable testaments to the power of faith and unwavering love. Marthe declared that she had prayed to St Theresa every day to protect her beloved Catherine: 'we have never prayed in vain. I look forward to the great day when I shall see you again, I kiss you with all my heart, how I love you. Please share this with dear Christian, who must be delighted.' Maurice Dior expressed himself with similarly devout emotion: 'My much loved darling Catherine, words fail me in expressing the immense and tender joy that I feel upon hearing of your resurrection. Knowing your courage, your bravery and your abnegation, I have never despaired, but I was distraught at the thought of the horrors you were suffering, and the implacable silence that surrounded your path of the Cross.'

Rereading Maurice Dior's letter to his daughter, as I have done many times, it seems to express the profound difficulties faced by families who were overjoyed by the return of their loved ones from Germany, yet could never fully comprehend the indescribable truth of the death camps. The challenge of giving voice to unspeakable experiences is also evident in Janet Flanner's second report for the *New Yorker*, dated 27 April, describing her encounter with one of the French survivors of Ravensbrück, a twenty-five-year-old resistant to whom she gave the pseudonym Colette. 'Her sorrowing blue eyes looked like the eyes of someone who has almost died . . . Her mind seemed quiet and clear. Her only trouble was loss of memory, which embarrassed her; she had suffered intermittent amnesia because she had been starved. She had lived through constant and humiliating horrors, some of which "*on ne peut pas nommer*."' Although there were nameless things too terrible to recount, Colette did speak to Flanner about the prisoners who had not yet been liberated from the camp, and those who would never return: 'Thousands of women dwelt and died at Ravensbrück, in terror, confusion, pain, and despair . . . Neither she nor any of the other women could forget what they had learned by heart and in body. On their minds, and in their memories, were the thirty thousand other women still in Ravensbrück.'

Denise Dufournier, who was in the first group of three hundred French-women to be freed from Ravensbrück, subsequently described her memory of the experience in an interview that appears in Anton Gill's book, *The Journey Back from Hell*. She was dressed in 'a silk black evening dress, deeply décolletée', that had been randomly allocated to her from the camp storeroom (a vast depository for the belongings of Holocaust victims) to wear on her journey home. 'It didn't strike me as anything other than a little odd at the time, but of course it was surreal. The surreal had become the normal for us – and maybe for the SS, too. None of us lived in the real world, but now it looked as if we might at last really be going back to it.'

Yet Denise's long-awaited return to Paris did not, and perhaps never could, live up to her expectations: 'leaving the train very quickly became a horrible, sad experience, because there were thousands of people there, and they were asking us for news of their loved ones, many of whom we didn't know, but also there were many whom we knew to be dead.' Her brother was waiting at the station to meet her: 'I was in a filthy temper. I think it was because I was so ill. My brother was certainly shocked when he saw me – he knew I'd been a prisoner, but he had no conception of how we'd been treated.' Denise remembered that several relatives subsequently asked her 'the most ridiculous questions, in ignorance', although she acknowledged that it was difficult for them to even begin to imagine the terrors of a concentration camp. She was aware, too, that her homecoming was less traumatic than those of many others: 'A friend discovered that the Nazis had shot her little sister in the street one day during the war. People returned to find that their whole families had died in air-raids; such discoveries, on top of what they'd been through, was too much to bear . . .'

Callian 29/5/45

Ma *bien* aimée Catherine Chérie,

Les mots me manquent pour t'exprimer la joie immense et si *pure* que je ressens en apprenant ta résurrection. Connaissant ton courage, ta vaillance, ton abnégation, je n'ai jamais désespéré, mais j'étais déchiré à la pensée des tourmens que tu subissais et un silence implacable entourait ils *montée* de ton calvaire.

Comment ta santé

a-t-elle pu supporter tant de choses, n'est-elle pas trop atteinte?

Les *Fromelin*, nombre de fois, lundi, merc. sont venus aux informations et la majorité du village se sont bien intéressés à ton malheureux sort.

Quand il te sera possible ton Papa sera bien heureux en te pressant sur son coeur.

Mes plus grandes affections aussi à Christian de votre

Dior

Maurice Dior's letter to Catherine, rejoicing at her safe return on 29 May 1945.

Another of the French survivors, Micheline Maurel, wrote a powerful testimony about her return home to Toulon, and the vast gulf that she felt separated her from people who had not experienced the Nazi camps, nor witnessed the mass rapes by the Soviet troops. 'The neighbours came from all over to meet the "deportee". I was the centre of attraction. Cousins came from afar to visit me. At first I was very excited, I greeted everyone, I answered all the questions. Then I became so exasperated that I shut myself in my room and refused to see anyone.'

The curiosity she encountered suggests that by this point, despite the taboo on discussing sexual violence, Micheline's family was aware of the possibility that it might have occurred. 'The questions I was asked were always the same: "Tell me, were you raped?" (This was the one question that was most frequently asked . . .) "Did you suffer much? Were you beaten? Were you tortured? What did they beat you with? Were you sterilised? And the Russians, were they so awful? Do you mean to tell me you had no other clothing? . . . And just how did you manage to survive?"' Micheline eventually asked herself an even more searching question. 'Officially, it is true, I did return. But in a real sense, was it I who came back home?' Her mother later observed that what had most disturbed her, more so than Micheline's gauntness, was the 'crazed look' in her eyes, while one of her brothers noticed that she appeared not to understand what people were saying.

For Micheline, as for so many other survivors, the camp could not be left behind in Germany, and the past still possessed her. 'For a long time the concentration camp had a reality more true and more definite than the world I was in. I was haunted, and sometimes I still am, by the faces . . . hundreds and thousands of faces, thin, twisted in pain, green with cold, full of hopelessness . . . I still instinctively feared a threatened blow, so that if someone moved too fast in my direction or brushed past me, I involuntarily winced and stiffened.' If she heard loud voices from the street or in an adjoining house, she thought they were speaking German, ordering her to run to roll call, shouting, *'Schnell, schnell!'*

Micheline also suffered the heartbreak of discovering that during her imprisonment, 'the man I loved had found another woman.' And, again like other returning deportees, she faced the further ordeal of telling families that their mothers, sisters, wives and daughters had died in Germany. 'I had not the right to feel unhappy,' she wrote, yet confessed that happiness eluded her, whenever she remembered the dead, and felt herself to be a ghost of the woman she once was.

Virginia d'Albert-Lake arrived in Paris on 27 May 1945, and described her own 'troubled state of mind' in her journal. This was not only because of her 'extreme physical weakness' (she weighed seventy-six pounds when she left Germany, having lost fifty pounds during her time in the camps, and now looked like a frail, elderly woman), but also because of her increasing ambivalence on the journey home. 'I had never experienced such joyful anticipation, but the joy was mingled with fear, fear of the unknown awaiting me . . . What had become of those I loved; my husband, my family, during this long year of unbroken silence?' As it turned out, her husband Philippe had survived, and was a member of the Free French, but her mother had died in America in April 1945, having desperately sought to discover the whereabouts of her daughter. Thus Virginia's reunion with her husband was darkened by the knowledge that her beloved mother had 'experienced only pain and anguish during those last days, and never knew that her efforts had not been in vain.' She was also haunted by the memory of her comrades who did not return: 'Of our group of 250 women, only twenty-five of us are living today. Some were shot, others were gassed . . . However, the majority died of cold and starvation. Of the twenty-five who returned, nearly all are suffering from tuberculosis, heart trouble, or some other physical or mental disorder resulting from the privations they endured. Many have lost all their material possessions or have come back to find their homes completely broken by deportation and death.'

Having battled to survive the camps, the returning women now had to adapt to a new way of life in France; a homeland they had fought for in the

Resistance, but which no longer looked or felt quite the same as before. And their presence was a painful reminder of the price that had been paid for victory, as Janet Flanner captured in her report on the shadow cast over the VE Day celebrations in Paris: 'France and the rest of Europe are tired to death of death, and of destruction. Much of the comfort which should have arrived automatically with the peace has been lost in the news of the German concentration camps . . . The stench of human wreckage in which the Nazi regime finally sank down to defeat has been the most shocking fact of modern times.' And however much France might have wanted to move on from the shame and humiliation of collaboration with the Germans, the deportees were visible evidence of the crimes that had been committed during the years of Occupation. 'The Nazi program of non-military destruction has not been affected by the peace,' Flanner concluded; 'it is still continuing in the bodies of the camp prisoners now home but still sick or still crazy or still mutilated or still stone-deaf from blows on the head or still malodorous with running sores.'

In a dark twist of irony, several of the returning women were at first mistaken for *femmes tondues* – those who had been punished for their sexual relationships with Germans by having their heads shaved during the *épuration sauvage*, the unofficial 'wild purge' that took place after the Liberation. One of these was Simone Rohner, a resistant who had been imprisoned in Ravensbrück, and wrote about her experience soon after arriving in France: 'Civilians looked at us with an air of disgust; some insults were flung at us . . .'

Along with the majority of the deportees, Simone was sent to the Lutetia, a grand hotel on the Left Bank that had been requisitioned by the Abwehr during the Occupation; it was now an official repatriation centre, where families and friends attempted to trace missing deportees. Simone described the crushing sense of unexpected sadness she felt when entering the Lutetia, making her way through crowds of people, desperately hoping to find their lost relatives: 'this was not what I had dreamed of . . . Life weighed on me. All joy was gone from my heart.' Similarly,

Jacqueline Marié, who had endured the same series of slave labour camps as Catherine, found the experience overwhelming: 'I have bad memories of the Lutetia which have stayed with me ever since – a kind of noisy hive where we were questioned for hours. We were so tired and anxious . . . the hubbub was intolerable, and we felt like we were on another planet.'

Meanwhile, Philippe de Rothschild was one of those who went to the Lutetia in search of information; he was still trying to find his wife Elisabeth, who had been deported to Germany on the last train out of Paris, alongside Catherine Dior and so many others. In his memoir, he wrote: 'A group of French women had just arrived, not long out of Ravensbrück. They looked as if they had just risen from the grave. Among them one recognised me. I looked again. It was Tania, Comtesse de Fleurieu, a brave woman in the Resistance. She had been very lovely but now all her teeth were smashed. They had beaten her across the mouth. She knew about Lili [Elisabeth], she had been there, in the same hut. Beaten, degraded, and too broken to move, Lili had been dragged from her plank bed by the hair of her head and thrown into the oven alive. She died because she had borne my name, there was no doubt about that . . . Poor pretty woman, until they came for her that morning her life had been so easy, all silk and roses.'

★

The Dior archives contain two pictures of Catherine that were taken after her return to France in 1945. In the first, more formal portrait, she is wearing two of her medals, presented in recognition of her outstanding courage and service. Catherine received some of the most prestigious national decorations: from France, a Croix de Guerre and the Croix du Combattant Volontaire de la Résistance; the Polish Cross of Valour; and the King's Medal for Courage in the Cause of Freedom, awarded by the British authorities. The citation for the Croix de Guerre, dated 10 November 1945, referred to her courage in volunteering for 'all the perilous missions', her exemplary 'prudence, sang-froid and decisiveness', her silence when subjected to 'the most particularly odious tortures', and her 'great valour and admirable spirit during her deportation to Germany'. In this photograph, Catherine's hair has grown back, but it is still much shorter than before the war. Her lips are sealed tight and down-turned; her dark eyes seem to meet mine, and the haunted look on her face is indescribably sad.

In the second picture, perhaps taken by her father, Catherine is framed in front of a doorway into Les Naÿssès, the family home in Provence. Her brother Christian and her lover Hervé des Charbonneries are on either side of her; Marthe is next to Christian. All four are very close, their arms linked together, but it is hard to interpret Catherine's faraway expression. It is as if she is gazing beyond the camera, and in this instant she looks older than her age (she was still only twenty-seven when she returned from Germany). And yet there she stands, flanked by two of the men who loved her, who waited for her and would cherish her forever.

Hervé's son Hubert, who was eight years old in 1945, recalled his father telling him that Catherine was unrecognisable when she first returned to Callian; another of his relatives said to me, simply, that Hervé wept when he told her about their reunion. Much to her family's relief, Catherine began to recover during the course of the summer at Les Naÿssès; on 1 July, in a letter to an organisation concerned with the welfare of deportees, she wrote that she was 'currently convalescing in Provence. I am benefiting from the sun and the calm of this beautiful region.'

By the autumn of 1945, Catherine was well enough to return to Paris with Hervé, and the couple moved into Christian's apartment at Rue Royale. Both needed to earn a living, and when Catherine was awarded a licence to trade in cut flowers, they began working together. The couple sold fresh flowers grown in Provence to florists in Paris, including the legendary Lachaume, founded in the nineteenth century and favoured by the leading couture houses. They also exported them to French colonies, even as far as Indochina. Hubert, who as a child developed a strong and

Hervé des Charbonneries, Catherine, Christian and Marthe Lefebvre
at Callian in 1945, after Catherine's return from Germany.

loving relationship with Catherine, remembered that she would rise at four o'clock every morning, without complaint, to go to the flower market at Les Halles. He also recalled the significance of 1 May, the day that lily of the valley is traditionally given in France as a symbol of good luck, when each year Catherine and Hervé would send great quantities of the delicate flowers to clients around the world.

The stoicism that Catherine displayed at work and her commitment to rebuilding her life become all the more evident in the context of her medical records, which form part of the official archives relating to the returned deportees. These note that she was still suffering from agonising injuries to her hips, back and feet, attributable to the months of slave labour as well as the death march, and from chronic arthritis, rheumatism and kidney problems. Catherine's psychological symptoms were equally severe: she battled with insomnia, nightmares, memory loss, anxiety and depression. Her dossier also reveals that she developed a need for 'isolation'; in common with many other survivors, she retreated into silence, rather than discussing her history of torture and the suffering she had experienced in the camps.

Catherine's silence was perhaps symptomatic of a more widespread reticence on the subject of the deportations. Soon after General de Gaulle's provisional government was established in Paris, Henri Frenay, who had been appointed the head of the Ministry for Prisoners, Deportees and Refugees, and charged with overseeing their return to France, issued a decree banning dissemination of information about the deportees, citing the unnecessary anxiety that it would cause for families. And while the heroism of the Resistance had been celebrated in the immediate aftermath of the Liberation, the stories of a relatively small number of courageous individuals swiftly evolved into a communal narrative of epic national achievement. For de Gaulle perceived that in order to try and unite France, it would be necessary to move on from the divisions between collaborators and their victims. Hence his famous victory speech, delivered when he entered the capital on 25 August 1944: 'Paris!

Paris outraged! Paris broken! Paris martyred! But Paris liberated! Liberated by itself, liberated by its people with the help of the French armies, with the support and the help of all France, of the France that fights, of the only France, of the real France, of the eternal France!'

De Gaulle's call for unity did not prevent spontaneous punishment from being meted out to collaborators: not only the shaving of women's heads and the daubing of swastikas on their faces, but also summary executions. Malcolm Muggeridge, who worked for British intelligence during the war, landed in France on 12 August 1944 and reached Paris at the same time as de Gaulle. His memoir provides a graphic account of the atmosphere in the city in the immediate aftermath of the Liberation. 'Paris was in a virtual state of breakdown, without organs of authority or law . . . By day, it was not so noticeable, though even then in places like the Palais de Justice and the prisons, which I had occasion to visit, there was total confusion; the judges having mostly disappeared or been arrested themselves, and the prisons being glutted with alleged *collaborateurs*, brought along by no one knew who, and charged with no one knew what. It was when darkness began to fall that one became aware of the breakdown; with no street-lighting, and the tall houses all silent and locked and boarded up, like sightless eyes. Inside them I imagined cowering figures, hopeful of surviving if they remained perfectly still and hidden. Then, as night came on, sounds of scurrying feet, sudden cries, shots, shrieks, but no one available, or caring, to investigate. It is unknown to this day how many were shot down, had their heads shaved, piteously disgorged their possessions in return for being released, but certainly many, many thousands . . .'

Muggeridge also witnessed for himself how some former collaborators were adept at switching sides and claiming to have been loyal to de Gaulle, as members of the Forces Françaises de l'Intérieur (FFI). He observed one such group at close quarters, having first met them at an Armistice Day parade at the Arc de Triomphe, where Churchill and de Gaulle laid wreaths on the Tomb of the Unknown Soldier. The

FFI band, whose leader was later discovered to have a collaboration-ist record, invited Muggeridge to their palatial headquarters on Avenue Foch, which bears a striking similarity to the apartment recently vacated by Friedrich Berger and his gang at Rue de la Pompe: it was 'formerly occupied by the Gestapo; large and elegantly furnished, well-stocked with champagne'. And the group itself sounds reminiscent of Berger's associates: 'They were a mixed lot who had come together by chance; the leader, I was told, an actor of sorts, and certainly given to striking attitudes – for instance, one arm in a sling, and flourishing a revolver with the other. His second-in-command was, I should say, an Algerian; rather vicious-looking, and probably a figure from the underworld . . . There was also a girl named Chantal; pretty, but ravaged-looking, in a khaki drill skirt and tunic, and wearing a cartridge belt.'

There were other parallels with Berger's gang, for the members appeared to regard looting as their right. 'They certainly took things from people – cigarette cases, jewels, money,' wrote Muggeridge. 'Equally certainly, they were given assignments; to go to such a house, conduct a search, interrogate such a person, make an arrest, and even – as they boasted, but I never saw them do it – carry out an execution. If a door was not opened to them, they would batter it down; everyone cowered before them, and did what they were told. Considering their youth, they behaved with horrifying callousness, arrogance, and brutality . . .'

Muggeridge's memoir also contains a telling account of his meeting with Henri Lafont, who like Friedrich Berger had combined a thriv-ing black-market operation with his activities on behalf of the Gestapo during the Occupation. Unlike Berger, who fled Paris before he could be arrested (and continued to extort, plunder, torture and murder as he made his way through eastern France to Germany in the autumn of 1944), Lafont had been captured five days after the Liberation of Paris.

Women in Chartres whose heads were shaved ('femmes tondues')
as punishment for collaboration with the Germans. Photograph by Robert Capa

By the time Muggeridge interviewed him, the notorious French gangster and *gestapiste* was already in the hands of the police and awaiting trial, but appeared intent on persuading the Allied Command – preferably General Eisenhower – to intervene personally in his case. Lafont told Muggeridge 'how he had hidden RAF pilots who had bailed out over France, and helped them to escape to Spain. This had become almost a routine reaction by now; I scarcely ever met a Frenchman who had not, at some point or another in the war, had at least one RAF pilot hidden in his attic. If there had been as many RAF pilots as these revelations would seem to suggest, I often reflected, our Air Force would have been so huge that we should have won the war almost before it began.'

Needless to say, the British did not intercede in Lafont's case; he was tried and found guilty by a court in Paris, and on 26 December 1944 was executed by a firing squad alongside his former right-hand man, the corrupt police inspector Pierre Bonny. 'The memory of my macabre encounter with him continued to haunt me,' wrote Muggeridge of Lafont; 'not because I had any particular pity for his plight, or sense of horror at what he had done. Rather, at the thought of that ego of his, lifting up its head, and darting out its cobra tongue; that vanity emerging, inviolate, fresh and new as a Pharaoh's treasure after centuries in a dark tomb . . .'

Several other high-profile trials followed those of Lafont and Bonny – most notably the leaders of the Vichy regime, Philippe Pétain and Pierre Laval. The marshal's ignominious exile to Sigmaringen Castle in Germany ended just before Hitler's suicide on 30 April 1945. His trial for treason began on 23 July at the Palais de Justice in Paris, and ended with him being convicted and sentenced to death on 15 August. Janet Flanner reported on the proceedings for the *New Yorker*: 'From the very first day of the trial, Pétain's haughty opening declaration that he would not deign to talk and that the special high court lacked authority to try him . . . told against him. The last straw was the Marshal's strange insistence that he, too, had been among "the first of the resistants," for, he asked, had he not held France for de Gaulle to recover, and what recovery could the General have effected for a France in ruins wrought by lack of German collaboration?' Flanner noted, too, that Pétain's letters to Hitler proved seriously damaging to his defence. On the anniversary of his now infamous meeting with the Führer at Montoire, where they determined the policy of collaboration, the marshal wrote to Hitler: 'France preserves the memory of your noble gesture.' And after an ill-fated Anglo-Canadian raid on Dieppe, in August 1942 (when nearly four thousand Allied troops were killed, wounded or taken prisoner by the Germans), Pétain wrote again to Hitler, thanking him 'for having cleansed French soil'.

The death sentence was commuted to life imprisonment by de Gaulle, due to Pétain's age (he was now eighty-nine), and he was sent first to Fort du Portalet in the Pyrenees, then transferred to another fort on the Île-d'Yeu, a small island off the French Atlantic coast. Having lapsed into senility, Pétain died in 1951 at the age of ninety-five and was buried on the island, thereby denied his wish to be interred among the fallen of Verdun.

Next came the trial of Pierre Laval; like Pétain, he had been exiled to Sigmaringen in Germany, although with the approach of the Allied forces, he escaped the final collapse of Germany by fleeing to Barcelona in a Junkers aircraft, complete with Nazi markings. Laval had hoped for political asylum in Spain, but was eventually taken into custody by the US army, handed over to the French authorities on 31 July 1945, and transferred to Fresnes prison.

By this point, the notorious prison that had previously been filled with members of the Resistance such as Catherine Dior was overflowing with alleged collaborators. Malcolm Muggeridge made a number of visits there, to attempt to unravel the claims of purported double agents. The new set of prisoners were 'an extraordinary collection', he remarked, of formerly eminent politicians, senior civil servants, military officers, diplomats, writers and journalists, alongside 'riff-raff from the streets accused of having been informers, agent-provocateurs or pimps for the Germans. They were all packed tight, five or six to a cell originally intended to accommodate a single prisoner. It was a kind of Beggar's Opera scene, in which it was difficult to distinguish between some immensely distinguished admiral or general, dishevelled, but still wearing his uniform and decorations, and rogues of the Lafont type; between some famous actress from the Comédie-Française and prostitutes who had found a lucrative clientele among German officers and other ranks. The only faces that were vaguely familiar to me were the politicians, and they mostly managed to get transferred to the infirmary, where one caught an occasional glimpse of them, seated with blankets around their shoulders like stalactites, and treated now with some degree of deference by the warders, even called M. le President again, as being on their way back to freedom and their former status.'

Yet Laval was not among those who evaded justice, despite the spirited defence he conducted for himself at his trial, which began on 4 October 1945. Laval's arguments were similar to those that Muggeridge heard from less senior figures at Fresnes: that he had played a double game, to deceive Germany and protect France. These statements enraged many in the Palais de Justice, including members of the jury, who hurled insults and threats at Laval, and the trial degenerated into a series of passionate denunciations and vociferous outbursts. Janet Flanner reported on the chaotic scenes in court: 'Judges, juries, lawyers, deputies, prosecution, a youthful visitor or two in the little gallery, and, above all, the accused himself, hemmed in in his narrow aisle on the crowded floor, all shouted as they undoubtedly never had before in public. It was probably sheer hatred of Laval, the physical as well as the symbolic *summum malum* of France's occupation, collaboration, and shame, that loosed the outcries against him. And there was something left in Laval that made him scream back. Physically and mentally, he completely dominated the court . . . When he started to talk, he was like quicksilver: no one could control him; his phrases, flashy or weighty, rolled in all directions through the court, separating, then coagulating, but always slipping through the fingers . . .'

In the end, after a trial that lasted less than a week and was regarded by his supporters as a travesty of justice, Laval was found guilty and sentenced to death. De Gaulle refused pleas for a retrial or an appeal, and the execution was set to take place at Fresnes on 15 October. Early that morning, Laval (who was by then suffering from cancer) attempted to kill himself with a cyanide pill that he had kept concealed inside the lining of his jacket. The poison did not kill him, however, and his stomach was pumped, reviving him sufficiently to be carried out and strapped to a chair for his official execution by a military firing squad.

Following the trials of Pétain and Laval, and that of the former head of the Milice, Joseph Darnand, public appetite for prosecutions of high-profile collaborators began to wane. The purge had not yet come to an end – eight hundred death sentences were carried out in the post-war period – but there seemed to be a growing sense of weariness with the process. After all, France was being encouraged to rebuild in unity, and the first democratic elections to the National Assembly, which would draft a constitution for the new Republic, took place towards the end of October 1945.

Philippe de Rothschild confirmed in his memoir that the angry cries for revenge were gradually silenced. After discovering the appalling circumstances of his wife's death in Ravensbrück, and that of his maternal aunt in the gas chambers of Auschwitz, de Rothschild had good reason to want to see justice done. He had also discovered, on his return to Paris with the Allied forces, that his home had been confiscated during the Occupation, and the locks changed. 'When the door was opened, who should be standing there, wearing my dressing-gown, but Henri Lillaz, a Cabinet Minister before the war, and a renowned collaborator.' De Rothschild ordered him to leave the house, but made the mistake of granting Lillaz a few days' grace: 'no sooner was my back turned than he brought a van and took away every stick of furniture I possessed, stripped the place down to the floorboards – he even took my night-shirts. Such games were all the rage just then: collabos playing hide and seek, skipping, fiddling, forging . . .'

Little wonder, he continued, that on VE Day in Paris, peace could not be celebrated, when 'the French were tearing each other's hearts out'. But even de Rothschild became disenchanted with the inconsistency of the legal attempts to impose justice. 'Many were let off, many had run off, others were kept locked up . . . Later, as the storm died down, de Gaulle started handing out pardons. That was when people like Paul Morand [the Vichy diplomat and writer] came drifting back, without having changed their opinions one iota.' As for de Rothschild himself, 'I couldn't sustain the loathing I had felt for the criminals,' he admitted. 'Angry feelings soon died in me. It's not that I'm a pacifist, far from it, but of what use is revenge? Shooting a man against a prison wall will not bring his victims back to life. But, of course, I was one of the lucky ones – I had escaped. Those of us who had been exiles were almost the only ones above suspicion, apart from the dead . . .'

★

Yet what of the exiles who had returned from the dead, such as Cath-erine Dior, and the ghosts of those who had died for the Resistance? Of the three hundred people arrested by Friedrich Berger and his gang, for example, more than half were deported to Germany, and 110 victims were known to have died. However, Irène Lewulis, the Polish resistant who was brutally tortured and sexually assaulted at Rue de la Pompe, had been left behind in a prison hospital when the Germans fled Paris, and was liberated by the Red Cross on 17 August 1944. Despite her griev-ous injuries, she was able to provide a damning witness statement just a month later before a judge at the Palais de Justice.

In time, the investigation into the various activities of the Rue de la Pompe Gestapo was assumed by the French military judiciary, and led by a dogged magistrate called Captain Mercier. Slowly, quietly, method-ically, Mercier's team began to track down other witnesses, including Catherine Dior, who gave her first substantive statement on 18 October 1945. She had no difficulty in identifying Berger and other key members of his gang from photographs, including his mistress Denise Delfau, and the men who had tortured her. For Catherine could never forget them, nor what they had done to her and her valiant comrades, some of whose voices had been silenced for ever.

Palais de Glace

Catherine Dior's return to her brother's apartment on Rue Royale brought her back into the heart of the Paris fashion district, a discrete world that had continued its activities throughout the Occupation and after Liberation. Just as Rue Royale was famed for its central position in the map of luxury landmarks – from Maxim's to Molyneux – so, too, the couture houses were part of the enchanted, intangible landscape of Paris, as they remain today. The legacy and prestige of each separate *maison* is fiercely protected from its competitors, yet together they seem to inhabit a vast and invisible glass palace, its mirrored arches stretching high above Place Vendôme and reaching along the grand boulevards, from Faubourg Saint-Honoré to Avenue Montaigne. The palace is well guarded, as are its treasures and secrets, but its gatekeeper is the Chambre Syndicale de la Haute Couture, which was established in 1868.

Surprisingly, the founding father of haute couture was an Englishman, Charles Frederick Worth. Born in Lincolnshire in 1825 and brought up in penury, he became an apprentice at a London department store and then worked for a textiles company, before moving to Paris at the age of twenty-one. There he married, set himself up as a dress designer using his beautiful wife as a model, and built a thriving business at 7 Rue de la Paix. By 1860, Worth was the chosen couturier for Empress Eugénie, the consort of Napoleon III; thanks to her patronage and the attendant publicity, the House of Worth attracted rich American clients, as well as members of the European aristocracy. When he died of pneumonia

The salon of the Worth couture house in Paris, 1910.

in 1895, his obituary in *The Times* noted, 'It is not a little singular that Worth . . . should take the lead in what is supposed to be a peculiarly French art.' Nevertheless, Paris played as great a part in Worth's fame as did his own prodigious talent and ambition. For it was Paris, rather than London, that was regarded as the capital of luxury and style, with its palaces and pavilions, theatres and opera houses, linked by the harmonious architecture of Georges-Eugène Haussmann, which Napoleon III had commissioned.

Couture houses, like all dynasties, rise and fall. Worth was eclipsed by Paul Poiret, who reigned over fashionable Paris in the early twentieth century with his theatrical Orientalism. Then Poiret sank into poverty, obscured by the legendary Coco Chanel, who swept away the furbelows and ornate embellishment of the Belle Epoque, introducing instead her alluring vision of streamlined modernity. Lucien Lelong was the same generation as Chanel, but did not achieve her global celebrity; as her own best advertisement, she embodied feminine chic in such a way that eclipsed her male contemporaries. Lelong was highly regarded, nevertheless, and possessed of a Russian princess for a wife: the glamorous Natalie Paley, who showed his clothes to perfection, at least until their divorce in 1937. He was also renowned for his unerring ability to pick talented designers to work for him, most notably Pierre Balmain and Christian Dior. And as the influential president of the Chambre Syndicale de la Haute Couture during the Second World War, Lelong was widely credited with saving the industry from being shut down by the German authorities, or forcibly moved to Berlin.

'Paris's haute couture is not transferable, either en bloc or bit by bit,' wrote Lelong in the autumn of 1940, in response to a plan that the ateliers and their highly skilled artisans should be sent to Germany. 'It exists in Paris or it does not exist at all.' Inevitably, however, his stalwart defence of couture brought him into close and regular contact with Nazi officials. When faced with the prohibition of exports from Paris, for example, Lelong decided to take a group show of twenty or so couturiers to Lyons in March

1942 (at a time when the city remained in the Unoccupied Zone, under Vichy rule). The hope was to attract buyers from the neutral territories, such as Spain and Switzerland; and in this aim, Lelong was successful. But in order to secure the necessary permission and documents to cross the demarcation line, Lelong attended a 'Round Table' lunch, one of a series of regular meetings held at the Ritz that brought together French businessmen and high-ranking German officials. After the Liberation, Lelong was accused of collaboration, as a participant in what were dubbed the 'Treason Lunches', but he was acquitted of all charges.

It might seem paradoxical that it was Lelong himself, in his role as president of the Chambre Syndicale, who called for an *épuration* commission to examine the record of the fashion industry during the Occupation. In the event, the committee investigated fifty-five cases of collaboration, none of which involved haute couture, and only the mildest of punishments, such as temporary suspensions, were imposed on those found guilty, who tended to be low-level employees. Jacques Fath, who had been a member of the Cercle Européen, the notorious club for collaborators, was not censured. Nor was his wife Geneviève, who was rumoured to have developed profitable business connections with the Germans as well as social relationships. Marcel Rochas, another member of the Cercle Européen, also avoided punishment, despite his reputation for opportunistic collaboration. One of his high-profile former clients was less fortunate: Corinne Luchaire, the young actress who had worn Rochas gowns to the most glittering Franco-German gatherings, spent several months in jail, while her father, Jean Luchaire, the head of the collaborationist press, was sentenced to death and executed in 1946.

According to the French fashion historian Dominique Veillon, the reason that couture escaped the purges unscathed was simple: at a time of economic uncertainty, when the country lay in ruins, there was 'a market to recapture, foreign currency to earn . . . In such conditions how was it possible to oust the "black sheep", those who had "compromised" themselves with the enemy but whose professional ability was undeniable?'

Outfit by Lucien Lelong. Illustration by André Delfau, 1942

Outfit by Marcel Rochas. Illustration by André Delfau, 1942

Thus it fell to Lelong, yet again, to promote the couture industry in the months after Liberation. This coincided with a bitterly cold winter, and limited supplies of rationed food, fuel and other basic commodities. The advancing Allies and retreating German armies had destroyed harbours, bridges and railways; fierce fighting continued in eastern France, while a number of key ports remained in German hands. As a consequence, there were dire shortages of all materials, including textiles for clothing and leather for shoes.

Lelong was supported in his endeavours by Carmel Snow, the redoubtable Francophile editor of *Harper's Bazaar* in New York, who was determined to return to her beloved Paris; it had been five years since her last trip, in September 1939. In her memoir she wrote that 'during the war, after France was occupied, there was a lot of loose talk to the effect that Paris was "finished" as the center of fashion. I was no more willing to concede the permanent fall of Paris than was General de Gaulle . . .' She requested a visa to travel to Paris, and was finally granted permission in December 1944. Her route was circuitous, and undertaken by air, because of the naval battle still being fought in the Atlantic: 'Instead of proceeding due east I had to fly south to Miami, thence via Trinidad and South America to West Africa, and from Dakar to Lisbon.' In Madrid, she had dinner with the revered Spanish couturier Cristóbal Balenciaga, and then set off by train to Paris. Upon arrival, she discovered that there were no taxis, because of the lack of fuel, and the only means to get about was on foot or by Métro. Snow was thrilled to be reunited with her friends, including Marie-Louise Bousquet, Christian Bérard and Janet Flanner (who also wrote for *Harper's Bazaar*), but she was appalled by the conditions in Paris: 'the old people looked shriveled and frozen and unutterably sad, with their clothes darned exquisitely and every scrap of old wool they could get on them.'

As Carmel Snow made her rounds of the jewellers and couture houses of Paris, she was struck by the lack of heat and light, even in these temples of luxury. At Cartier, she admired the beautiful creations and talked to their designer, Jeanne Toussaint, 'a remarkable woman, full of force. Around her neck were three strings of magnificent pearls; on her feet, embroidered Russian boots dating from the *ancien régime* . . . The shop was freezing, and the incongruity of looking at the most extravagant jewels in the world in an icy room can't be imagined . . . It was so cold that everyone wore gloves, and as Jeanne Toussaint said, "It's bad for us, but imagine the workmen up on the sixth floor, using their hands all day long for the finest of work."' When Snow went to Balenciaga for a long-awaited couture fitting, an apologetic seamstress kept dropping her pins, so stiff were her fingers in the arctic temperatures. 'Coal was almost non-existent, and electricity was shut off at eight-thirty in the morning,' she wrote. 'At five in the afternoon, when all the offices and shops closed because no electricity could be used in them, you could tell the time by the sudden clack-clack-clack of hundreds of wooden shoes on the streets.'

Aside from her cheerleading for the couture industry, Snow undertook an expedition beyond Paris with the great photographer Henri Cartier-Bresson, to report on the Allies' progress across France. 'There were villages we passed through where there wasn't a breath of life: houses, stables, churches blown to atoms . . . But of course it was the wounded in the hospitals that broke your heart.' She was equally moved by the experiences of several of her French peers who worked for the Paris edition of *Vogue*, which had ceased publication during the war. The editor, Michel de Brunhoff, had lost his only son, a teenager killed by the Gestapo on suspicion of being in the Resistance; so too had the fashion editor, Solange d'Ayen, whose son died in October 1944, at the age of nineteen, on his way to join the French army. Solange had endured solitary confinement in Fresnes for several months, while her resistant husband, the Duc d'Ayen, had been deported and held prisoner in a series of German concentration camps. He died at Bergen-Belsen on 14 April 1945, the day before it was liberated.

Bettina Ballard, the Paris correspondent for American *Vogue*, had left France after the outbreak of war and subsequently joined the Red Cross;

she arrived back in the city soon after Carmel Snow, and heard the same terrible stories of suffering from her former colleagues. In her autobiography, she wrote that Michel de Brunhoff had aged twenty years since they had last met, and could not comprehend the death of his son. 'He seemed completely dazed by it still, by the uselessness of it . . . He had hated this war from the first, I remembered, and now the horror of it had descended, never to leave, on his shoulders . . .' When Bettina visited Solange d'Ayen, she felt that she was 'seeing her ghost', and realised that if she tried to speak about the death of her son, 'it was a tragedy too raw for her to face.' Instead, Solange talked about the beige jersey Balenciaga dress she was wearing when she was arrested, which she washed carefully every morning in prison: 'It has been cleaned now, and still looks very well.'

At first, wrote Bettina, 'I had no desire to involve myself in *Vogue* activities in Paris, partly because fashion seemed so remote from the war.' But the presence of Carmel Snow, proclaiming her faith in French fashion, was sufficient competition to prompt her to re-establish her pre-war relationships with the couturiers, or at least those who remained in business. (There had always been a rivalry between *Harper's Bazaar* and *Vogue*, which was heightened when Snow left *Vogue* in 1933 to become editor of *Bazaar*.) Bettina's first appointment was at Balenciaga's couture house: 'His salons looked much the same, except that the white paint had yellowed and the white-satin curtains were dingy. His famous seventeenth-century Spanish chairs were still standing elegantly around the room like a group of proud Spanish grandees. The only strange note was a group of noisy, fat, fancy-hatted women with hard, vulgar voices . . . One of the women was counting out thousand-franc notes from her purse, paying cash for a dress that she was carrying away with her in a white-and-blue Balenciaga box . . . These were black market customers, Balenciaga explained to me later, apologetically . . . They would buy anything . . . and at any price, always paying cash out of bulging purses . . .' Apart from his disapproval of these customers, whom he regarded as unrefined, 'Balenciaga himself seemed very little touched by the war, or, for that matter, the Liberation . . . As always, he led his own secluded life, busying himself with the only thing that he really knew anything about – clothes.'

Bettina also met Lucien Lelong, and was genuinely impressed by his efforts as 'the go-between with the Germans whom he had persuaded to encourage the talent in the couture [houses] and to give them enough fabrics to work with on the grounds that it would be good for the morale of Paris in general'. And she endorsed an unlikely-sounding theory that was being promoted at the time, claiming that the French couturiers who sold to German customers during the Occupation had somehow tricked them into buying ridiculously lavish clothes. 'The Germans, Lucien explained, had such an inferiority complex about French fashions that almost anything could be put over on them. The more extravagant the French fashions, the more the Germans liked them.' In fact, the percentage of 'couture ration cards' that had been reserved for German clients in Paris remained very low: only two hundred, out of a total of 13,625 issued in April 1944. Thus the wealthy customers who were buying extravagant couture were far more likely to be French than German.

Before long, Bettina found herself drawn back into the customary pre-war conversations – 'about hats, about clothes, and the usual fashion-world gossip'. She visited Schiaparelli's couture salon in Place Vendôme, and discovered it 'very much in need of paint and heat', but she was delighted with her purchase of a striped turban there, 'to wear with my only black suit'. As she dashed around Paris, Bettina marvelled at the vast and complicated hats that were now in fashion; in particular a towering one that she spotted on the head of an elegant woman on the Métro, made of pink felt 'in which little birds nestled and over which there was a beautiful haze of tulle . . .'

Bettina noted, too, that Parisian society was 'antique mad, art mad, house mad. Collecting treasures had become the smart way to place their money during the war, and art and antique dealers were among the *nouveaux riches* of Paris.' Her memoir does not comment on the

Model in an outfit by Jacques Fath, Paris, 1944.
Photograph by David E. Scherman

Model wearing a hat by Legroux Sœurs, Paris, 1944.
Photograph by David E. Scherman

fact that many of these treasures would have been looted from Jewish families during the Occupation; she did nevertheless observe that 'Paris was made up of contrasts: the people who had suffered, almost beyond bearing, lost everything, even their hope, and the countless others who drifted through the war keeping their lives intact.'

After this relatively brief visit to Paris, Bettina went home to America for several months, and then returned to her job at the *Vogue* office in Paris in the summer of 1945. She moved back into her former flat, which had been inhabited during the Occupation by a German officer and his French mistress, and resumed her comfortable pre-war domestic routine. 'The same maid, Marcelle, brought my breakfast, her hair by now grown out from the shaving it had been subjected to after the Liberation to be frizzed into its habitual tight curls.' Meanwhile, the concierge, who washed Bettina's linen sheets, wore a pair of silver high-heeled sandals from first thing in the morning until last thing at night: 'The shoes were an indulgence that she permitted herself from the profits of the black-market eggs and butter smuggled in from Normandy by her old taxi-driver father.'

Yet Bettina was dismayed by the 'tired lethargy' of her colleagues at *Vogue*: 'There was no momentum; the office was like a house full of clocks that hadn't been wound.' She enjoyed the more cheerful atmosphere at Marie-Louise Bousquet's weekly salons at her home on the Place du Palais Bourbon, which had continued without interruption after the Liberation. The German guests who used to join the sociable gathering every Thursday had vanished, and were never mentioned. They were replaced by Allied war correspondents, who were amused by their hostess's repartee.

Aside from Mme Bousquet's convivial salon, Bettina observed that 'the hard core, the nugget of social life' in Paris was now centred at the British embassy, thanks to the charms of its new ambassador Duff Cooper and his stylish wife, Lady Diana Cooper, who had arrived in September 1944. 'Here was to be found the "little group", the type of inner exclusivity that Paris loved so dearly, the closed set where conversation was in a particular jargon, almost incomprehensible to the outsider.' The key members of this select circle, she reported, were Marie-Louise Bousquet, Christian Bérard, Georges Geffroy and Louise de Vilmorin, a literary femme fatale with whom Duff Cooper began an affair.

Malcolm Muggeridge, who had remained in Paris after the Liberation as an intelligence officer for MI6, found himself in a difficult position, as the guest list of those entertained at the embassy 'caused some head-shaking and eyebrow-raising' among his colleagues. In his memoir, Muggeridge wrote that the Coopers 'had raised the banner of pre-war smartness, and many flocked to it, some of whom for various reasons had been lying low since the Liberation. Every social situation produces its appropriate phraseology, and any vague – or, for that matter, actual – anxieties felt by millionaires, actors, writers, dress-designers, *vicomtesses* and others, coming into the gossip-writer's category of *tout Paris*, about their behaviour during the occupation, were described as *des ennuis*. The Duff Coopers' salon was a great place for shedding *ennuis*, and much frequented accordingly.'

One of Duff Cooper's former lovers, and a regular guest at the embassy, was Daisy Fellowes, who was as famed for her malicious tongue as for her great elegance and priceless collection of jewellery. In the words of Carmel Snow, she was 'the personification of the hard Thirties chic that came in when Schiaparelli became the rage', and she would retain her position as a supreme arbiter of taste in the fashion world. A Paris correspondent for *Harper's Bazaar* in the early 1930s, Daisy had no real need or inclination to work: she been born into wealth in 1890, the only daughter of a French duke and an American heiress, Isabelle-Blanche Singer. Her first husband was the Prince de Broglie, with whom she had three daughters, two of whom were accused of collaboration during the war, and punished during the *épuration sauvage*. The oldest, Emmeline, spent five months in Fresnes, while the youngest, Jacqueline, who was married to an Abwehr espionage agent, had her head shaved.

Daisy's second husband was Reginald Fellowes, a cousin of Winston Churchill, and the couple spent the war in England; upon her return to Paris, she resumed her previous position in high society, as did her daughters. This process was eased with the help of Duff and Diana Cooper, both of whom were well aware of the charges of collaboration against Daisy's daughters. Duff spent a morning reading the intelligence file relating to Jacqueline and her husband, and noted in his diary that it was 'a thrilling story'. But he saw little reason to take heed of what he dismissed as 'gossip', particularly when it came to his mistresses, including Louise de Vilmorin, who was regarded with suspicion for her war record. According to Philippe de Rothschild, 'she was by no means free from taint, having spent a good deal of her war careering around Germany with a Hungarian husband'; while Duff himself admitted in his diary that he had quarrelled with Louise because 'she is so anti-American and anti-Jew'.

As for Diana Cooper, she tended to be less forgiving about people who bored her than those who had collaborated with the Germans. In the words of her biographer Philip Ziegler, she 'sometimes put friendship before the dictates of discretion. When the daughter of Daisy Fellowes was released from the Parisian prison where she had been incarcerated for her relationship with a German officer, she was at once invited to the Embassy. Diana was fascinated to know how Emmeline had got on with the four prostitutes with whom she had shared a cell for the past five months and who were apt to stand by the window with bared breasts waving to passers-by. "I asked her if she had got fond of any of them (I know I should have). She said no emphatically. She's an unlovable woman and I hope I shall never go to prison with her."'

As it happens, it was Daisy's other daughter, Jacqueline, who called upon Malcolm Muggeridge to help with the case of P. G. Wodehouse. The novelist and his wife had been denounced as traitors and arrested while staying at Le Bristol in Paris, on the basis of several ill-advised radio broadcasts which Wodehouse had delivered from Berlin in 1941, about his experiences as an internee in Germany. Muggeridge had already looked into the case, on behalf of MI6, and decided that Wodehouse was innocent. 'The broadcasts . . . are neither anti- nor pro-German,' he observed, 'but just Wodehousian.' Having secured the release of Wodehouse, his wife and their Pekingese dog, and settled them into a discreet hotel near Fontainebleau, Muggeridge then took the opportunity to meet Coco Chanel, a similarly controversial figure in Paris at the time.

Chanel had been summoned for questioning after the Liberation, due to her wartime relationship with a German intelligence officer, Hans Günther von Dincklage. She was swiftly released, possibly because of her longstanding friendship with Winston Churchill, which dated back to the 1920s, when Chanel had been the lover of Churchill's friend the Duke of Westminster. Unlike a number of her other friends, including Jean Cocteau and Christian Bérard, who had openly attended high society gatherings with German guests during the Occupation, Chanel tended to keep a low profile during the war. She did not reopen her couture house until the early 1950s, although she continued to sell her sought-after perfumes, including Chanel No. 5.

Muggeridge recalled being invited to have dinner with Chanel 'by an old friend of hers, F, who had appeared in Paris, covered in gold braid, as a member of one of the numerous liaison missions which were by now roosting there. So I went along with F to Mme Chanel's lavish haute couture and perfume emporium with a sense of being on duty as well as pleasure bent . . . If Mme Chanel felt any uneasiness at my presence, she gave no indication of it . . . Nor had she, as a matter of fact, any cause for serious anxiety, having successfully withstood the first *épuration* assault at the time of the Liberation by one of those majestically simple strokes which made Napoleon so successful a general; she just put an announcement in the window of her emporium that scent was free for GIs, who thereupon queued up to get their bottles of Chanel No. 5, and would have been outraged if the French police had touched a hair of her head. Having thus gained a breathing space, she proceeded to look

Paris fashion after the Liberation. Photograph by Bob Landry

for help *à gauche et à droite*, and not in vain, thereby managing to avoid making even a token appearance among the gilded company – Maurice Chevalier, Jean Cocteau, Sacha Guitry, and other worthies – on a collaborationist charge.'

Afterwards, Muggeridge attempted to draft an intelligence report on his evening with Chanel, but as he concluded in his autobiography: 'really there was nothing to say except that I was sure the *épuration* mills, however small they might grind, would never grind her – as indeed, proved to be the case.'

★

Against this backdrop of moral ambiguity, it is perhaps unsurprising that haute couture appeared to some observers to have gone astray in the months after Liberation. In his memoir, Christian Dior wrote that following his sister Catherine's return to Paris, 'An unhappy chapter of my life had ended. On the fresh, still unblemished page before me, I hoped to record nothing but happiness.' Yet the aftermath of the war was impossible to ignore: 'Traces of it were all around me – damaged buildings, devastated countryside, rationing, the black market, and less serious, but of more immediate interest to me, hideous fashions. Hats were far too large, skirts far too short, jackets far too long, shoes far too heavy . . . For lack of other materials, feathers and veils, promoted to the dignity of flags, floated through Paris like revolutionary banners. But as a fashion I found it repellent.' The *New York Times* was no less scathing in January 1945, when Lucien Lelong commented in an interview that Paris continued to be the inspiration for couture. The newspaper's response was dismissive: 'To be inspired by Paris at this time . . . might mean reflecting the exaggerated psychoses of a city that is still emerging from the humiliation of defeat with the resentful sensitivity of a convalescent that is plaintively miserable without heat or light and buys its moments of comfort and gaiety on the black market.'

Carmel Snow, too, was bemused by the state of couture that she discovered on her return to Paris; always an astute interpreter of the ways in which fashion expresses the mood of the moment, she observed that it now 'reflected the confusion the French had been going through since the Occupation. The people who were buying . . . were the new black-market rich, with a vulgarity that was too dreadful to be believed. They were the people who had traded with the Germans and were still making fortunes trading among themselves, and they were the explanation of much that went on in Paris: the awful hats, the women in expensive clothes whom you wouldn't be seen dead with . . .' She did, however, admire Dior's work at Lelong, and remained loyal to Balenciaga. Above all, she still had trust in the timeless art of Paris couture, and its place in what General de Gaulle had hailed in his Liberation speech as '*la vrai France, la France éternelle*'.

Yet for all Carmel Snow's consistent support of the French fashion industry in the pages of *Harper's Bazaar*, a more powerful, if unexpected, boost came about as a consequence of philanthropy. Towards the end of 1944, Raoul Dautry, who had been appointed Minister of Reconstruction and Urban Development by General de Gaulle and was the president of L'Entraide Française (the umbrella organisation for French war charities), approached the Chambre Syndicale de la Couture with a request that it should put on a fundraising exhibition. Lelong agreed, and a plan was conceived to show a collection of couture outfits on dolls, inspired by the historic tradition of French dressmakers, who had used miniature models to present their wares at the royal courts of Europe. Robert Ricci, who with his mother Nina Ricci had co-founded a couture house in 1932, was put in charge of the organisation of the project, and he asked a young artist named Eliane Bonabel to design the dolls. She had come to fame as a teenager with her illustrations for Céline's modernist novel *Journey to the End of the Night*. Her previous association with the fascistic Céline – who was at this point still exiled in Sigmaringen Castle in Germany, with the remnants of the

Vichy regime – did not appear to concern Ricci, nor indeed anyone else involved in the exhibition.

Bonabel devised sculptural wire figurines, twenty-seven and a half inches tall, with white plaster heads, and Robert Ricci came up with the concept of a series of little theatres to act as backdrops for the mannequins; hence the title of the exhibition, Théâtre de la Mode. Christian Bérard was appointed art director, and he enlisted the help of his friends, including Jean Cocteau and Georges Geffroy. Each of the couture houses embarked upon sewing individual outfits, complete with tiny belts, gloves, hats, jewels and feather trimmings, hand-stitched with the same loving attention to detail as their full-scale wares. Textile rationing was still in force, but the most precious fabrics were used to ensure that 220 dolls would display the expertise of thirty-seven leading maisons and their teams of seamstresses. Only Chanel was notable for her absence, but her couture house remained closed. The results were enchanting, and the exhibition opened to immense acclaim on 27 March 1945 at the Pavillon de Marsan in Paris.

Looking at photographs of the superbly dressed mannequins in their theatrical settings, they seem threaded through with a powerful undercurrent of the uncanny; even today, they retain an eerie quality, like gothic automata or mechanised dolls. Indeed, they seem to me reminiscent of Freud's essay 'The Uncanny', written in 1919, four years before Cocteau was inspired to draw an imaginative portrait of the psychoanalyst. Freud describes the unsettling effect of a beautiful doll that appears in E. T. A. Hoffmann's gothic masterpiece of 1816, 'The Sandman', and goes on to define the uncanny as mingling a sense of unease with that of the familiar. The association is captured in the German word for the uncanny, *unheimlich*, which derives from *heim*, meaning home. Thus the supernatural may be all too close to home, and therein lies its strange appeal.

Cocteau's haunting set design for the Théâtre de la Mode was entitled '*Ma femme est une sorcière*' (taking its name from René Clair's 1942

Hollywood movie, *I Married a Witch*). It shows a half-destroyed room, the ceiling open to the night sky, as if after a fire or explosion. Inside, a group of dolls wear full-length evening dresses; one of them is in an ivory satin wedding gown designed by Marcel Rochas, with white kid gloves. The dolls are looking up towards the wrecked roof, where a bewitching figure hovers on a broomstick – *la sorcière* herself; she is wearing a long dress of grey tulle embroidered with dark iridescent beads, created by Pierre Balmain.

Unlike Balmain, who had recently founded his own couture house, Christian Dior was still working for Lucien Lelong at this stage. Three of the most memorable outfits in the exhibition are believed to have been designed by Dior for the house of Lelong; one is a strapless floor-length evening gown in ivory tulle, its full skirts embroidered with a delicate blue floral pattern. The second is a day dress of turquoise and white polka-dot chiffon, and the third is just below the knee, a 'dance dress' with a romantic pink crêpe bodice, adorned with matching fabric roses, and a contrasting black full skirt. The evening gown appeared against the backdrop of Christian Bérard's hand-painted theatre, which evoked the romance of France's great dramatic tradition, and the day dress in a tableau of the Palais-Royal, alongside striking designs by Balenciaga and Schiaparelli. The dance dress had a more unusual setting: '*Le Port du nulle part*' ('The Port of Nowhere'), with the torn sails of a ghost ship beside a nameless harbour, where a group of mannequins stand in line on the quay. This tableau was the work of a Russian émigré named Georges Wakhévitch, an acclaimed art director and set designer for opera and film, who worked with Cocteau among others.

As I examine the faded photographs of the exhibition, I cannot help but think of Christian Dior working on these fragile dresses in March 1945, at a time when he was waiting anxiously for news of his sister who had disappeared into the darkness of the Third Reich. The war against Germany was still raging: an air battle was fought in the skies over Berlin on 18 March, and the Western Allies launched their operation to cross

A Lucien Lelong dress, believed to have been designed by Christian Dior,
for the Théâtre de la Mode exhibition in March 1945.

Previous page: Théâtre de la Mode, Paris 1945. Photograph by Robert Doisneau
Above: Théâtre de la Mode, Paris 1945. Photograph by Ralph Morse

the Rhine on the 23rd, the same day that Elisabeth de Rothschild, formerly a doyenne of the fashion world, died at Ravensbrück.

And yet in Paris, the show went on. The Théâtre de la Mode was accorded such importance that the Garde Républicaine provided a guard of honour in full ceremonial uniform on the opening night, and it ran until 10 May (two days after victory was proclaimed in Europe), having been extended by several weeks because of the sheer number of people who were eager to see it. More than a hundred thousand visitors came, and the entrance fees raised a million francs for war relief charities, while also reminding its audience of the immeasurable value of couture.

On 8 May, Raoul Dautry wrote to the French ambassador in London, asking for his help in arranging for the Théâtre de la Mode to come to England: 'France has little, alas, to export, but she has her appreciation of beautiful things and the skill of her couture houses.' It opened in London in September 1945 – the first foreign exhibition since the outbreak of the Second World War – with a private view arranged for the Queen. In six weeks, 120,000 visitors queued to see what was called 'The Fantasy of Fashion'; and the Théâtre de la Mode then went on tour to Leeds, Copenhagen, Stockholm and Vienna. In 1946, an updated version was sent to New York and San Francisco, where it did much to re-establish the reputation of French couture in America.

Lucien Lelong, hailing the great success of the Théâtre de la Mode, wrote: 'This is Paris and nothing but Paris: this theatre of fashion! Its smile, its strength, its spirit, its charm . . .' And the silent white-faced dolls were the very opposite of the vulgar customers who had brought their black-market cash into the couture salons; their perfect mannequin faces untouched by brash make-up; their blank eyes having seen nothing of the horrors and humiliations of the war; their wire limbs immune to starvation and injury. If couture was drawing on its hallowed past in the exhibition, it was also readying itself for the future; dressing not to kill, but to survive.

Magical Thinking

'The maintenance of the tradition of fashion is in the nature of an act of faith,' wrote Christian Dior in the final page of his memoir. 'In a century which attempts to tear the heart out of every mystery, fashion guards its secret well, and is the best possible proof that there is still magic abroad.' His words suggest that the origins of the couture house that he founded – a tale that he told many times – are cloaked in mystery; perhaps to create a more beguiling fable than a prosaic, business-like account. And while he had a thorough grounding in the commercial aspects of fashion, thanks to his experience as a freelance designer and his years working for Lucien Lelong, he also believed in the power of intuition and enchantment. Dior repeatedly references the importance of fate and fortune-telling in his auto-biography, beginning with a prediction he received at the age of fourteen, when he was living in Granville. 'It was in 1919, at a bazaar near my home, organised to raise funds for the soldiers. There was every kind of sideshow and we all took some part in it. I dressed myself up as a gypsy . . . and sold lucky charms. In the evening, when the crowds were thinning out, I found myself next to the fortune-teller's booth. She offered to read my palm. "You will suffer poverty," she said. "But women are lucky for you, and through them you will achieve success. You will make a great deal of money out of them, and you will have to travel widely."'

The encounter remained in his mind, although at the time the prophecy seemed unlikely. Yet after his period of impoverishment in the early

Lenormand fortune-telling cards (as used by Christian Dior), named after a French psychic from the Napoleonic era, Marie Anne Lenormand.

1930s, when his father lost a fortune and his own art galleries collapsed, Christian was more inclined to trust the advice of clairvoyants. His faith deepened when Catherine returned from Germany: an event that he believed had been foreseen by his favourite fortune-teller, Mme Delahaye. And in April 1946, he felt that fate intervened very literally in his life, when he happened to meet a childhood friend from Granville, whom he had not seen for many years, while he was walking to his apartment on Rue Royale. The friend was a director of the Gaston couture house, based nearby on Rue Saint Florentin, who explained to Christian that the somewhat faded establishment was now owned by Marcel Boussac. A leading industrialist and racehorse owner who had made a fortune in textile manufacturing, Boussac was looking for a new designer to revive his couture house. When the friend asked Christian if he knew of a suitable candidate, 'I thought hard for a few moments before telling him regretfully that I could think of no one who would do.'

Several days later, Christian and his friend met each other for a second time, on exactly the same stretch of pavement between Rue Saint Florentin and Rue Royale, and had the same conversation; yet again, Christian did not suggest himself. But on the third occasion, believing that destiny had surely led him to his friend, he finally put himself forward for the job, spurred on by what he saw as a lucky omen, a small cast-iron star that he found on the street, and picked up and put in his pocket. However, when he visited the dusty Gaston couture house soon afterwards, he was convinced that it could not be rescued; as he said, with surprising vehemence, 'I decided that I was not meant by nature to raise corpses from the dead.'

What happened next was unexpected: Christian went to see Marcel Boussac, fully intending to turn down the job and remain in his comfortable position at Lucien Lelong, but rather to his surprise, he found himself outlining an altogether different plan. 'I suddenly heard myself telling him that what I really wanted to do was not to resurrect Gaston, but create a new couture house under my own name, in a district of my

Christian Dior's lucky star, found by him on a Paris pavement in April 1946.

own choosing. I wanted a house in which every single thing would be new . . . All around us, life was beginning anew: it was time for a new trend in fashion.' Yet in order to achieve this, he continued, 'French couture would have to return to the traditions of great luxury.'

Having reflected on the proposal, Boussac agreed, which threw Christian into a state of apprehension. He therefore made another appointment to see Mme Delahaye: 'She ordered me sternly to accept the Boussac offer at once.' He confided the news to a close friend and colleague at Lelong, Raymonde Zehnacker (known as 'Mme Raymonde', whom he fondly regarded as his 'guardian angel'). She in turn consulted a different fortune-teller, 'the Grandmother', who provided further reassurance that the plan was destined for success. It was only at this point that Christian felt confident enough to proceed. The timing, he believed, was fortuitous; it also coincided with his sister's resumption of life in Paris. If Catherine had miraculously returned from the dead to Rue Royale, her arms filled with the flowers that signified her new career, then Christian could now take this important leap of faith in his own career, and establish a *maison* that epitomised the beginning of a fresh era.

★

As I write about Christian Dior's belief in clairvoyance, I can imagine sceptics wrinkling their noses in derision, and I feel torn between defending his attitude and distancing myself from it. My sister used to tease me gently about my propensity for magical thinking; yet when she died, I needed to believe that the bond between us was not severed, even though I felt broken myself. Was it the experience of my sister's death that made me more sensitive to the ghosts that seem to haunt the world of fashion? And not just fashion, as anyone will understand who has kept a piece of clothing of a loved one; unwilling to discard the fabric that lay close to their skin, and survives as material proof of their existence, long after their body has turned to dust.

I hope that those readers who have walked with me into the glass palace of Parisian couture will understand that its rituals and history include a belief in magic, and a respect for the ghosts whose reflections flicker in the mirrors of its salons. 'Time works for those who place themselves outside of time,' wrote the French poet and artist Jacques Yonnet in 1954. 'No one can be *of Paris*, can know that city, who has not made the acquaintance of its ghosts.' A former member of the French Resistance, Yonnet described Paris during the war as an otherworldly terrain occupied by phantoms as well as German forces, where the uncanny continued to be present in day-to-day life. Yonnet's territory was the shadowy alleys of the Left Bank, but his observations are as relevant to the grand couture *maisons* on the other side of the Seine. The inhabitants pride themselves on being able to see into the future, to imagine what their followers will most desire to wear in a coming season; hence the widespread practice of palmistry, astrology and tarot-reading. Yet couturiers also revere the past, for as Christian Dior observed, their citadel is not 'merely a Temple of Vanities: it is a charming outward manifestation of an ancient civilisation, which intends to survive.'

Dior was certainly not the first couturier to be drawn to the mysteries of an unseen realm. Coco Chanel's imagination was shaped by her perception of the supernatural, and a graveyard was central to her own account of her childhood. 'Every child has a special place, where he or she likes to hide, play and dream,' she said to her friend Paul Morand soon after the war, when both had sought refuge in Switzerland (he would later set down her memories in his book *L'Allure de Chanel*). 'Mine was an Auvergne cemetery . . . I was the queen of this secret garden. I loved its subterranean dwellers. "The dead are not dead as long as we think of them," I would tell myself.' Chanel even brought her favourite dolls to the graveyard – rag dolls that she had sewn – to introduce them to the dead, while she decorated the tombstones with wildflowers.

Chanel's great rival Elsa Schiaparelli was similarly fascinated by the paranormal. Despite Schiaparelli's brief and ill-fated early marriage to a vaudeville performer of so-called psychic phenomena (who in 1915 was found guilty in a London court of 'pretending to tell fortunes'), she did not stop believing in a magical universe. Its symbols were threaded through Schiaparelli's fantastical creations, most notably in her Zodiac couture collection, created at the pinnacle of her power in the winter of 1938–39, and inspired by astrology and celestial constellations. Chanel loathed Schiaparelli, and both women were caustic about Christian Dior as he became ever more renowned; yet all three shared a tendency towards superstition. Schiaparelli regarded four as her lucky number; Chanel attached great weight to the number five; Dior favoured number eight. They were similarly enthralled by fortune-telling cards. Chanel's precious set of cards still lies on the desk in her private apartment, alongside an array of talismanic objects that surrounded her in life and continue to be preserved after her death.

Carmel Snow, too, was an ardent disciple of soothsayers and seers, and regarded by some as possessing her own sixth sense. When Snow died at the age of seventy-three, the *New York Herald Tribune* published a tribute by Eugenia Sheppard, who described her as 'a bit of a witch. The slim little woman . . . was in her time feared, catered to, and almost superstitiously respected for her uncanny insight into unhatched fashion trends. ("She knows," they used to say as they studied her poker face at fashion shows.)' Snow's favoured astrologer in New York was named Evangeline Adams, and she always consulted her before making an important decision; in her memoir, she gives much credence to Adams, while confessing that this belief was at odds with her devout Catholicism. 'I'm susceptible to the supernatural, I freely admit, and because my Church frowns on fortune-telling, I try to treat my "vice" as a diversion.'

Whenever Snow was in Paris, she would attend mass at least once a day, as well as finding the time for card readings with various fortune-tellers in the city, including Mme Delahaye, to whom she had been introduced by Christian Dior. She also commissioned her friend Janet Flanner to write a lengthy piece entitled 'Prophecies and Portents' for the February 1940

Christian Dior at home with his clairvoyant, Mme Delahaye, Paris, 1954.
Photograph by Willy Maywald

issue of *Harper's Bazaar*. 'Never before have so many people urgently wanted to know what history has in store for them,' observed Flanner. 'Some of the men who are making history are apparently equally curious. A university president, returned from Germany, affirms that Herr Hitler, in order to approximate what the future is laying up for him, employs a staff of five astrologers (perhaps all in uniform).'

★

Whether through mystic foresight or her own experienced eye, it was Carmel Snow who predicted that Christian Dior was on the cusp of fame in early 1946, while he was still working for Lucien Lelong. Snow was so impressed by his couture collection in February that year that she declared: 'Lelong has a new designer whose collection was sensational – full of ideas. His name is Christian Dior.' The fact that he had been working at Lelong for four years was irrelevant to Snow; she had deemed him 'new', and therefore he was. She promptly commissioned Henri Cartier-Bresson to take a portrait of Dior for *Harper's Bazaar*, and the rest of the fashion world took note.

By this point, Bettina Ballard had transferred to the New York office of *Vogue*, but she travelled to Paris in February 1946 to cover the couture collections, and was struck by the sudden interest in the house of Lelong. 'I was curious as to whose hands behind the scene had given this fresh and tempting look to clothes in the lethargic post-war fashion atmosphere that pervaded Paris at the moment.' Having hailed it as the best collection of Lelong's career, Bettina was introduced to 'a pink-cheeked man with an air of baby plumpness still about him and an almost desperate shyness augmented by a receding chin. "This is Christian Dior," Lucien said, as if he were producing a rabbit from a hat. The small mouth of the blushing man in front of me curled sideways in a disarmingly sweet but rather sad smile as he murmured politenesses in reply to my compliments.'

So taken was Bettina with the collection that she ordered an outfit: 'an evening costume, a very new conception with a calf-length black satin skirt, [and] a pale mauve chiffon off-the-shoulder bodice'. Her description sounds similar to the 'dance dress' designed by Christian Dior for the Théâtre de la Mode exhibition the previous spring (the only difference is that the original had a rose-pink crêpe bodice), and its silhouette is a forerunner of the 'Miss Dior' dress that would appear three years later, in Dior's 1949 spring collection.

But not everyone was ready for Dior's fresh take on fashion, as Bettina discovered when she wore her gown on a visit to London, only to be barred from entering the 400 Club (the most fashionable nightspot for British high society). 'Englishwomen swept by me in their trailing pre-war chiffons, shedding beads as they walked, but in my new Paris creation for the evening I was considered underdressed. The young guardsman with me kept threatening the man at the door that the whole incident should be brought up in Parliament, that it was outrageous that England should be so backward in fashion, and more outrageous that an editor of *Vogue* should be turned away from the 400.'

Despite Dior's design not passing muster in London, his talent was creating a stir in Paris. 'By the summer collections of 1946,' wrote Bettina, 'Christian Dior was a much-talked-about personality owing to the extraordinary news that Marcel Boussac, the cotton king of France and a great racing figure, was to back him in a couture house . . . Lelong told me sadly that he could not help encouraging his star designer to branch out on his own with the talent he had. Suddenly it was popular to claim Dior as an "old friend". Bébé [Christian] Bérard, the artist, and Georges Geffroy, the decorator, proclaimed themselves his personal advisors and hovered around him. The smell of fame was strong, attracting not only friends, but workers who felt the stir of something happening in the couture and were willing to take a chance on this lucky man.'

Dior's first step was to hire Raymonde Zehnacker as his right-hand woman and director of the design studio. 'Raymonde was to become my second self,' he wrote in his memoir, 'or to be more accurate, my other half. She is my exact complement: she plays Reason to my Fantasy, Order to my Imagination, Discipline to my Freedom, Foresight to my Recklessness, and she knows how to introduce peace into an atmosphere of strife.'

He then recruited Marguerite Carré as 'technical director'; in other words, the leader in charge of a skilled team of couture seamstresses. She had worked at the house of Patou for many years, and Dior described her as 'Dame Fashion in person . . . If the world came to an end while she was poring over a dress, I really did not believe she would notice it . . .' It would be 'Mme Marguerite', as he called her, who turned his sketches into the white cotton toiles that formed the patterns for Dior's couture creations, and oversaw their painstaking realisation into finished products.

The third member of his female coterie was Mizza Bricard, who had previously worked for the house of Molyneux on Rue Royale until war broke out. She was ostensibly employed as head of the millinery department, but fulfilled a wider and more nebulous role that appeared to be integral, if not indispensible, to his creative approach. Dior provides a vivid description of her appeal. 'We had become great friends: Mme Bricard is one of those people, increasingly rare, who make elegance their sole *raison d'être*. Gazing at life out of the windows of the Ritz, so to speak, she is superbly indifferent to politics, finance, or social change.'

His choice of words is intriguing, especially in the context of his sister's wartime experiences, and the Occupation of Paris, when much of the Ritz was occupied by high-ranking Nazi officers. Hermann Goering moved into the Imperial Suite, and found it a convenient base during his regular trips to Paris, when he combined his official duties with the acquisition of looted art and shopping for jewellery. And, infamously, Chanel lived at the Ritz with her German lover.

Indeed, Dior's account of Mme Bricard suggests that she was in every way the opposite of Catherine. 'In August she allows herself to spend a month at a fashionable watering-hole in order that she may be seen in the square or the casino, but on the whole her love of the country and nature does not go further than the flowers with which she decorates her hats and her dresses.' How different from Catherine Dior, and from Christian himself, with their shared love of gardening and growing roses, not to mention their commitment to the annual harvest of flowers in Callian.

Dior's homage to Mizza continues: 'Her high standards are inflexible: in fashion she aims immediately for the most marked expression of that indefinable, and perhaps slightly neglected thing called chic. Mme Bricard is completely cosmopolitan in her elegance, and I felt that her remarkable character, her inimitable extravagances of taste, would have had an excellent effect on the phlegmatic temperament which I had inherited from my Norman forebears. I knew that her presence in my house would inspire me towards creation, as much by her reactions – and even her revolts – *against* my ideas, as by her agreements. Her deep knowledge of the traditions of *haute couture* and her refusal to compromise seemed the best possible stimulants for a temperament such as mine, so inclined to be discouraged by the *laissez-faire* spirit of our age. In her personal tradition of elegance, Mme Bricard seemed to personify that motto which I already wanted to take for my own: *I will maintain . . .*'

Christian Dior's memoir makes no explicit link between his sister and the trio of women who came to work for him; yet in the chronology of events that led to the establishment of his couture house, Catherine is an intangible presence. His breakthrough collection for Lelong – shown in February 1946 – would have been designed in the winter of 1945, when Catherine was living with her brother at Rue Royale. The timing seems significant – as if the safe return of Catherine allowed Christian to commit to his own future. And as Christian fully embraced his ambition as a couturier, his vision of beauty and femininity surely encompassed his sister, the woman he loved most in the world. Yet while Catherine was recognised by those who knew her as a true heroine who exemplified the best and bravest spirit of French resistance during the war, she was not a fashion muse for her brother, nor would she ever seek the limelight.

Above: Christian Dior and Mizza Bricard, choosing ties. Photograph by Willy Maywald
Opposite: Mme Bricard, wearing a mink wrap designed by Dior, accessorised with her
seventeenth-century Hindu necklace, Cartier bracelets and earrings.
Photograph by Horst P. Horst for *Vogue*, 1950

Her innate modesty and quiet discretion were clad in the silence that surrounded her wartime suffering; her face still showed the sadness and pain that she had endured, and her body bore the scars of her torture and punishing imprisonment. Instead, Catherine would become associated with the scent of Miss Dior, a perfume launched at the same time as the couture brand.

Such was the gathering excitement around Christian Dior in 1946 that, even before he opened his own couture house, he had already been approached by another childhood friend from Granville, Serge Heftler-Louiche, with the idea to set up a perfume company together. Serge had been a director for many years at the Coty perfume company, and he suggested to Christian – a godfather to his son – that they should go into business together. Ultimately, it would be Marcel Boussac who provided the capital to finance the venture, but Serge became director of the Christian Dior perfume company, and owned 35 per cent of the shares, while Boussac had 40 per cent, and Christian held 25 per cent.

Dior was directly involved in the creation of the first scent, asking an expert 'nose', a highly regarded perfumer named Paul Vacher, to make 'a perfume that smells of love'. Vacher duly came up with the distinctive formula, using Provençal jasmine and roses: two of the flowers most cherished by Christian and Catherine. Legend has it that Mizza Bricard played a part in the naming of the scent. The source for this story was another of Christian's confidantes, Alice Chavane, a fashion editor for *Le Figaro* who had commissioned him during the war as a freelance illustrator for the newspaper, while he was living with Catherine in Callian. According to Alice (whose handwritten account of the origins of Miss Dior is kept in the Dior archives), Christian was musing about what the perfume should be called, when Catherine walked into the room. 'Madame Bricard said: "*Tiens! Voilà Miss Dior!*" This is why Catherine, a flower dealer at Les Halles, where she went at four o'clock every

Original designs for the Miss Dior perfume bottle.

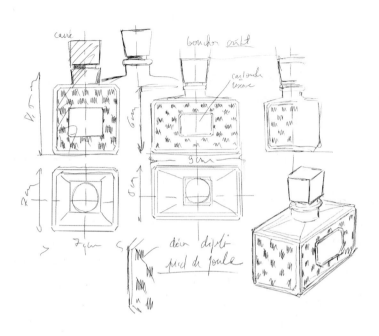

morning, became, one evening, the unforeseen godmother of a little bottle that contains lily of the valley, the springtime and love under the name of Miss Dior.'

Alice Chavane's lyrical description (in the original French, '*un petit flacon qui enferme le muguet, le printemps et l'amour*') has a tinge of poetic licence; after all, lily of the valley is only a minor ingredient in Miss Dior, although it was regarded by Christian as his lucky flower, and was sewn into the hemlines of his couture wedding gowns. Yet in the creation myth of Miss Dior, it is intriguing that both Mizza and Catherine are present at the birth. For the contrast between these two women, both so vital to Christian, was deeply pronounced. Catherine was seventeen years younger than Mizza, and defined by her integrity, her valiant commitment to freedom, and her principled ideals. Certainly, Catherine knew something about fashion, having worked in a boutique in Paris before the war, and because of her closeness and loyalty to her brother, but she drew more inspiration from her garden than a couture salon. Mizza was famed for her glittering collection of fine jewels; Catherine possessed the prestigious medals she had been awarded for courage, but she only wore one treasured bracelet, given to her by Hervé's mother, with two gold circles etched in Roman numerals marking the dates of her arrest and release from imprisonment. Above all, Catherine was always described as 'honourable' by those who knew her; a word that would never be used about Mizza. If the floral scent of Miss Dior was inspired by Catherine, and still survives as a timeless tribute to the tenderness of Christian's love for his sister, then a perfume that embodied Mizza would be darker and more sensual.

Mizza swathed herself in mystery and leopard print, as if she had something to hide. Even the spelling of her name is uncertain – she is sometimes referred to as Mitza or Mitzah. In fact, she was born Germaine Louise Neustadt on 12 November 1900 in Paris, and her parents' names on the birth certificate are listed as Max Neustadt and Agnes Sussman. Mizza was married three times (confusingly, her maiden name is spelled differently again in the Paris city archives: the records of her first and second marriages – in 1923 and 1930, respectively – show her as Neudstadtl). Her first husband, Alexandre Bianu (also known as Biano), was a Romanian banker who would become a diplomat in Paris from 1944 to 1946. No one seems to know the identity of her second husband, but the archives reveal that her third marriage took place on her birthday in 1941 to a businessman called Hubert Bricard, whose only appearance in the tale of Mizza is when he dutifully carried a handbag containing her evening shoes.

Her closest friends were aware that the romantic past she described to them was likely to be founded in fantasy. One of those friends, Jane, Lady Abdy, writing about Mizza after her death in December 1977, observed, 'Sometimes Madame Bricard talked to me of her early life, though I feel there was more than an element of mythology in it. She was, as Anita Loos commented of another beauty, "a girl who has been historic for fifty years", and in none of her reminiscences was she on oath.' With those caveats in place, Lady Abdy continued, 'her father was Viennese, her mother English . . . and her childhood memories included a visit to the garden of water lilies which Monet made at Giverny . . . When she was seventeen, she made the obligatory fairy-tale marriage, to the Russian Prince Narishkine, but this trailed away – and the former princess was soon working in her true métier, in the house of the greatest couturier in Paris, Jacques Doucet.'

It was Doucet who gave Mizza a piece of advice that she took to heart for the rest of her life: 'When a man wants to send you some flowers, always say to him, "My florist is Cartier."' And it was in his ateliers that Mizza learned the importance of using only the finest materials, for Doucet was renowned for the extravagant luxury of the dresses that he designed for his clients, including Sarah Bernhardt. But Jane Abdy also suggests that Mizza's ambition to create beautiful clothes had arisen before she joined Doucet; as a child she had been taken to the races at Longchamp, where she was inspired by 'the supreme elegance of the *demi-mondaines* . . . looking like flocks of lacy butterflies'.

Mizza's acolytes swooned over what they regarded as her exquisite taste, which she continued to refine when she moved from Doucet to work for Molyneux. But her detractors thought she was a *demi-mondaine* herself, with a streak of vulgarity, and as such, she was not quite *comme il faut*. During her decade at Molyneux (from 1930 to 1940), her path crossed with that of the young Pierre Balmain, who had joined the couture house as an assistant designer in 1934. Balmain's ambivalence about Mizza emerges in his memoir, where he described her as 'Madame B'. 'She had made few friends, but she seemed to amuse Molyneux. In the studio she wore a white overall to which she pinned three big stars of platinum and diamonds that made it gape open and reveal her black lace lingerie. Her legs were rather thick but were clad in fine black stockings, set off in very high-heeled shoes. One of her hands bore traces of vitriol burns . . . She intimidated, but also fascinated, me. I could see her playing the role of a central European spy, or as one of the cocottes who revolutionised Maxim's in 1900.'

Balmain was not alone in speculating that Mizza could have been a spy as well as a courtesan, although her reputation for intrigue, and possible duplicity, seems not to have concerned the world of haute couture. When Bettina Ballard first encountered Mitza (as she called her) in the 1930s, she was Molyneux's assistant. 'She was a legend in those days,' wrote Bettina, 'sitting at Maxim's in a clinging black, very low V-necked gown, her famous diamond star pins accentuating the lowness, and yards of black tulle trailing from her head.' When they met again, after the war, at Christian Dior's Rue Royale apartment, along with Christian Bérard and Marie-Louise Bousquet, Bettina once more noted 'the Maxim's type of elegance' that defined Mme Bricard; in other words, she was not quite as 'socially impeccable' as those with whom Dior came to surround himself later, but beautifully dressed nonetheless.

Tellingly, in his conversations with Bettina, Christian himself referred to Mizza as 'an assistant': neither he nor Bettina uses the term 'muse', so often attributed to her subsequently. He explained Mme Bricard's value as someone 'to whom elegance was a religion, whose mind and body were dedicated to feeling, thinking, and breathing fashion. Mitza was a rare phenomenon in that she had eliminated all other interests in her life.' She also had the capacity to be exasperating; Bettina observed that she was 'difficult, temperamental, egotistical to a degree that isolated her from all simple relationships, obsessed with her jewels, with which she covered herself even in the morning'. Yet she represented something 'deeply Parisian; the heart of Paris . . . I remember once when she came to lunch in Connecticut, wearing what she termed her "country jewels" (sapphires), her perennial veil over her eyes, a bois de rose shantung dress – the latest Dior model – her high-heeled shoes in pale alligator, "for the country". She looked at the flagstones of my terrace and visibly drew her toe back onto the familiar parquet of the living-room floor. Sunlight, earth, stones, air – none of these belonged in the fashion life of Mitza Bricard.'

History does not relate the nuances of the relationship that existed between Christian, Catherine and Mizza; certainly, it seems unlikely that his sister and his assistant had anything in common, other than Christian himself. But René Gruau, who knew all three (and had first met Christian and Catherine during the war in Cannes), created an evocative visual representation of their strange dynamic in his illustrations for the Miss Dior perfume. In an interview in 1984, Gruau described Mizza as 'the most elegant woman I have ever met . . . she was a fabulous design herself.' Like Mizza's other admirers, Gruau was unsure of the truth about her origins. 'We speculated endlessly about her nationality, which we never managed to discover,' he said; but the assumption was that she was Slavic. In 1949, Dior commissioned Gruau to produce a series of advertisements for Miss Dior, and their elliptical appeal is such that they remain timeless. The first is a white swan, with a large black bow and three strings of pearls at the base of its shapely, sinuous neck. 'The swan is curvaceous like a young girl,' said Gruau; 'it is white, like lily of the valley, Christian's favourite flower. It symbolises elegance, freshness and purity all at the same time. The bow and pearl necklace are there to add a touch of sophistication.'

I have an original print of Gruau's swan beside me as I write. As I look at it again, I marvel at the delicacy of his brush-strokes, and then close my eyes and imagine Mizza at work, adorning Catherine's slim neck with pearls and a black bow. The second illustration is in a book that is open on my desk; it depicts a woman's sinuous white hand resting on a leopard's paw. It needs no caption, but summons up '*la Belle et la Bête*'. One of the stories told about Mme Bricard was that the scar on her wrist – which she sometimes covered with a leopard-print scarf – was the result of an attack by another woman, angered by Mizza's seduction of her husband. The third illustration by Gruau shows a white-gloved feminine hand holding a black fan. The fan is surprisingly large – it fills half the page – and its darkness appears almost at odds with Gruau's characteristic light touch. 'Whose is the hidden hand in the glove?' the picture seems to ask. The unseen woman remains elusive, enigmatic, compelling; and just like the Miss Dior scent, her mystery will never fade with age.

René Gruau, *Le Cygne*, illustration for Miss Dior, 1949.

René Gruau, *L'Eventail*, illustration for Miss Dior, 1949.

René Gruau, *La Main*, illustration for Miss Dior, 1949.

The New Look

The house of Dior stands at 30 Avenue Montaigne, facing the Hôtel Plaza Athénée and the Théâtre des Champs-Elysées, both of which opened in 1913, drawing fashionable visitors to the tree-lined street. Christian had already admired the townhouse in 1945, when he stopped to look at it with his friend Pierre Colle. 'I pointed out [the] neat, compact proportions, and air of sober elegance without the least hint of ostentation.' The following year, after he had concluded his negotiations with Marcel Boussac, Christian discovered that the lease was coming up for sale, and was determined to make it his own. The location was convenient for both Parisian and foreign clients, and the building's attractive nineteenth-century architecture appealed to him. There was only one problem: the property was not available until 16 December 1946, less than two months before the scheduled unveiling of Dior's first collection on 12 February 1947. Christian had agreed to remain at his job at Lucien Lelong until 1 December 1946, which meant that he and his chosen team would have to work fast to ensure that the *maison* opened on time.

After leaving Lelong, Christian went to stay with Pierre Colle and his wife Carmen (she would soon be employed to run the boutique at Avenue Montaigne). The Colles had a country home south-east of Paris, in the middle of the forest of Fontainebleau, which was covered in snow at the time. And it was there, in icy midwinter, that Christian Dior conceived the romantic vision of beauty that would make him legendary: a spring collection inspired by the corolla, the delicate grouping of petals

The New Look, 1947. Illustration by Christian Bérard

that forms a flower. As he wrote in his memoir: 'We were just emerging from a poverty-stricken, parsimonious era, obsessed with ration books and clothes-coupons: it was only natural that my creations should take the form of a reaction against this dearth of imagination . . . In December 1946, as a result of the war and uniforms, women still looked and dressed like Amazons. But I designed clothes for flowerlike women, with rounded shoulders, full feminine busts, and hand-span waists above enormous spreading skirts.'

On 9 December, while he was in the midst of finalising his sketches for the collection, Christian received the news that his seventy-four-year-old father had died. He immediately took the train to the south of France, to attend the funeral at Callian with Catherine. Their siblings Raymond and Jacqueline were also there for the ceremony, along with their old governess, Marthe Lefebvre, who had cared for Maurice Dior until the end. (Bernard, however, was still institutionalised in the mental asylum in Normandy where he had been committed at the age of twenty-two, and would remain until released by his own death in 1960.)

When Christian took possession of his first couture house, just a week after his father's death, it marked a momentous transformation in both his personal and professional life. 'I felt as if I had come of age for the second time,' he wrote. 'I was no longer a child to anyone: it was my turn to provide comfort and support for those who were coming after me. I had to step out of the warmth and intimacy of the family circle and welcome into the world that forbidding stranger – Christian Dior, *couturier*.' This idea forms an underlying theme of his memoir, and gives rise to its title, *Christian Dior et moi*. It indicates there are two Christian Diors: one the shy, private individual, and the other the grand couturier, who inhabits the *maison* that bears his name.

Yet the couture house was suffused with nostalgia for Christian's Belle Epoque childhood, before the intrusion of war and the subsequent di-

Facade of 30 Avenue Montaigne, 1947. Illustration by Christian Bérard

Hommage
a Christian
Dior

ferd 47

sasters that beset his family. His team included two longstanding friends from Granville, Suzanne Luling, who had helped him try to save Catherine from deportation, and Serge Heftler-Louiche. Serge's role would be to launch and run Dior Parfums, Suzanne's to manage sales and publicity for the couture side of the business. Christian commissioned another friend, Victor Grandpierre, to oversee the decoration of the *maison*. Despite having told Marcel Boussac that his overriding ambition was for it to appear 'new', he seemed more intent on looking back to his past. In his memoir, he spoke of his wish to recreate a style that he remembered from his parents' first apartment in Paris, which 'had since gone completely out of fashion. From 1900 to 1914 decoration *à la Louis Seize* was all the rage . . . white woodwork, white enameled furniture, grey hangings, glass doors with square panes and bronze light brackets with small lampshades . . . I felt it would be the ideal background against which to show my collections . . . I was determined that my décor should not degenerate into elaborate decorations.'

Grandpierre and Dior had met in Cannes in the early 1940s, during the Vichy years. They shared a similar artistic sensibility and a respect for tradition; indeed, Grandpierre had been born into the Parisian world of the Belle Epoque. His father was a well-regarded architect, whose commissions included a neoclassical townhouse for Winnaretta Singer, the aunt of Daisy Fellowes; as a talented young photographer, Victor was responsible for a flattering portrait of Daisy. After the Liberation, Grandpierre was befriended by Lady Diana Cooper, and collaborated with Louise de Vilmorin, Duff Cooper's mistress, on a project combining his own photography and her poetry.

One might have expected that Christian would turn to his better-known friend Georges Geffroy to decorate the premises. Before the war Geffroy had proved his talent by devising the private salon in Robert Piguet's couture house, and in 1944 he had been commissioned by the couturier Marcel Rochas and his wife Hélène to design their home in Paris. Most recently he had helped with the creation of a handsome new library for Duff Cooper at the British embassy. But Christian's choice of Victor Grandpierre was very deliberate; as he explained in his memoir: 'my friends who were professional decorators were either too purist or too much in love with their ideas to listen to mine: I did not want an authentic *Louis Seize* interior – I wanted a 1910 version of *Louis Seize*, a notion which most of them would have considered mere folly.' Grandpierre understood the effect that he was seeking: 'our tastes coincided wonderfully, and we were both equally happy recapturing the magic years of our childhood. He created the "Helleu" salon of my dreams, all in white and pearl grey, looking very Parisian with its crystal chandeliers . . .'

★

To walk into 30 Avenue Montaigne today is to step into Christian Dior's dream world: through the imposing front entrance, across a limestone hall and up the broad steps of the central, circular staircase. The walls are still painted the distinctive pearl grey that he made his own, and the floral scent of Miss Dior wafts through the air, just as it did when the *maison* first opened its doors. As in every couture house, some areas are more private than others: in particular, the ateliers on the top floor, where the '*petites mains*' perform their painstaking craft, hand-sewing the exquisite creations. Then there is the *cabine*, a dressing room that is no longer in use today, but was once the place where the models readied themselves for the couture shows that were staged across the corridor in the high-ceilinged salon. I have slipped into this room before now and imagined how it must have felt, crowded with models and their dressers, with Christian Dior himself making last-minute adjustments, before they stepped out in his latest designs. The wall clock has stopped in the *cabine*, though time does not stand still here; instead, it seems to circle in on itself, its invisible currents stirred by the ghosts of the beautiful girls who once shimmied within these walls.

Above: Christian Dior standing in the dressing room at his Paris couture house before
a presentation of his collection. Photograph by Loomis Dean
Opposite: Backstage at a Dior fashion show; elevated view of the dressing room. The designer
stands on the left, as a gown is lowered for a model. Photograph by Loomis Dean

Today, I have been granted a unique privilege: to write at Dior's own desk in the private salon that remains at the heart of the *maison*. Beside me there is a picture in a gilt frame of Christian as a young boy in the garden at Granville. The black-and-white photograph shows a child in a sailor suit, standing on the lawn, one hand in his pocket, hair neatly brushed; his gaze direct, yet innocent. The salon is the place where the boy finally became world famous, as a forty-two-year-old man; it is here, in a hallowed temple of Parisian elegance, that Christian Dior worked on his couture creations, surrounded by his faithful team, and where his clients were seated to watch each spectacular presentation. Today is a quiet midweek afternoon in February and the *maison* is calm after yesterday's show: a glorious collection by Maria Grazia Chiuri, the first female creative director of Dior, and a woman who has placed sisterhood and feminism at the forefront of her inspiring work as a designer. All is hushed, yet I am trying to envisage the feverish excitement of a long-ago morning, when this room was crowded with guests who had gathered at 10.30 am on 12 February 1947 to witness Christian Dior's launch.

The decorators had been working through the night, and when Christian arrived at dawn, the velvet carpet was still being tacked down. 'As Mme Delahaye had predicted,' he recalled, 'the last bang of the last hammer was actually heard as the first visitor entered.' There are photographs hanging in the corridor, taken on the day of Dior's debut collection: the stairwell crammed with onlookers and well-wishers; the grand salon filled with gilded chairs, a name card on each one highlighting the strict hierarchy of the front row, in accordance with the protocol that still governs the fashion world today. Lady Diana Cooper was here at that first show; so too were Jean Cocteau, Georges Geffroy and Christian Bérard; and in prime position, seated on a gilded throne, Carmel Snow, accompanied by her loyal courtier Marie-Louise Bousquet. Bettina Ballard recalled in her memoir that an expectant crowd had gathered on the street outside, while inside there was a sense of 'electric tension' that she had never before experienced in her years of working for *Vogue*. 'The

Christian Dior drawing, 1948. Photograph by Willy Maywald

Pencil sketches by Christian Dior; legacy left by Catherine Dior
to the Christian Dior Museum in Granville.

first girl came out, stepping fast, switching with a provocative swinging movement, whirling in the close-packed room, knocking over ash trays with the strong flare of her pleated skirt, and bringing everyone to the edges of the seats in a desire not to miss a thread of this momentous occasion . . . We were given a polished theatrical performance such as we had never seen in a couture house before. We were witnesses to a revolution in fashion and to a revolution in showing fashion as well.'

Ernestine Carter, then the fashion editor for the British edition of *Harper's Bazaar*, subsequently described the show as the most memorable of her long and distinguished career: 'the model girls arrogantly swinging their vast skirts (one had eighty yards of fabric), the soft shoulders, the tight bodices, the wasp-waists, the tiny hats bound on by veils under the chin. To us in our sharp-shouldered (a legacy from Schiaparelli), skimpy fabric-rationed suits, this new softness and roundness was positively voluptuous. All round the salon you could see the English tugging at their skirts trying to inch them over their knees.'

Each model sashayed through the salon, moving at speed, then returned to the *cabine* and reported back to the anxious designer. He had ordered that the salon be filled with garlands of fresh flowers – including his lucky lily of the valley – and sprayed throughout with the scent of Miss Dior. The perfume would not go on sale until later that year, but the formula had already been finalised, and Dior decreed that the entire *maison* should be enveloped with its floral fragrance. Catherine, for whom it had been named, was sitting quietly in the audience. 'It really was euphoric,' she told Stanley Garfinkel, an American historian, in 1983, in a rare interview. 'Everyone was a little surprised by the triumph – yet this was a triumph for French fashion, and for an artist.'

Her brother himself seemed more surprised than anyone, as the applause increased throughout the presentation, swelling to a standing ovation for the finale. 'I blocked my ears, terrified of feeling confident too soon,' he wrote in his memoir, 'but a series of short bulletins from the battlefield confirmed that my troops . . . had triumphed.' Christian was led into the salon to take a bow, surrounded by a tumultuous throng of friends and admirers, all congratulating him at once. It was then that Carmel Snow came up with the phrase that would define Dior: 'It's quite a revolution, dear Christian. Your dresses have such a new look.'

'After the opening,' recalled Bettina Ballard, 'some of us stayed and tried on the extraordinary new clothes, slightly punch-drunk with the excitement of it all. Bébé Bérard tried a tiny side-slanted hat on his permanently dirty little white dog, while Georges Geffroy made Proustian speeches on the theory of design and on Dior's genius. Everyone insisted that I order the dress called "1947" immediately, which, when I returned to New York, gave me a brief moment of fame. Even taxi-drivers asked me, "Is this the 'new look'?" so quickly did the expression become part of our everyday vocabulary.' Yet at the moment of his greatest triumph, as his friends celebrated in the salon after the show, Bettina noted how Christian Dior himself stood apart from them, 'with his teasing, slightly sad smile . . .'

What became of Catherine in the multitude, I wonder. There is no written account of her presence; no surviving photographs record the look on her face. Catherine was the only member of the Dior family who was present that day to witness Christian's success; although the memory of their mother might have been a hidden ingredient within the scent of Miss Dior, and the sound of her rustling dresses echoed in the swishing silks of the New Look collection. Cecil Beaton, one of the most discerning observers of fashion, recognised that Dior had conjured up an exhilarating sense of delight 'after a gloomy interval of war', but he also perceived the couturier's homage to the past: 'With an impeccable taste, a highly civilized sensitivity, and a respect for tradition that shows itself in a predilection for the half-forgotten, Dior creates a brilliant nostalgia.'

A sepia photograph of Madeleine Dior still stands on her son's desk, and I find myself glancing at it as I write these words. She is wearing a high-necked, intricately embroidered dress, with a tiny corseted waist, her dark hair pulled back and arranged in a bun in the elaborate style of the Belle Epoque. This was, perhaps, a new look at the time, at the

A Christian Dior fashion show in the salon of his couture house, *c.*1950.
Photographs by Eugene Kammerman

dawn of the twentieth century; certainly the image suggests a thread of continuity with her son's subsequent vision of female beauty. The portrait shows a wistful-looking woman, her face turned slightly away from the photographer, her lips a little compressed, as if in displeasure. Gazing at the picture, I am reminded of the handful of clues that Catherine provided about her mother, more than half a century after Madeleine Dior's death. 'My mother, who was a very elegant woman, had a great influence on the work of my brother,' she told Garfinkel, 'and my brother's interest in women's outfits was in some sense thanks to my mother . . . She was a charming woman, who liked to entertain guests and dress up, and when my brother was very young he started taking an interest in the gowns that she wore. When he was a bit older, he would accompany her to the couturière, Rosine Perrault, on Rue Royale . . . They enjoyed talking about fashion, they liked discussing artistic questions. My brother had great affection for our mother and they had a lot in common.' Then there was Catherine's interview with Christian's biographer Marie-France Pochna, in which she referred to the maternal discipline that prevailed in their childhood: 'my mother was severe with the boys, and even more so with the girls.' Pochna believes that it was Madeleine Dior – a distant yet haunting figure – who would be her son's muse; a maternal ghost 'present in every fold, in every yard of fabric unfurled by the designer in his yearning for *le temps perdu*. She was both his critic and his inspiration.'

On the eve of Dior's first show, referring to the facade of the couture house that bore his name in discreet black lettering (just as it does today), he confessed, 'If mother had lived, I would never have dared.' His comment was a tacit acknowledgement that his mother would have disapproved of his career, having made it clear that she did not want him to go into trade. For even though the original Dior fertiliser business carried the family name, Christian's mother had forbidden him to use it on his initial commercial venture, the avant-garde art gallery that he co-founded in Paris in 1928. Yet was he still trying to please her with the *maison* he created at Avenue Montaigne? Despite the trail-blazing art that Dior showed as a

First sketches of Dior's New Look, 1947. Illustration by Sam

gallerist, no such modernism is evident within the private salon of his couture house. A graceful Renoir hangs between the tall windows overlooking Avenue Montaigne, while Christian Bérard's charming sketches adorn the other walls. I count eleven ceramic swans dotted around the salon – decorative reminders of the Miss Dior illustration. The panelling, painted a soft grey, is embellished with curlicues, cherubs, classical goddesses carved on the edges of the ceiling, and leafy tendrils garlanding the doorframes.

If there are ghosts in this room, they seem to have retreated; through the looking glass, perhaps, that hangs above Monsieur Dior's desk. The silvery mirror is placed too high to reflect my face as I write, but it does reveal another version of the salon, itself reflected in a second mirror on the opposite wall, over the marble fireplace. The reflections merge into each other, creating a parallel space; the gleam of the crystal chandelier hanging between the two mirrors shimmers into infinity. If I close my eyes, just for a few seconds, I can imagine the china swans taking flight. They soar up and away from their roosts on the heavy furniture, beyond my reach, and vanish into the looking glass.

Christian Dior seems to have noticed them too; not the little boy in the first picture, nor the solemn teenager captured in another photograph on the desk, but the young man in a third frame. He is with a younger, unnamed woman: I'd like to believe it is Catherine, though her face is in shadow. Her eyes are downcast, away from the camera; she has a smile on her lips, and he is smiling, too. He looks at me again, as if amused, but also with a hint of encouragement.

Go on, he seems to say, follow the swans. Find them, and you might find us. And then he is gone, as a black-suited security guard walks into the room, muttering to himself.

Models wearing the latest designs by Dior, in the couture salon, 1957.
Photograph by Loomis Dean

A model wearing Dior is attacked on Rue Lepic in Paris, October 1947.
Photograph by Walter Carone

The impact of Dior's inaugural show, with the display of luxury in both his designs and the couture house, seemed all the more extraordinary given that rationing was still in force across Europe, and the exceptional severity of the winter weather had caused further hardship and suffering. As Christian himself observed, referring to the bullet holes that scarred the fabric of the city, 'Paris had still not forgotten the war. The wounds in its walls were still there.' These circumstances may explain the outrage that was expressed in some quarters of Paris, and elsewhere, about the extravagance of the New Look. A notorious incident took place during a Dior fashion shoot on Rue Lepic, a market in Montmartre, when a model had her couture outfit ripped apart by several angry women, who were still enduring the privations of post-war austerity and were incensed by the sight of such profligacy on the street. Photographs of the confrontation, taken by Walter Carone, appeared in *Paris Match* in October 1947; there has been some speculation that the episode was staged as a clever publicity stunt, but the pictures do possess a sense of spontaneous drama.

The author Nancy Mitford, who had moved to Paris after the war, was a Dior enthusiast from the start. She ordered a 'Daisy' suit from the New Look collection in February, and joked in her correspondence about the perils of being seen in Dior couture on the streets of Paris. In a letter to her sister Diana Mosley, dated 29 October 1947, Nancy described an encounter while she was wearing her new suit: 'a strange woman said would I excuse her asking but does it come from Dior? This was in the bistro I go to – and of course everyone knows about Dior's prices. So I made up a sort of speech about how I saved up the whole war for a new coat etc.! But I know mine will soon be the same fate of *l'élégante de la rue Lepique* [sic]. Between the Communists and the *ménagères* [housewives] one's life is one long risk.'

Writing to her friend Edward Sackville-West in the bitter cold of December 1947, Mitford asked, 'Have you heard about the New Look? You pad your hips & squeeze your waist & skirts are to the ankle – it is bliss. So then you feel romantic like Mme Greffulhe [Elisabeth, Countess

Greffulhe, a renowned Parisian beauty] & people shout *ordures* at you from vans because for some reason it creates class feeling in a way no sables could.'

In London, the president of the Board of Trade, Sir Stafford Cripps, denounced Dior couture as an inexcusable waste of material at a time of textile rationing. Ernestine Carter was summoned to a meeting at the Board of Trade, with several other British fashion journalists, at which it was made clear to them that 'Dior's New Look was the work of the Devil . . . Sir Stafford banged the table and snorted, "There ought to be a law."'

Carter, however, recognised that no amount of disapproval would counteract the New Look's universal and enduring appeal: 'Tall women, short women, large women and small women, older women, young women, the New Look suited them all.' The sheer prettiness of Dior's first collection also seduced Susan Mary Patten, the twenty-eight-year-old wife of an American diplomat posted to Paris. 'We are saved, becoming clothes are back,' she wrote to her friend Marietta Tree on 23 February 1947. 'And such well-made armor inside the dress that one doesn't need underclothes; a tight bodice keeps bust and waist small as small, then a crinoline-like underskirt of tulle, stiffened, keeps . . . the ballet skirt tutu effect that Monsieur Dior wants to set off the tiny waist.'

Nancy Mitford remained steadfast in her support for the flattering silhouettes. On 4 September 1947, she reported to her sister Diana: 'Yesterday I stood at Dior for two hours while they moulded me with great wadges of cotton wool & built a coat over the result. I look *exactly* like Queen Mary – think how warm though! Ad [Adelaide Stanley, a cousin of the Mitfords] says all the English newspapers are on to the long skirts, & sneer. They may, but all I can think of is now one will be able to have knickers over the knee. Now I'm nearly fifty I've decided to choose a style & stick to it, & I choose Dior's present collection. Simply, to my mind, perfect . . .'

The New Look Bar jacket and skirt, Paris. Photograph by Willy Maywald

Yet for all its beguiling femininity, the New Look was a complicated, sculptural affair, involving sturdy corsets, copious padding and stiff linings of cambric. As Dior himself explained, 'An ethereal appearance is only achieved by elaborate workmanship: in order to satisfy my love of architecture, and clear-cut design, I wanted to employ quite a different technique in fashioning my clothes, from the methods then in use – I wanted them to be constructed like buildings.'

Little wonder, then, that Coco Chanel, who had stripped away constrictive corsets with her fluid designs and introduced trousers more than three decades previously, was outraged by the New Look. 'Dior doesn't dress women,' she declared. 'He upholsters them.' A woman could not ride a bicycle or dash to the office in a Dior gown, and the iconic Bar jacket of his debut collection was the antithesis of the soft, loose-fitting cardigans that were characteristic of Chanel. Pierre Cardin, who came to work for Dior as a tailor in the winter of 1946, still remembered the meticulous fittings for the Bar jacket when I interviewed him at his home in Paris in 2019. At the age of ninety-seven, Cardin drew several deft sketches of the ivory shantung jacket, emphasising the tiny waist, and describing how it would be pulled tight on the already slender models to achieve the desired shape. As his pen brought the original jacket to life again, Cardin caught his breath and glanced at me. 'The girl had to hold her breath,' he said, 'just like this. Even the very thinnest girl, she had to breathe in for the Bar jacket.'

★

In 1996, the author Francine du Plessix Gray wrote an essay for the *New Yorker* to mark the fiftieth anniversary of the house of Dior. Her diplomat father had been killed in 1940, when his plane was shot down as he attempted to join the Free French forces; her stepfather, Alexander Liberman, was art director of American *Vogue* and a friend of Christian Dior's. Perhaps it was this family history that made Gray particularly receptive to the nuances of the New Look. She was seventeen in 1947, and her memories were reawakened as she examined a navy silk taffeta cocktail dress named '*Chérie*' from Dior's first collection, preserved in the Costume Institute of the Metropolitan Museum in New York. Gray admired the colour – 'the most ethereal blue imaginable, only a speck darker than the iridescent plumage of a pheasant's neck' – and 'the wizardly craftsmanship' by which a full skirt with almost fourteen yards of fabric flared out from a twenty-inch waist, in 'the shape of an inverted Martini glass'. And yet she confessed to being 'filled with ambivalent emotions of recollected pleasure and stern reproach. It was not so much the archaic coquetry of the dress that I was questioning as, rather, the collective past self of my generation . . . who had enthusiastically capitulated to the Dior style; who had laced themselves, groaning, into the torturous waist cinches demanded by the likes of *Chérie*; and who had turned their backs on almost five decades of fashion that had gradually unfettered women's bodies.'

In retrospect, the timing of the New Look might seem perverse; Gray dismissed the name as 'the dumbest misnomer in the history of finery'. Frenchwomen had finally achieved the right to vote in the elections of 1945, and Coco Chanel was certainly not alone in seeing Dior's designs as reactionary. Diana Vreeland admired the romance of the New Look, and promoted it in the pages of *Harper's Bazaar*, but was not willing personally to don a corset to be able to wear Dior's early collections. 'Oh I couldn't stand [the clothes] myself,' she finally admitted to a journalist in 1977; 'all that wiring and . . . trussing.' And when their creator visited America for the first time in the autumn of 1947 (having been invited to receive the prestigious Neiman Marcus Award in Dallas), the mild-mannered couturier was met by scenes of protest, as well as popular adulation. He described the demonstrators as 'suffragette housewives brandishing placards on sticks, bearing the words: "Down with the New Look", "Burn Monsieur Dior", "Christian Dior, Go Home".' The controversy made headline news. *Newsweek*, for example, quoted a woman who said that 'long skirts are dangerous. With today's speed, you can't even catch a streetcar in a long skirt. And how can you drive an auto?'

By this point Dior was already famous, and he was astute enough to appreciate that the debate would be good for business. 'The battle of the New Look is all the rage,' he wrote from New York to Jacques Rouet, the general manager of the *maison*. 'It's wonderful publicity. I don't think our name has ever been as widely known as now.'

Dior's instinct was proved right, as was evident in his soaring commercial success, even if the sartorial emancipation that had been represented by Chanel's designs was lost in the rush to embrace the New Look, right across Europe and America. 'It turned the clock back to the restrictive folderol of La Belle Epoque,' wrote Francine du Plessix Gray, 'and evoked alarmingly regressive models of femaleness: women as passive sex objects, displayers of their men's wealth and status – women who needed to be helped into cabs, who required huge trunks in order to travel with their finery, and maids to help them dress.'

Gray also placed Dior's stated desire to return French style to its 'traditions of great luxury' within its historical context: 'Luxury in 1947 was both a form of exorcism and an economic imperative: exorcism of the privations and constraints imposed upon the West by the Second World War, and an ambitious attempt to restore France to its centuries-old role of the capital of Western style . . . Moreover, if couturiers, like poets, express the subconscious longings of their peers, France's particularly tricky record of collaboration may have been all the more conducive to a nostalgia for a safely *distant* past: the guiltless hedonism of La Belle Epoque was an ideally soothing choice.'

There is much in Gray's analysis that resonates today; yet somehow, the genius of Christian Dior still resists such scrutiny or deconstruction. One could argue that the architectural nature of his clothing represents protection, not restriction, or that the padding and layering might be construed as armour against attack rather than a means to reduce women to docile submission. And even if Dior's first collection included evening dresses of burdensome proportions, the models that wore them at Avenue Montaigne swished through the salon with the grace and confidence of liberated young women.

As always, Dior himself provides a thoughtful account of why the New Look was such a success. 'A golden age seemed to have come again,' he wrote in his memoir. 'War had passed out of sight and there were no other wars on the horizon. What did the weight of my sumptuous materials, my heavy velvets and brocades, matter? When hearts were light, mere fabrics could not weigh the body down . . . All this took place in the year of grace 1947. 1937 had danced in the ospreys and furbelows of Schiaparelli, on top of a grumbling volcano. Ten years later, people were dancing in the New Look on a volcano extinguished, we hope, forever . . . Maison Christian Dior profited from this wave of optimism and the return of an ideal of civilized happiness. I insist on using the word happiness . . . Women have instinctively understood that I dream of making them not only more beautiful, but also happier.'

Rising from the Ashes

On the morning of 5 December 1946, as Christian Dior was sketching his first couture collection, intent on creating the most beautiful clothes in the world, a group of seven women filed into the dock of the War Crimes Court at Hamburg in Germany. Among the observers was Jerrard Tickell, who was writing a biography of Odette Sansom, the SOE agent formerly imprisoned at Ravensbrück concentration camp. Tickell observed that the women, who were facing a British military tribunal for crimes they were accused of committing at Ravensbrück, 'looked about them with self-conscious curiosity. Though it was bitterly cold in the freezing rubble of the streets outside, the courtroom was pleasantly warm. There was nothing physically abnormal about any of these women. Each of them might have stepped out of any bread queue in any German city.' One was more noticeable than the others: Carmen Mory, a Swiss national and former *Blockova*, a 'black-haired woman on whose breast was displayed the neutral emblem of Switzerland. She adjusted her red fox fur, the better to show the disarming white cross.'

After the women had sat down, nine men were escorted to the dock. Tickell noted that their appearance was similarly unremarkable, apart from Dr Percy Treite, who been a member of the medical staff at Ravensbrück, and looked as if he 'would have been more at home in a Harley Street consulting-room' than a German court. All the accused wore on their chests a white number on a square of black cardboard. 'As this number was sometimes obscured by the level of the dock, they were

Defendants in the dock at the first Ravensbrück trial in Hamburg.

invited to raise it and, with deprecating gestures, each of them tightened the string around his or her neck, unaware of the macabre symbolism of what they did.'

The hearing that followed was the first of seven Ravensbrück trials in Hamburg; the last of the proceedings took place in July 1948. In total, there were thirty-eight defendants, of whom twenty-one were women. Given the large number of staff who had worked at Ravensbrück in its six-year history as a concentration camp, the trials were necessarily representative, even symbolic. An estimated 3,500 female guards, known as *Aufseherinnen*, had passed through the camp, many of them training there before being sent to other postings. The majority never faced prosecution, nor did their male counterparts. The first camp commandant, Max Koegel, disappeared at the end of the war, and was not arrested until 26 June 1946; he committed suicide the following day in his prison cell. Koegel's successor, Fritz Suhren, fled the camp at the end of April 1945, as Soviet troops approached; he drove to an American base, taking Odette Sansom with him, hoping that her presence would save him. Suhren had been charged with war crimes and was due to stand trial along with his subordinates in Hamburg, but somehow escaped from prison just days before the first trial started. Hans Pflaum, who had been in charge of the slave labour system at Ravensbrück, escaped at the same time as Suhren. Both men were finally recaptured in 1949 and executed in 1950, after a French military trial held at Rastatt, near Baden-Baden.

Odette Sansom gave evidence at the first trial in Hamburg, and the graphic drawings of the French nurse Violette Lecoq were also exhibited by the prosecution. Violette and her friend Dr Louise Le Porz, who together had witnessed so much horror at the camp, were called as witnesses, and described in detail the cruelty of the medical staff in the 'hospital' block.

Another of the Ravensbrück survivors, Germaine Tillion, was present at the trial as a representative of the French deportees. She later observed that the crimes committed in the 'abnormal world' of the concentration camp were incomprehensible to those who had not experienced them,

Carmen Mory when she was sentenced to death on 4 February 1947,
following the Ravensbrück trial.

including the judges and lawyers conducting the legal proceedings. For as Germaine stared at the accused in the dock, she too was struck by their apparent normality. Dorothea Binz, who had been feared throughout the camp for her murderous brutality, was still only twenty-six at the time of the trial, and her blonde hair was as neatly styled as it had been during her time as a guard. Her former colleagues in the SS looked similarly respectable. 'There they were,' recalled Germaine, 'well-dressed, well-groomed, well-scrubbed, proper. A dentist, doctors, a former printer, nurses, middle-level workers. No criminal records, normal educations, normal childhoods . . . Ordinary people.'

Germaine Tillion attended every day of the trial, which went on until 3 February 1947. All of the sixteen defendants pleaded not guilty to the charges of ill-treatment and killing of Allied prisoners interned at Ravensbrück; all were found guilty (although one, a doctor named Adolf Winkelmann, died of a heart attack two days before sentencing). 'During the recesses,' Germaine wrote, 'with the courtroom almost empty, I remained there facing them, looking at them silently, overwhelmed with pain and sorrow before these creatures who had committed so much evil and who now, aligned only a few yards from me, were having to answer for the thousands of cold, deliberate murders of defenseless women.' The experience reinforced her sense that the sheer scale of the suffering was so unfathomable that it would be impossible to ensure justice for the victims, or to explain why the perpetrators had behaved with such savage inhumanity. 'I was very aware that what I knew personally barely scratched the surface of their crimes, and that no man, no legal proceeding, nor any historical study could ever give the complete account. And they, the best-informed, the only ones who had known the entire story, had already forgotten part of it . . . I became all too aware of the widening gap between what really happened and that imprecise representation known as "history".'

Of the fifteen surviving defendants, eleven, including Dorothea Binz, were sentenced to death by hanging. Percy Treite and Carmen Mory committed suicide in April 1947, before they could be executed. The rest received prison sentences. One of these was Martin Hellinger, a dentist who had joined the SS in 1933, and whose principal duty at Ravensbrück was to extract gold teeth from the living and the dead, which was why he had been present at the shooting of the SOE agents Violette Szabo, Denise Bloch and Lilian Rolfe in January 1945. Hellinger was sentenced to fifteen years' imprisonment, but he was released in May 1955 and, with the aid of a German government grant, re-established his dental practice.

★

The sentencing of the Ravensbrück defendants on 4 February 1947 was captured on film by a British Pathé cameraman; there is no sound, but the silent black-and-white footage is as compelling as it is strange. Each of the defendants is marched separately to the bar of the court, all wearing their numbers around their necks, apart from two women in fur coats: Vera Salvequart, a German nurse, described by Tickell as having an air of 'lazy carnality', and Carmen Mory, dressed in her flamboyant fox jacket. Mory is the only one who does not look impassive as she is sentenced to death; she surveys the courtroom with apparent insouciance, and theatrically makes the sign of the cross. When the guards discovered Mory's corpse, after she had slit her wrists with a razor hidden inside her shoe, it was surrounded by dozens of items of her clothing, including her signature red fox fur, like an actress's discarded costume after the final act.

If the Ravensbrück trials were a show of justice against a very small minority of the individuals involved in running the camp, they also reflected the widespread challenges in bringing Nazi perpetrators to account for their crimes. Hitler, Goebbels and Himmler committed suicide before they could be tried, and although Hermann Goering was found guilty at the most prominent of the post-war trials, he too killed himself rather than face his death sentence. Goering had been tried at the International Military Tribunal at Nuremberg, as one of twenty-four leading figures in the Third Reich. This was the first and best known of the Nuremberg trials, and was held in the city's Palace of Justice between 20 November 1945 and 1 October 1946. The Allies had agreed to co-operate for these proceedings; hence there were judges and prosecutors from Britain, the United States, the Soviet Union and France. Three of the intended defendants did not appear in court: Martin Bormann, Hitler's personal secretary, had vanished at the end of the war and was tried and sentenced to death *in absentia*; the Nazi politician Robert Ley killed himself in prison before the trial started; and the senior industrialist Gustav Krupp was judged medically unfit to stand trial, and died at home in 1950. In the event, three defendants were acquitted, twelve were sentenced to death, and the remainder received prison terms of varying lengths.

The International Military Tribunal, like the series of war crimes trials that followed it, was intended not only to prosecute individual defendants but also to highlight the terrible extent of Nazi atrocities. As Robert Jackson, the Chief of Counsel for the United States, declared in his opening address at the first Nuremberg trial: 'The wrongs which we seek to condemn and punish have been so calculated, so malignant, and so devastating, that civilisation cannot tolerate their being ignored, because it cannot survive their being repeated.'

Key to the prosecution's case was the testimony of Marie-Claude Vaillant-Couturier, who gave evidence on 28 January 1946. A photo-journalist and member of the French Resistance, she had been one of the first people to report on the concentration camp at Dachau in 1933, and she survived Auschwitz and Ravensbrück. Her account of the camps was devastating. As dignified as she was articulate, Vaillant-Couturier provided the tribunal with precise details of gas chambers, slave labour, medical experiments, forced sterilisations, late-term abortions, starvation, epidemics, and the SS guards' constant and sadistic violence. And yet, at the end of her testimony, she told the court, 'It is difficult to convey an exact idea of the concentration camps to anybody, unless one has been in the camps oneself, since one can only quote examples of horror . . . If asked what was worst of all, it is impossible to answer, since everything was atrocious. It is atrocious to die of hunger, to die of thirst, to be ill, to see all one's companions dying around one and being unable to help them . . . there were times when we asked whether our life was not a living nightmare, so unreal did this life appear in all its horror . . . for months, for years, we had one wish only: The wish that some of us would escape alive, in order to tell the world what the Nazi convict prisons were like everywhere, at Auschwitz as at Ravensbrück. And the comrades from the other camps told the same tale; there was the systematic and implacable urge to use human beings as slaves and to kill them when they could work no more.'

Marie-Claude Vaillant-Couturier was a communist, and she went on to have a long and distinguished political career in France after the war; but she had been born into a family that was at the heart of fashionable Paris society. Her father, Lucien Vogel, was unusual in that he was as committed to left-wing politics as he was to the art of couture; and as a publisher, he promoted both causes with vigour. Vogel had launched his original fashion magazine, *Gazette du bon ton*, in 1912, the same year that Marie-Claude was born. Her mother Cosette became the first editor-in-chief of French *Vogue* in 1920, and her maternal uncle, Michel de Brunhoff, succeeded to the role in 1929. Meanwhile Lucien Vogel went on to establish an illustrated news magazine, *Vu*, which campaigned against fascism in the 1930s. Indeed, it was in *Vu* that his daughter Marie-Claude's 1933 report on Dachau appeared. In June 1940 Lucien Vogel found himself in grave danger, as a well-known anti-fascist, and fled with his wife to New York. There he did some work for his friend Condé Nast, and continued his political activism, promoting the cause of Charles de Gaulle. In November 1944 they returned to Paris, where Lucien helped his brother-in-law Michel de Brunhoff to re-establish *Vogue*, after it had ceased publication during the Occupation. The Vogels and de Brunhoff were close to Christian Dior, and among the honoured guests at his debut show in February 1947. Their presence – when Michel de Brunhoff was still grieving for his only son, killed by the Gestapo in 1944 – seems to highlight the threads of family and friendship that linked Dior's post-war salon with the events of the recent past, and all its attendant losses and tragedy.

★

At the time of Dior's New Look presentation in Paris, the first Ravensbrück trial had just finished in Hamburg, but another war crimes trial was continuing in Nuremberg: this one against the German doctors accused of taking part in Nazi medical experiments and the mass murder of concentration camp inmates. One of the twenty-three defendants was Karl Gebhardt, formerly SS Chief Surgeon, president of the German Red Cross, and personal physician to his friend Heinrich Himmler. The 'Doctors' Trial', as it became known, had started on 9 December 1946 (the same day as Maurice Dior's death), and it continued until 20 August 1947. Horrific details were revealed at the trial. One of the Polish witnesses, Jadwiga Dzido, appeared on the stand to show the scars on her leg, and the disfigurement and disability that had resulted from the operations she had endured as a prisoner at Ravensbrück, under Gebhardt's direction. Gebhardt was sentenced to death, along with six others, and executed in June 1948. The sole female defendant, Herta Oberheuser, a qualified doctor who had assisted Gebhardt in all the experiments at Ravensbrück, was sentenced to twenty years' imprisonment. But in common with the majority of those punished with prison terms for their war crimes, her sentence was later commuted, and she was released in 1952 having served only five years. Oberheuser then simply resumed her former career, and became a family doctor in West Germany. However, when she was recognised by a Ravensbrück survivor, there was international outrage that she was still practising, and after pressure from

Britain, her medical licence was eventually revoked in 1960. She died in 1978 at the age of sixty-six.

★

Catherine Dior could never bring herself to return to Germany after the war; she could not bear to hear German voices, and even the sight of cars bearing German number plates on the roads in France would make her angry and upset. So implacable was her attitude that when she inherited a portrait of her brother as a young man by a German artist, Paul Strecker, she scratched out his signature, even though he and Christian had been friends, and he had painted the picture in 1928, while living in Paris. After Catherine's experiences in the Nazi slave labour camps, she would not countenance having a German product in her own home, nor buy any of the industrial brands for which she and her comrades had toiled, and which continued to thrive after the war, such as Siemens and BMW.

Three trials of German industrialists who had benefited from the use of slave labour were held by an American military tribunal at Nuremberg. The first ran from 19 April until 22 December 1947, prosecuting the magnate Friedrich Flick and five other directors of the Flick group of companies. In his many enterprises spanning the iron, coal and steel industries of the Third Reich, Flick had exploited forty-eight thousand slave labourers, the majority of whom did not survive. Three of the accused were acquitted and the other three received relatively lenient prison sentences. Friedrich Flick served less than three years of a seven-year jail term, and after his early release in 1950, he went on to rebuild a colossal fortune, with significant holdings in the French steel industry and the German car manufacturer Daimler-Benz. At the time of his death in 1972, Flick was one of the richest men in the world, yet had not given a single penny of compensation to any of his former slave labourers.

The IG Farben trial followed, from 27 August 1947 until 30 July 1948. Twenty-four directors in the chemical firm that had manufactured Zyklon B, the poison used in the Nazis' gas chambers, were accused of war crimes including mass murder and enslavement. Ten of them were acquitted, one was removed from the trial for medical reasons, and thirteen were found guilty, receiving prison sentences ranging from one to eight years (including time already served). One of the witnesses at the IG Farben trial was Norbert Wollheim, who had studied law and politics at Berlin University before the war. Wollheim's wife and three-year-old son were gassed at Auschwitz; he had been a slave labourer in the IG Farben chemical factory that was built close to the camp. In a subsequent interview with the writer Anton Gill, Wollheim said that 'the process of the trial was coloured by the Cold War – US politicians would come over and urge the prosecution to go easy, especially on German industry in case it was needed in the new Allied campaign against the Soviets. And indeed the majority of the industrialists implicated got lenient sentences if they got any at all.'

The case of Fritz ter Meer, a chemist and board member of IG Farben, is just one example: he had been closely involved in the planning of an Auschwitz satellite camp that would provide twenty-five thousand enslaved workers for one of the company's factories, and was sentenced at Nuremberg to seven years' imprisonment. After his early release 'for good behaviour' in 1950, he rapidly rose to become chairman of Bayer AG (part of the IG Farben conglomerate), and took on directorships at several leading German banks and businesses.

The last of the industrialists' trials, which was heard by a panel of three American judges, lasted from 8 December 1947 until 31 July 1948. It saw the prosecution of twelve directors of the Krupp group, including the CEO of the company, Alfried Krupp (the son of the elderly Gustav Krupp, who had been deemed medically unfit to participate in the first Nuremberg trial). The company had flourished during the war, producing heavy armaments and using an estimated one hundred thousand slave labourers. But Alfried Krupp denied any guilt, stating: 'We Krupps never cared much about [political] ideas. We only wanted a system that worked well and allowed us to work unhindered. Politics is not our business.' Yet the Krupp business had become indelibly linked with Nazism, as Alfried himself acknowledged: 'The economy needed a steady or growing development . . . We thought that Hitler would give us such a healthy environment. Indeed he did do that.'

Gustav Krupp, who had been chairman of the company since 1909, had initially been sceptical about the rise of National Socialism, but after Hitler won power in 1933, he became a loyal supporter. Hitler appointed him Chairman of the Reich Federation of German Industry, in which role he expelled all Jewish industrialists. On four occasions Hitler visited Gustav at the Krupp family property, Villa Hügel, a vast nineteenth-century mansion near Essen, presenting him with the golden badge of honour of the Nazi party on his seventieth birthday in 1940, and conferring upon him the title 'Pioneer of Labour'. By this stage Gustav was showing signs of dementia, and he suffered a stroke in 1941. His son Alfried assumed sole ownership and control of the company in 1943.

The younger Krupp was himself a devoted supporter of the Nazi party, having joined the SS aged twenty-four in 1931 as a 'sponsoring member'. Like his father before him, he was appointed a *Wehrwirtschaftsführer* (official military economic leader of the Third Reich). According to William Manchester, in his book *The Arms of Krupp*, Alfried was instrumental in the policy of 'extermination through labour'. Citing the Nuremberg trial records, Manchester wrote: 'Krupp put it to the Führer . . . he said that every party member favoured liquidation (*Beseitigung*) of "Jews, foreign saboteurs, anti-Nazi Germans, gypsies, criminals and anti-social elements" (*Verbrecher und Asoziale*), but that he could see no reason why they shouldn't contribute something to the Fatherland before they went. Properly driven, each could contribute a lifetime of work in the months before he was dispatched.'

It was no surprise, therefore, that one of the four charges against Alfried Krupp and the other defendants related expressly to slave labour: 'Crimes against humanity by participating in the murder, extermination, enslavement, deportation, imprisonment, torture, and use for slave labour of civilians who came under German control, German nationals, and prisoners of war.' One defendant was acquitted; the others were sentenced to between seven and twelve years' imprisonment. Krupp himself received twelve years, and all of his property was confiscated. However, in January 1951 the American High Commissioner for Germany, John J. McCloy, under pressure from the German government led by Chancellor Konrad Adenauer, pardoned Krupp (and dozens of other convicted war criminals), reducing his sentence to the six years he had served, and revoking the property confiscation order. The decision gave rise to widespread criticism, even prompting Eleanor Roosevelt, the widow of the previous president, to write to McCloy and ask, 'Why are we freeing so many Nazis?' One of the judges who had conducted the Krupp trial, Justice William J. Wilkins, later recorded that he had 'felt impelled to write to Mr McCloy', noting that 'trial judges are very often reversed, but at least they have the opportunity to know the reasons.' Wilkins concluded that the decision had been dictated by political expediency, a view shared by many at the time. Alfried Krupp was released from prison, his fortune restored, and resumed his role as head of the company; two of Krupp's former directors, who had been convicted at the original trial, also rejoined the firm.

★

Despite the immense amount of meticulous legal work that had gone into the post-war trials, the emerging tensions of the Cold War brought the process in Germany to an end. The 'denazification' initiative, which had been launched by the Allies to rid German society of members of the Nazi party and the SS, was soon recognised as being impractical. More than eight million Germans had joined the Nazi party, and hundreds of thousands were involved in the system of concentration camps and slave labour factories. The SS had set up twenty-seven main camps and more than 1,100 satellite camps during the course of the Third Reich. Not only would it be administratively impossible to punish all of these people, but the economic urgency of rebuilding Germany was becoming a far greater priority. The western Allies could not afford the exorbitant costs of running the country; in any case, they were now more concerned about the rise of the Soviet Union. Indeed, the Americans and the Soviets had already spirited away hundreds of Nazi scientists to work on their rocket programmes and atomic projects. The Soviet 'anti-fascist' purges tended to be more extensive, and were ruthless in the eradication of 'subversive elements', but there were many former Nazis who proved themselves to be obedient Stalinists, when required, in the new East Germany. 'Looking to the future had to take precedence over a more thorough cleansing of the past,' concludes the leading historian Professor Sir Ian Kershaw. 'Collective amnesia was the way forward.'

Thus Ernst Heinkel, whose aircraft factories had vied with those of IG Farben and Krupp in the use of slave labour, managed to avoid being put on trial. Not a single member of the Siemens board, or its staff, was charged with crimes committed at Ravensbrück, nor were the SS officers and guards who ran the satellite camps where Catherine Dior had worked as a slave labourer. Zahava Szász Stessel, who had been a fourteen-year-old slave at Markkleeberg with her younger sister, having lost their entire family at Auschwitz, wrote in her memoir that 'it was unbearable to think that our tormentors had escaped punishment'. Yet when Zahava was given the opportunity to testify against a Hungarian SS guard whom she had recognised in a displaced persons' camp, she could not bring herself to do so, knowing that he would be turned over to the Soviet authorities who would probably execute him. She had not known his name, but could never forget his face: 'I still occasionally see the man's haunting "wolf eyes" in my dreams.' But even now, she says, she does not regret her decision: 'The feeling of pity and compassion is easier to bear and lighter to carry than the burden of revenge and retribution.'

Other survivors were less able to forgive. Denise Dufournier, a lawyer by training before she joined the French Resistance, wrote a memoir in 1945, in which she declared that 'when, here or there, I hear expressions of indulgence towards our enemies, my heart hardens, for I remember the agonised faces of all those who will never come back and who were, under our impotent gaze, tortured to their last breath.' Dufournier married a British diplomat in 1946 and had two daughters, but did not resume her legal career. 'I was too ill,' she told Anton Gill, 'and too disfigured, morally and mentally . . . What I wanted above all was "earth" things, a home, and a family.' Yet she was forever aware of the gulf that would separate her from those who had not shared her imprisonment. 'The memory of the camps never fades, not even slightly, not for any of us . . . The thing is totally imprinted upon us, and one remembers always the friends who survived, but whose minds were destroyed. What world do they live in still, and for the rest of their lives?'

★

On 1 October 1955, Christian Dior flew to Germany for a six-day tour that would include business meetings in Lippstadt, where the Werner Uhlmann company had been licensed to manufacture Dior stockings since 1953, and Pforzheim, the home of Henkel & Grosse, a firm that produced Dior costume jewellery. Lippstadt had been the site of a sub-camp of Buchenwald during the war, where women had worked as slave labourers in munitions and aircraft manufacture; but by 1945, as was the case right across Germany, the town's factories and infrastructure lay in ruins. Then came the announcement in June 1947 of a wide-ranging European Recovery Programme, otherwise known as the Marshall Plan, after its instigation by the US Secretary of State, George C. Marshall.

This led to a generous programme of financial aid: $12 billion, intended to rebuild a devastated Europe and counteract the threat of Soviet communism. As Marshall made clear in his speech introducing the project: 'Under the arbitrary and destructive Nazi rule, virtually every possible enterprise was geared into the German war machine . . . The breakdown of the business structure of Europe during the war was complete.' By restoring capitalism, Marshall suggested, democracy would be strengthened; and bolstering European trade relationships with the US was the best weapon against Soviet expansionism. The Marshall Plan also provided financial support to Britain and France; indeed, the UK was the greatest beneficiary, receiving more than twice the amount of money provided to West Germany. But its symbolic importance was most obvious in West Germany, Italy and Austria. In the words of Ian Kershaw, 'These countries were now made to feel that they were no longer enemies, but part of an American-sponsored project that offered the prospects of long-term recovery and political stability.'

The Marshall Plan was immense in its scope and ambition, and its effects on a small local community could be significant. Gregor Ziemer, an author who had worked in Berlin until 1939, then fled to the United States, before returning to Europe as a correspondent embedded with the US army, wrote a memorable eyewitness account of how the Marshall Plan enabled Werner Uhlmann to re-establish his hosiery business in a disused artillery workshop. 'The scene is a former Nazi armaments plant, well hidden among the oak forests on the outskirts of the medieval town of Lippstadt, Westphalia. Once the buildings buzzed with secret activity as Hitler's mechanics finished off delicate parts of heavy guns. Today it's a dismantled war plant . . . But on the adjoining [railway] track are rows of cars heavy with pine-board boxes 45 feet long, each weighing more than 12 tons.' The emblems on these boxes, observed Ziemer, proved this to be a truly historic moment, for the labels revealed that they had been sent from the United States. Ziemer went on to quote the speech made by Werner Uhlmann to his workers: 'Men, you have just witnessed a great occasion. This is the first of 20 full-fashioned hosiery machines which are coming to us from America under the Marshall Plan.' Uhlmann described Hitler as 'a tyrant' who had enforced their submission, then spoke of the loss of his family-owned hosiery factory in Saxony when it became part of the Soviet zone in 1945. 'Our plant, like hundreds of others, was dismantled, shipped to Russia. My family and I got away with one suitcase each. Many of you had to steal across the border into the Bizone [the American and British occupied territory] with less than that. But here, through the help of the Marshall Plan, we are going to work again . . . There is one characteristic we Germans all have in common. We can work.' Less than ten days after the arrival of the machines from the US, the factory was producing its first batch of high-quality nylon stockings, and the excellence of Werner Uhlmann's products led to his company winning Dior's first licence deal in Germany.

When he arrived in Lippstadt, Dior made a graceful speech in German. 'For several years now I wanted to be able to take a study trip to Germany; unfortunately I was never able to realise that plan; today I have done so,' he said in his opening remarks, and continued with his customary diplomacy. 'Permit me to express the sincere wish that the exchange between the Paris fashion industry and the German textile and garment industry may substantially contribute to the further improvement of German–French relations and thus a further element of European unity will be created, on which we all hope that our two countries, which are already united in mutual appreciation and admiration, will co-operate to the utmost.'

Even before Christian Dior's trip to Germany, a number of his fashion collections had been presented there, beginning as early as April 1949, as part of charitable and diplomatic initiatives. The first show came about thanks to a request made by three wives of American generals stationed in Heidelberg, and it was a US military aircraft that flew the Dior models and couture outfits from Paris to Germany, to appear at an event for officers' wives and 'other distinguished guests'. A letter of gratitude sent by one of the organisers to Christian Dior reveals the continuing challenges of life in post-war Germany. 'Your charming and generous presentation of those creations, which represent the highest form of creative art, has encouraged everyone and uplifted the spirits of those who at times have . . . despaired at the living conditions prevailing here. Some people can scarcely imagine what comfort a show like the one you have held might give to a woman. She will never forget it nor will she forget you.'

The next Dior event was staged in Hamburg in December 1949, at the instigation of a German fashion magazine called *Constanze*, and with the patronage of the French consul-general and the British deputy commissioner for the city. Three sold-out shows took place, attended by a total of three thousand spectators. The proceeds went to a local welfare charity in the city, and the publicity was extremely positive, with a Hamburg newspaper publishing an exhaustive report under the headline: 'Edifying and Instructive Clothing Show'.

Another round of gala shows was organised in March 1952 at Bad Godesberg and Dusseldorf, again to raise money for charity (this time the French Association of War Widows and Orphans), and at the invitation of the wife of the French High Commissioner to Germany. The Dior press officer, who accompanied Suzanne Luling and the models on this trip, reported afterwards that the seven hundred guests at the Dusseldorf show were mostly 'bigwig' industrialists: 'They are once again enjoying prosperity, travel, particularly to Switzerland and England, and work. They laugh without making much noise, appear well-heeled and are decent citizens.'

In May the following year, two Dior couture shows were held on consecutive days at a Munich hotel, the Bayerischer Hof; much of the building had been destroyed in an Allied bombing raid in 1944, but its famous 'hall of mirrors' had survived. The patrons were the French consul-general and the Bavarian economics minister, and the proceeds from ticket sales went to the Red Cross of France and Germany. Jean

Cocteau was in the audience (perhaps because one of the dresses in the show had been named in his honour), and he cast a critical eye on the proceedings. His diary for 9 May 1953 reads: 'Yesterday, Dior dress night at the Bayerischer Hof. Contrast between mannequins and tables. At one table, there was a fat red lady wearing a massive hat covered in shaggy white feathers and the same white feathers around her neck. The mannequins who circulated as though they were wafting around unseeing and in quite another world could see the room very well and described it to me afterwards. I was in the middle . . . at the minister's table, between two little princesses . . . who were blown away by this parade of dresses.'

The last of Dior's shows in Germany in the 1950s was the grandest, a gala evening held on 12 December 1953 at the Krupp family home, Villa Hügel. Alfried Krupp had been held there for several weeks after his arrest in 1945, after which it was appropriated by the American and British members of the Allied Commission set up to control post-war Germany. With the reversal of the property forfeiture order against Krupp in 1951, Villa Hügel had returned to his ownership. There is no record of Alfried attending the Dior show, but his mother Bertha and his brother Berthold were certainly there. So, too, was the French ambassador to West Germany, André François-Poncet, who had himself been arrested by the Gestapo during the Occupation and imprisoned for three years. The ambassador's wife was named on the invitation as patron of the event; and as before, the money raised by the show went to French and German charities. The mayor of nearby Essen and the French ambassador both praised the occasion as an important contribution to reconciliation between the two countries.

The arrival in Germany of Christian Dior caused an even greater stir in October 1955. In purely personal terms, it was a momentous decision on his part, given his sister's feelings; but Catherine's loyalty to Christian was such that she never spoke openly about his trip to a country she loathed, nor questioned his genuine commitment to post-war European unity and democracy. By this point, the company had expanded across five continents, with landmark licensing arrangements and fashion shows taking place from Canada to Cuba, Scotland to South America, while the Miss Dior perfume was sold in eighty-seven countries around the world. The crucial role that Christian Dior had played in the revitalisation of the French economy, and his unique contribution to France's cultural prestige at home and abroad, was recognised when he was awarded the Légion d'Honneur in 1950. Even so, Dior's contract with Henkel & Grosse had initially aroused concerns in Paris; the French Minister of Industry intervened to request that the licensing agreement be revoked, due to the political sensitivities of such a high-profile deal with a German manufacturer. Eventually, however, the transaction went ahead in the summer of 1955, because of its economic value to France, and was therefore already in place when Christian Dior landed in Germany.

After visiting the stocking and jewellery factories in Lippstadt and Pforzheim, Dior made brief tours of Frankfurt and Heidelberg, before flying to West Berlin on 3 October. Dozens of photographers and journalists were awaiting him at Tempelhof airport, and during the two days of his stay in the city, the Berlin newspapers gave widespread coverage to the French 'fashion tsar', remarking on his famous clients, including the German film star Marlene Dietrich. One radio interviewer introduced Dior as 'the man who created the New Look in 1947 and whose revolutionary ideas have since then kept the fashion world stirred up', yet observed afterwards that he 'doesn't seem all that extravagant, rather shy and reticent in fact . . . You might take him for a bank manager or a university professor.' During the radio interview, Dior said a few words in German, and then switched to French. He told the listeners: 'I was very interested in seeing what life looks like in Berlin and my primary concern was to renew contacts with a capital that still has something to say to the world and is known for its exuberance.'

Another journalist described Dior as 'the archetypal diplomat', and there were more compliments for his graciousness and courtesy as he shook hundreds of hands at a reception for Berlin businessmen and

Above: Alfried Krupp while under house arrest for war crimes, standing beneath a family portrait at Villa Hügel, July 1945. Photograph by Margaret Bourke-White
Opposite: The Dior fashion show at Villa Hügel in December 1953.
Photograph by Ralph Crane

industrialists. Heinz Mohr, the chairman of the Berlin Ladies' Garment Industry, delivered a speech thanking 'the most honoured Mr Dior' for undertaking a visit to Berlin that 'represents a substantial contribution to the union of Europe which we are all striving for . . . We hope that you will take a very good look at our city of Berlin, which we all love so much . . . The atmosphere of this city is imbued with a great desire for reconstruction.' In his reply, Dior also referred to the need for 'an ultimately united Europe'.

The fulsome newspaper reports of Dior's visit ran alongside the other important headlines of the day: the first German prisoners of war were returning home from internment in Soviet camps; the West Germany economy had achieved nearly full employment, and there was continuing debate on whether a forty-eight-hour week should be made mandatory.

A decade after the end of the Second World War, the German economic miracle, or *Wirtschaftswunder*, was already in full swing, and Christian Dior had played his part in it. 'I believe that there is a logic in fashion,' he declared in the last chapter of his book *Talking about Fashion*, and reiterated his belief that 'tradition and enduring values' would sustain Western Europe. 'In an era as serious as ours, where national luxury means artillery and jet aircraft, we must defend every inch of our own personal luxury . . . I believe it answers to an underlying necessity. Everything beyond warmth, food, and a roof over one's head is a luxury. Our civilization is a luxury and we are defending it . . . My simple duty is not to give in, to set an example, to create in spite of everything.'

Marlene Dietrich wearing Dior, 1948. Photograph by Horst P. Horst

The Flower Girl

So we are finally alone together, Miss Dior and I, in the quiet archives of Christian Dior. She has returned home to Paris after a long trip to America, where she was on show in the Dallas Museum of Art. Now, just for a few hours, she is allowed out of the darkness of the subterranean chamber where she has been resting, a silent Sleeping Beauty. Miss Dior stands upright, on a headless white mannequin. Her tiny waistline is as trim as the day she made her debut, more than seven decades ago; her calf-length skirt still elegantly flared, its six layers of petticoats intact beneath. Gently, I reach out to touch the flowers on her bodice: they are soft and yielding, faded, like ageing skin. It seems intrusive to be so close, my fingertips an invasion of Miss Dior's privacy.

Christian Dior once said that he cherished his dresses, as if they were children; hence they were each christened with a name. 'The baptism of a dress has a sort of sacramental quality,' he wrote, and the naming of the Miss Dior dress therefore seems particularly significant. It appeared in his spring couture collection presented on 8 February 1949, two months after the Miss Dior perfume had launched with great success in the United States. I don't usually think of dresses as people, although perhaps they contain a fleeting memory of those who made them, wore them, loved them. But the Miss Dior dress seems different – neither human nor inhuman, but nevertheless a mysterious creature.

The blinds in the archives are drawn against the sunlight. Outside, the

Barbara Mullen wearing the 'Miss Dior' dress from the spring/summer 1949 collection.
Photograph by Lillian Bassman for *Harper's Bazaar*

sky is clear and blue over Paris, on a bright winter's morning at the beginning of a new decade. By chance rather than design, I am here on 21 January, Christian Dior's birthday. Given his own propensity for magical thinking and his lifelong belief in the power of talismans and symbolic numbers, it seems a propitious date for my visit. There are, however, no mystical signs to be seen in the room where I am working; its pale grey walls are blank, the space empty, apart from a pristine white table and black chair opposite the mannequin. Beside me, I have the original programme for the couture collection where Miss Dior made her debut at Avenue Montaigne. Each outfit is numbered, in alphabetical order; Miss Dior is number 89, out of a total of 170 ensembles, and described as an evening gown embroidered with '*mille fleurs*'.

The delicate fabric flowers that cover the dress are exquisite: hundreds of hand-sewn petals in silken shades of rose, lilac, lily of the valley and forget-me-not blue, entwined with tiny green satin leaves. Christian Dior would have conceived the spring gown in winter, sketching it in the old mill in the countryside that he had bought the previous year. Le Moulin du Coudret was in Milly-la-Forêt, not far from his friends' home in the forest of Fontainebleau, where he had sketched the New Look collection.

'The seasons determine the rhythm of nature,' observed Dior in *Talking about Fashion*; 'the new dresses must bloom just as naturally as the blossom on an apple tree.' Yet as is always the case in the Paris couture collections, a spring dress is designed in midwinter (and vice versa). 'But this soon becomes second nature to us,' continued Dior. 'For fashion comes from a dream and the dream is an escape from reality. On a warm summer day it is delightful to imagine a brisk winter morning. When the leaves are falling, it makes me happy to remember a spring garden.'

Dior said that he knew a sketch had worked if it seemed 'to hail you like a friend . . . you feel a sense of conspiracy between you, based on the fact that you have always known her.' He preferred to design in solitude, in a quiet country retreat; but then came the time to return to Paris, and hand over his precious drawings to Mme Marguerite. Under her supervision, the sketches were turned into white cotton *toiles* in the expert hands of the *premières* and their teams of seamstresses. 'The *première* examines her appointed sketch,' wrote Dior in his memoir, 'pulls it to pieces, takes it away with her, gets the feel of it, and finally drapes her *toile* around a dummy figure . . . When a *toile* is successful, one personalises it immediately; if it is a failure, it is just "that dress" – impersonal and contemptuous phrase.'

Once a *toile* had been accepted by Dior as the appropriate expression of his original design, and he had taken infinite care over the choice of fabric, there would be a series of painstaking alterations as the pattern was transformed into a finished couture piece. 'Imagine a manuscript perpetually erased, and indefatigably recommenced,' he explained; but rather than working with his pencils and paper at this stage, Dior directed his team like an orchestral maestro, giving directions with the aid of a wooden cane, pointing out flaws or indicating where he wanted adjustments. Then the design would go back to the ateliers, to be worked upon again by the seamstresses. Throughout this meticulous process, he wrote, 'I will follow the progress of each dress like an anxious father – proud, jealous, passionate, and tender – suffering agonies on their behalf. They have absolute power over me, and I live in perpetual dread that they will fail me.'

Clearly, Miss Dior did not fail him. She was one of the stars of the collection, a glorious creation that would continue to dazzle innumerable admirers, long after her contemporaries were forgotten. Now she is back in the house of her birth, and where she will remain in her final resting place.

Did Christian Dior have his sister Catherine in mind when he designed this superb dress, as a tribute to her love of flowers? The name would suggest so, and he certainly gave Catherine outfits from each of his collections, yet it seems unlikely that she would ever have chosen to wear the Miss Dior dress. By 1949, Catherine and Hervé des Charbonneries had moved out of Christian's apartment on Rue Royale, and were living nearby in a home of their own, at 49 Rue Montorgueil. It was close to the market at Les Halles, and convenient for their fresh-flower business; although they continued to spend every summer at Les Nayssès, which Catherine had inherited after her father's death. There, she tended her garden and the fields of jasmine and roses that were key ingredients for the production of Dior perfume. The pictures that I have seen of Catherine in her post-war life show her at ease in linen trousers and shirts in Provence, or discreetly attired for work in Paris. Occasionally, there are surprises in these photographs: a bold plaid jacket worn on a city street, as Catherine walks arm in arm with Hervé; a striking leopard-print Dior coat, donned for the wedding of two close friends (the groom a former comrade in their Resistance network; the bride a relative of Hervé's). Catherine looks well dressed, but there is little evidence of the elaborate padding and traditional corsetry that were essential elements of Dior couture, which he dubbed 'ephemeral architecture, dedicated to the beauty of the female body'. Instead, she appears to be wearing her clothes simply to get on with life, rather than as a means to display her brother's consummate artistry. Hence the intriguing juxtaposition that exists in a photograph of Catherine taken in 1987 at a retrospective exhibition of her brother's work at the Musée des Arts Décoratifs: she is wearing a modest dark coat, and standing beside a mannequin in an extravagant Dior ensemble, complete with a cartwheel hat. Catherine is gazing at the flamboyant outfit with the faintest hint of a quizzical expression on her face.

At first, as I began to explore Catherine's history, and realised that she was more or less invisible to Christian's acolytes, I felt angry on her behalf. And then I wondered how Catherine had navigated the arena of Parisian fashion, with its brittle etiquette, guarded cliques and whispered gossip. Was she received with respect when she came to see her brother's couture collections at Avenue Montaigne, amidst the chattering swarm of journalists, editors, celebrities and socialites? Did they even recognise her as Christian's sister, or appreciate her association with Miss Dior?

But I have come to believe that Catherine was possessed of a rare grace and inner strength that would have protected her from the jostling fashion crowd, with their sharp elbows, narrowed eyes and stiletto heels. Catherine knew who she was. She had walked to hell and back. She loved her brother, and applauded his success, but she did not need the protection or disguise of his clothes. In the images that show Catherine wearing a Dior dress – for example, in the garden at Les Naÿssès, a glass of wine in her hand, or at the christening of her godson Nicolas, cradling him close – she still looks entirely herself.

As for the uncertainty regarding Catherine's relationship with the Miss Dior dress: a clue may lie in the name of the collection where the gown first appeared, which Christian himself baptised the 'Trompe-l'œil' line. The literal translation of the phrase is 'deceiving the eye'; what might be the visual illusion at work here? That the flowers of the Miss Dior gown were real? That the original Miss Dior was untouched by the horrors of war, remaining safely in the past, an innocent young girl in the rose garden of Granville? Or is it simply as Dior described it in the programme notes for the collection: 'There are two principles on which the "Trompe-l'œil" line is founded: one is to give the bust prominence and breadth, at the same time as respecting the natural curve of the shoulders; the other principle leaves the body its natural line but gives fullness and indispensable movement to the skirts.'

Yet the calm professionalism of this explanation is at odds with the emotional intensity that Dior reveals in his memoir, when he declares that he is 'obsessed' with the clothes he creates: 'They preoccupy me, they occupy me, and finally they "post-occupy" me, if I can risk the word. This half vicious, half ecstatic circle, makes my life at the same time heaven and hell.' The passionate art of his couture therefore resists being fully dismantled, and examined as a logical, rational craft. His most precious designs may have seemed alive to him – whether as beloved daughters or trusted friends – but they also possessed him, embodying an idealised version of femininity that could never exist in a real woman. Miss Dior is

Above: Catherine Dior with her godson Nicolas Crespelle at his christening on
15 February 1948. She wears a couture outfit from Dior's spring/summer 1947 collection.
Opposite: Catherine Dior and Hervé des Charbonneries.

born of a dream, a compulsive desire to create perfection. Adored by her maker, she seems more than an artefact. But like the alchemist's treasured doll in Hoffmann's eerie tale of 'The Sandman', she is unable to take on a life of her own.

★

It feels cold in the archives; the air conditioning chilled to keep the fragile dress from being damaged. I stand up, walk around the grey room to stop myself from shivering, and then kneel down beside the dress, to look at the stitches more closely. Miss Dior remains silent; but could the loose threads reveal her distant past, whirling through a midsummer evening, dancing until dawn?

This was Christian's favourite dress in the collection, according to a contemporaneous magazine story that has been kept in the archives, together with the original black-and-white illustration of the gown. The article features a picture of Monsieur Dior in a grey suit, standing halfway up the central staircase in Avenue Montaigne, looking down, with a serious expression on his face, towards an impassive model wearing the embroidered floral gown. The photograph is in colour, and the dress seems brighter and bolder than today, but the camera might have lied.

Suddenly I remember the remarkable pencil portraits that I first saw at Ravensbrück, of women in their striped concentration camp uniforms. The pictures were drawn in secret by Jeannette L'Herminier, who was imprisoned there at the same time as Catherine. She used a pencil that she had found on the ground; at first, she drew on abandoned scraps of newspaper, then on cardboard torn from the boxes used for the machine-gun bullets that she and her comrades were forced to manufacture in a munitions factory. What makes the drawings so arresting is that all the faces are blank. Yet the undrawn expressions are somehow integral to

Sketch for the 'Miss Dior' dress from the spring/summer 1949 collection.

the power of these clandestine images, which to my eye are filled with sensitivity and love. The faceless women are bestowed with a dignity that seems miraculous, given the Nazi regime's aim of destroying every vestige of humanity in the camps; inexplicably, they suggest the possibility of life, even when surrounded by death.

Unlike many of her models, Jeannette L'Herminier survived, as did her drawings, and she returned to Paris in May 1945. Although she said little on the subject of her pictures at the time, she explained in an interview in 1997 that she'd had to sketch very quickly, to avoid being discovered and punished by the SS guards, and that she didn't have the time or the confidence to draw faces. She also revealed that she had made the women appear less emaciated in their portraits than they were in reality. This, she said, was an attempt to improve the morale of her companions in the camp; it would have been too dispiriting to depict them as they really were: dirty, their hair shaved, abject in ragged, filthy uniforms. By portraying them more as they had been before they were deported to Germany and forced into slave labour, she tried to instil hope in her comrades, and the belief that they would 'remain French, in spite of everything'.

It might seem perverse, sacrilegious even, to contemplate these portraits while looking at the picture of Christian Dior with his model, and the illustration of the Miss Dior dress. But I can't help myself. I don't want those images to dwell alongside each other in my mind: I try to push them apart. There should be a vast gulf between them – a chasm created by the war – and yet they co-exist, if only in my own thoughts. For they emerged out of moments of time that feel too close to be separated, connected by their makers' urge to create beauty.

What did Christian Dior see in the face of his sister when she returned to Paris at the end of May 1945? He left no written account of meeting her at the train station, but later confessed that he did not recognise her. I remember the description of the first convoy of Frenchwomen arriving at the station on a spring day in April 1945. Some of the survivors were still clad in the striped uniforms they had worn in the camp; others were in rags or wearing the clothes of the dead. Such was the shock of the waiting families that they dropped their welcoming bouquets to the ground, the scent of the spring flowers mingling with the stench of dirt and disease.

These, then, are the images that accompany me into the empty room in the Dior archives; the shorn women, the blank faces, the lilacs crushed underfoot at the railway station. How could anyone imagine an enchanting dream after a time of such madness and horror? And yet Christian Dior did. This is the audacity – the improbable daring – of the New Look. And therein lies the illusion of the *Trompe-l'œil* collection, whereby Miss Dior emerged out of the darkness of winter, a young woman bedecked with eternal flowers, looking ahead to the coming of spring. If Christian Dior was a father to this astonishing dress, then it also represented his hope for the future, and his belief in the transformative power of couture. Thus his name would become famous throughout the world, synonymous with the alchemy of fragrance and fashion. In the words of his friend Jean Cocteau, 'Dior is that nimble genius unique to our age with the magical name – combining God and gold [*dieu et or*].'

Princess Dior

In May 1949, Christian Dior's status as fashion royalty was confirmed as a result of a visit by Princess Margaret to his couture salon. She was eighteen years old, and on her first European holiday. The young princess created a sensation wherever she went, attracting swarms of photographers and journalists, for as Christian recalled in his memoir, 'she crystallised the whole popular frantic interest in royalty . . . She was a real fairy princess, delicate, graceful, exquisite.' Such was the frenzy surrounding Margaret that she had been pursued throughout Italy in the preceding days by paparazzi, who captured images of her in a bikini on the island of Capri, which were then published around the world. Meanwhile, an intrepid female journalist slipped into Margaret's hotel suite, and reported that it contained a detective story by Dorothy L. Sayers called *Busman's Honeymoon*, a bottle of Tweed perfume and a phial of Peggy Sage nail polish.

The princess arrived in Paris on 28 May, and in between sightseeing and socialising, she visited four couture houses: Jean Dessès, Jacques Fath, Edward Molyneux and Christian Dior. Margaret was already perceived as being fashion-conscious. For the silver wedding celebrations of her parents, King George VI and Queen Elizabeth, the previous year, she had worn an outfit designed by the royal dressmaker, Norman Hartnell: a full skirt and fitted jacket in forget-me-not blue that had been much admired in the press. The *Daily Express* hailed it as 'outstanding', and 'the

Princess Margaret wearing her Dior gown for her twenty-first birthday portrait in 1951.
Photograph by Cecil Beaton

first all-out new look [*sic*] dress to appear in the Royal Family'. Margaret was also ravishingly pretty, with big blue eyes, a soft, peach-like complexion, and a voluptuous hourglass figure that was perfectly aligned with the New Look silhouette.

On 31 May, the princess was filmed arriving at 30 Avenue Montaigne and being met by Christian Dior. After a tour of the couture house, she was shown dresses from the latest spring collection, the *Trompe-l'œil* line that included Miss Dior, and chose a romantic evening gown for herself. Many years later, she recalled, in an interview with her friend Angela Huth, 'My favourite dress of all was never photographed. It was my first Dior dress, white strapless tulle and a vast satin bow at the back. Underneath the huge skirt there was a kind of beehive, fixed like a farthingale. It meant I could move any way, even walk backwards, without tripping up.'

Dior was delighted, of course, to have secured such a high-profile client, and impressed by Margaret's sartorial confidence, which he saw in the course of this first meeting and on subsequent occasions. In his memoir, he noted that she 'was keenly interested in fashion, and also, unlike many women, knew exactly the sort of fashions which suited her fragile height and Titania-like figure'.

The Dior dress, however, caused raised eyebrows when Margaret returned to England and wore it for the first time at a private dinner party given by her father; apparently her mother suggested that shoulder straps should be added and the low-cut neckline raised to a more demure level. Princess Margaret's mother was certainly well versed in the perils and power of royal dressing. Born Elizabeth Bowes-Lyon in 1900, when she first emerged into public view as the fiancée of the Duke of York (the second son of King George V), she was regarded as charming but not especially stylish. At the couple's pre-wedding ball in April 1923, the prime minister, H. H. Asquith, described 'the poor little bride' as being 'completely overshadowed'; while her somewhat shapeless wedding dress was – in the words of her biographer, Hugo Vickers – 'abysmal in its dowdiness'. Virginia Woolf, observing the Duchess of York at the theatre one evening in December 1929, was dismissive with faint praise: 'a simple, chattering sweet-hearted little woman in pink: but her wrist twinkling with diamonds . . .'

The contrast could not have been more pronounced with Wallis Simpson, the American socialite who in 1931 entered the orbit of Elizabeth's brother-in-law, the Prince of Wales. Wallis was not a conventional beauty, by her own admission: 'Nobody ever called me beautiful or even pretty,' she wrote in her memoirs. 'My jaw was clearly too big and too pointed to be classic. My hair was straight when the laws of compensation might at least have provided curls.' But she was undeniably chic, with an air of polished sophistication that Cecil Beaton described as 'alluring', her skin 'incredibly bright and smooth like the inside of a shell, her hair as sleek as only the Chinese women know how to make it'. The Chinese reference may not have been coincidental, for the twice-married Mrs Simpson was rumoured to have seduced the heir to the throne with sexual techniques that she had picked up in Shanghai at the time of her first marriage. This was not the least of the lurid speculation that surrounded Wallis Simpson: she was suspected by the FBI, amongst others, of being a Nazi sympathiser, and of having been the mistress of Joachim von Ribbentrop, later the Nazi foreign minister, when he was the German ambassador in London in 1936. Disapproving courtiers variously described Mrs Simpson as a vampire and a witch, whose dark arts had hypnotised the heir to the throne and turned him into a masochist. Whatever the truth of the fervid gossip, by the summer of 1934, Wallis appeared fully in charge. The prince's equerry, John Aird, described the situation as 'most embarrassing . . . [he] has lost all confidence in himself and follows W around like a dog.'

As the relationship continued, it seemed increasingly peculiar to those who knew him that the future king was behaving with such flagrant disregard for protocol, and debasing himself with a woman who appeared not even to love him. The strangeness of the affair is reflected in Cecil Beaton's photograph of Mrs Simpson wearing a Schiaparelli dress

Wallis Simpson, 1936. Photograph by Fayer

printed with a giant lobster (the result of the couturière's collaboration with Salvador Dalí). The wonder is that Wallis chose to wear this surreal dress because she thought recent portraits had made her look hard, and she wanted to appear softer and more appealing; hence the pastoral backdrop, and the bouquets of spring blossom that she dangles in each hand.

The Duchess of York, who would no more have donned a Schiaparelli lobster dress than run naked down the Mall, considered Wallis to be 'the lowest of the low, a thoroughly immoral woman', and did her best to avoid meeting her. When the two women did happen to encounter each other in 1935 – at Fort Belvedere, the Prince of Wales's retreat in Windsor Great Park – it was in embarrassing circumstances. The Duchess of York walked into a room, only to discover Mrs Simpson doing an unkind imitation of her. Wallis dubbed Elizabeth 'the Dowdy Duchess', or 'the fat Scottish cook', while Elizabeth simply called her 'that woman' or 'a certain person'. Their mutual antipathy hardened into distrust, bitterness and lasting resentment, following the death of George V in January 1936.

When the Prince of Wales succeeded his father to the throne as Edward VIII, Mrs Simpson continued to dominate his life. In August that year, he set off with Wallis on a yachting cruise around the Mediterranean, and Duff and Diana Cooper were invited to join the party. Rather to their surprise, the Coopers witnessed the King getting down on all fours to release the hem of Mrs Simpson's dress from under a chair, while she berated him in contemptuous tones. Diana Cooper soon wearied of Wallis and her wiles, but she also believed that the relationship wouldn't last. 'The truth is,' she wrote, 'Wallis is bored stiff by the King.'

Nonetheless, by November 1936, it became clear that Edward could not be dissuaded from marrying Wallis, despite the constitutional crisis that would arise if he were to wed a woman with two living ex-husbands. The King's scandalous relationship had already been broached in the US press, including the American edition of *Harper's Bazaar*, which ran a portrait of Wallis in its May 1936 issue, with the knowing caption: 'Mrs Ernest Simpson, the most famous American in London, wears a Chinese dinner dress.' But British newspapers did not publish the story until the beginning of December, at which point the negative publicity was so overwhelming that the King decided that Mrs Simpson was no longer safe in London, and should be sent to stay with friends in Cannes. He asked an old friend, Lord Brownlow, to accompany her on the journey; Brownlow noted in his diary that the King was 'rather pathetic, tired, overwrought, and evidently dreading Wallis's departure, almost like a small boy being left behind at school for the first time'.

A few days after Mrs Simpson had left England, Edward told his younger brother that he had made the decision to abdicate; and on 11 December, the former king, who would now take the title of Duke of Windsor, delivered his momentous abdication speech to a shocked nation. The coronation of George VI was set for 12 May 1937; the Duke of Windsor's wedding would take place in France three weeks later, on 3 June. But there would be no royal reconciliation: the Duke of Windsor was enraged that none of his family proposed to attend the event, and that the title of Her Royal Highness was to be withheld from Wallis.

Amidst this emotional turmoil, Wallis pressed on with the fittings for her wedding dress, even though the decree absolute for her divorce from her second husband was not yet finalised (it eventually came through on 3 May). She ordered a trousseau of eighteen outfits from Schiaparelli, but for her bridal gown she selected a pale blue silk dress by Mainbocher, with a matching hat adorned with an angelic halo of tulle. Wallis's choice of couturier was as precise as her sleek hair and immaculate maquillage: Mainbocher was a house founded in 1929 by Main Rousseau Bocher, an American based in Paris who had worked as an illustrator for *Vogue* after the First World War, and was appointed editor of the French edition of the magazine in 1927. According to Bettina Ballard, who became an admirer of his work after she joined *Vogue* in the 1930s, 'His clothes have always been important fashion trend setters, the women who wear them

The Duke and Duchess of Windsor at their wedding in France, 3 June 1937.

important fashion leaders.' Mainbocher's clientele valued the subtlety and assurance of his designs, and such qualities were evident in the Duchess of Windsor's wedding gown, which was made in a specially dyed shade known as 'Wallis blue'. Her bridal dress would often be copied that year, but the original, which is now in the archives of the Costume Institute in New York, has lost its signature colour, and faded to the dull blotchy beige of weather-beaten skin.

Despite the couple's reputation as highly polished paragons of style, their choice of wedding venue was misjudged. On 11 May 1937, the eve of his brother's coronation, the Duke of Windsor held a press conference at the Château de Candé in Touraine, to announce his formal engagement. The château was owned by a multi-millionaire entrepreneur named Charles Bedaux, an acquaintance of one of Wallis's American friends, who had offered to host the wedding; an invitation that appealed to the Duke of Windsor, who always preferred it when someone else picked up the bills. Bedaux was born in France in 1886 and emigrated to the United States in 1906, where he took citizenship and made a fortune as an expert in industrial efficiency. He had renovated the sixteenth-century castle at vast expense, and it provided a luxurious venue for the Windsors' nuptials. But their association with Bedaux, like so many of their others, was questionable, given that he was already regarded with suspicion by the intelligence services of Britain, the United States and France. (Bedaux was later arrested by the Americans in Algeria in 1943, and charged with treason for his commercial dealings with Nazi Germany and the Vichy regime. He killed himself before he could face trial.)

Cecil Beaton arrived at the château to take photographs of the couple the day before the wedding ceremony, and wrote in his diary that he found Wallis 'especially unlovable, hard and calculating and showing an anxiety but no emotion'. As for the duke, Beaton observed that 'His expression, though intent, was essentially sad, tragic eyes belied by impertinent tilt of nose . . . His eyes, fiercely blue, do not seem to focus properly – are bleary in spite of their brightness . . .'

Meanwhile, Bettina Ballard recognised that ever since the abdication, Wallis Simpson had become 'the major preoccupation' for the American edition of *Vogue*, whose avid readers 'couldn't get enough information about every detail of her fashion technique'. She also noted that the British edition of the magazine 'felt it was in very bad taste to pay any attention' to her at all. For Bettina herself, the poignancy of the Windsors' wedding could not compete with the pageantry of the coronation procession, which she watched from the vantage point of a London party held by Elsa Schiaparelli. To Bettina, it looked like 'a fairy tale', and afterwards she joined the cheering crowds outside Buckingham Palace. 'I forgot all about *Vogue* and acted like an urchin . . . We screamed for balcony appearances. The shy King, the charming Queen, the blaze of diamonds and ribbons against the backdrop of crystal chandeliers were wonderful rich fare for the people . . .'

While the Duke and Duchess of Windsor seemed somehow reduced in their subsequent exile abroad – she thinner than ever, he more shrunken than before, like an ageing Peter Pan – the new King and Queen appeared to have grown into their roles, and they and their two little daughters were esteemed and popular figures with the British public. The King had battled to overcome his shyness and stammer, and the Queen's wardrobe choices became more confident, with the help of Norman Hartnell, who designed a superb all-white wardrobe for her state visit to France in July 1938. Elizabeth's mother, the Countess of Strathmore, had died the previous month, but black was deemed too funereal for her to wear to Paris; the choice of white, however, accorded with the historic precedent of French queens in mourning to adopt *le deuil blanc*.

In his memoirs, Hartnell attributed the transformation of the Queen, and 'the regal renaissance of the romantic crinoline', to her husband, who had taken him on a tour of Buckingham Palace and pointed out the flattering portraits of European empresses by the nineteenth-century court painter Franz Xaver Winterhalter. This, said the King, was how he wanted the new queen to appear, and so Hartnell fashioned full skirts for the forthcoming state visit, in white satin, tulle and organdie. As an image, it suggested tradition and dignity; the graceful antithesis of the hard-edged modernism embodied by Wallis Simpson.

The French were unexpectedly impressed by the Queen's elegance; Duff Cooper, the future ambassador to France, observed: 'Everyone says that the Queen has something magnetic about her which touches the masses as well as the lucky few who know her.' But the Duke and Duchess of Windsor were nowhere to be seen, having been advised that the royal couple would not receive them in Paris or elsewhere.

The rift had been deepened by the Windsors' trip the previous year to Germany, where they had met Hitler and other Nazi leaders. The ostensible reason was for the duke to study the housing and working conditions of the German labour force, but his official biographer, Philip Ziegler, observes that it was more likely inspired by the desire to impress Wallis: 'He wanted to prove to the Duchess that, even though she had not married a King, she was at least the wife of someone who commanded the respect of a major power. He could never do that in Britain and, following the lead of his family in London, the French aristocracy and ruling class treated him with cautious restraint. In Germany at least he could be sure of a proper welcome and, more significantly, so could the Duchess.'

The trip was arranged by Charles Bedaux, who had significant business interests in Germany and would soon be appointed an economic advisor to the Reich. The German authorities paid for the tour and organised the itinerary, some of which involved travel on Hitler's private train. When the Windsors arrived at Berlin station on 11 October, Pathé News filmed them being greeted by Robert Ley, the head of the German delegation, bullish in his Nazi uniform; the Duchess of Windsor wore an impeccably tailored royal blue suit and dazzling jewels.

The duchess was referred to throughout as Her Royal Highness, and met with curtsies; the duke was greeted with Nazi salutes, which he appeared to return. Ribbentrop was confident that the Windsors were already pro-German, and hosted a reception for them in Berlin, where

The Duke and Duchess of Windsor arrive in Berlin in October 1937,
where they are greeted by Nazi politician Robert Ley.

The Duke and Duchess of Windsor meet Adolf Hitler, 22 October 1937.

they were introduced to Albert Speer, Hitler's architect and ally. They had congenial dinners with a number of leading Nazis, including Joseph Goebbels and his wife Magda; the duchess is said to have described Magda as 'the prettiest woman I saw in Germany'. 'What a delight to talk to him,' wrote Goebbels in his diary. 'We discussed a thousand things.' The Windsors also visited Hermann Goering at his country estate; there, the duke and the commander-in-chief of the Luftwaffe played happily together with a model railway and a miniature aircraft that flew across the room on a wire, dropping little wooden bombs on the toy trains below.

The itinerary included a trip to the Krupp armaments factory in Essen, which was already producing tanks and U-boats, and an inspection of SS troops, but the highlight was their meeting with Hitler at Berchtes-gaden, his mountain retreat in the Bavarian Alps. The Führer and the duke spent some time talking privately together, while the duchess took tea with Hitler's deputy, Rudolf Hess. Photographs show the Windsors with the Führer, the duchess smiling radiantly as Hitler bows and clasps her hand in his, the swastika emblazoned on his sleeve at the forefront of the images.

By the beginning of the Second World War, Queen Elizabeth was expressly comparing Edward to the Nazi leader (at least in a letter to another brother-in-law, the Duke of Kent): 'Odd creature, he is exactly like Hitler in thinking that anybody who doesn't agree with him is auto-matically *wrong*.' And she remained implacably opposed to the Duchess of Windsor. Writing to her mother-in-law Queen Mary on 26 September 1939, after the Windsors had briefly visited England, Elizabeth declared: 'I trust that she will soon return to France and STAY THERE. I am sure she hates this dear country, & therefore she should not be here in war time.' In the event, the Windsors did return to France, and the duke found an opportune moment in March 1940 to visit Cartier in Paris, where he commissioned a striking piece of jewellery for his wife: a large diamond brooch in the shape of a flamingo, with plumage of rubies, sapphires and emeralds.

Following the German invasion of France in May, the Windsors crossed into Spain, where Wallis was photographed wearing the flamingo brooch on the duke's forty-sixth birthday at the Ritz hotel in Madrid. From there, they moved onwards to Portugal, and dined with the American ambassador, who noted that they were outspoken against the British government. At the same time, the German ambassador in Lisbon sent a confidential memo to Ribbentrop, saying that the duke 'definitely believes that continued severe bombing would make England ready for peace'. And in London, a damning British intelligence report was received on 7 July, and passed directly to the King and the prime minister, stating: 'Germans expect assistance from Duke and Duchess of Windsor, latter desiring at any price to become Queen. Germans have been negotiating with her since June 27th.' It was against this background, as the Battle of Britain began in the skies, that Churchill, who before the abdication had been sympathetic to Edward's cause, dispatched the Windsors by ship from Portugal to the Bahamas, where the duke was installed as governor in August 1940.

Meanwhile, the King and Queen remained steadfastly in England, and were nearly killed on 13 September 1940, when a German plane bombed Buckingham Palace – one of sixteen occasions that the palace and grounds were struck. Throughout the Blitz, as London suffered appalling casualties and widespread destruction, the royal couple often visited the victims of the nightly air raids. The King wore military uniforms, but the Queen followed the advice of Norman Hartnell to wear light colours, so that she would stand out in the crowds. In his memoir, Hartnell recalled the problem of how the Queen should be dressed when visiting the scenes of devastation. 'In black? Black does not appear in the rainbow of hope. Conscious of tradition, the Queen made a wise decision in adhering to the gentle colours, and even though they became muted into what one might call dusty pink, dusty blue and dusty lilac, she . . . never wore black. She wished to convey the most comforting, encouraging and sympathetic note possible.'

Queen Elizabeth talking to Londoners about the air raids that had hit their area,
11 September 1940. Two days later, a German plane bombed Buckingham Palace.

The Queen was also careful to abide by the rules for clothes rationing, and ensured that her two daughters did so too. Elizabeth and Margaret had been dressed in matching attire throughout their childhood, despite the five-year age gap; even in 1940, when Princess Elizabeth was fourteen, she was photographed wearing the same outfits as her younger sister. This might have looked twee, were it not for the fact that it underlined a message of reassurance that was deployed throughout the war: here was a united royal family, with a devoted queen, a stalwart and responsible king, and two well-brought-up daughters. It was only towards the end of the war that the difference between the two princesses became more apparent: in February 1945 Elizabeth joined the Auxiliary Territorial Service, where she was trained as a mechanic and driver, and photographed in her uniform in front of an army ambulance. The ultimate expression of the royal family's significance and solidarity came on 8 May 1945, as the kingdom erupted in VE Day celebrations, when its four members appeared on the balcony of Buckingham Palace to greet the cheering crowds; the King was in military uniform, as was Princess Elizabeth, while Margaret and her mother wore the customary feminine pastels.

By this point, Elizabeth was already in love with her distant cousin Prince Philip of Greece, and in August 1946, while they were both staying at Balmoral, she accepted his proposal of marriage. Her father consented, on the condition that they keep their engagement a secret until after her twenty-first birthday the following April. When the time came for Princess Elizabeth to choose her wedding dress, she turned to her mother's favourite designer, Norman Hartnell. For reasons of patriotism – the wedding took place in November 1947, when post-war rationing and austerity were still in force – it was imperative that her ivory silk-satin gown, embroidered with a pattern of white York roses, should be British. Hartnell sourced a suitable material from a Scottish

King George VI, Queen Elizabeth, Princess Elizabeth and Princess Margaret in the grounds of Windsor Castle, 21 April 1940 (Elizabeth's fourteenth birthday).

firm, but, as he disclosed in his memoir, 'then the trouble started. I was told in confidence that . . . the silk worms were Italian, and possibly even Japanese! Was I so guilty of treason that I would deliberately use *enemy* silk worms?' Further investigation revealed that these were in fact Chinese – which was apparently acceptable.

Needless to say, the Duke and Duchess of Windsor were not invited to the royal wedding. They had returned to Paris after the war, where their lives appeared to revolve around shopping for clothes, the duchess's daily hair appointments, and adding to her priceless collection of jewellery. Susan Mary Patten described the conversation she had with the duke at a dinner party. 'He is pitiful,' she wrote to her friend Marietta Tree. 'I never saw a man so bored . . . "You know what my day was today," said the Duke. "I got up late and then I went with the Duchess and watched her buy a hat . . . I had planned to take a walk, but it was so cold that I could hardly bear it . . . everyone I saw looked green with cold and their coats were so shabby that I became overcome with depression, in fact I saw one fellow who had no socks on and his ankles were blue, and I thought, 'What would happen to me if I didn't have my fur-lined slippers?'" . . . I thought this description of a day was pretty sad from a man who used to be Edward VIII.'

Their presence in Paris was also a source of tension and embarrassment for the British ambassador, Duff Cooper, and his wife Diana. 'The two poor little old things were most pathetic,' wrote Diana, when she saw them in the autumn of 1945. 'She is much commoner and more confident, he much duller and sillier.' Duff Cooper, meanwhile, wrote to Sir Alan Lascelles, the King's private secretary, to say that the Windsors would be better off living in the United States. 'He can do no good in this country . . . here he can only find a place in that cosmopolitan little world, the existence of which in Paris will probably always continue, and which can never do anything but harm.'

It was inevitable, in this shallow yet glittering realm of café society, that the Duchess of Windsor would be lauded as a queen of fashion, with the magnificent jewels and couture outfits to match her status.

In the Windsor set, ugly politics were no hindrance to what was considered beautiful. Wallis's loyal friend Diana Mosley had married her second husband, Sir Oswald Mosley, the leader of the British Union of Fascists, at Goebbels's home in October 1936, with Hitler as guest of honour. Diana now wrote admiringly of how Wallis outshone the dowdy royal family: 'The Duchess in her Paris clothes looked like the denizen of another planet among the flowery toques and pastel overcoats.' Diana's sister Nancy Mitford was less impressed; she remarked in a letter that the duchess was 'like the skeleton of some tiny bird, hopping in her hobble skirt', and that the couple were both 'ravaged with misery'. Nevertheless, when Pierre Balmain opened his couture house in October 1945 and acquired the duchess as one of his early clients, she was regarded as conferring a regal seal of approval. In his memoir, Balmain recalled, 'The salon had to be used for both displays and fittings, and we installed folding screens at the far end to serve as dressing cubicles. One day the Duchess of Windsor's screen collapsed on that of the Comtesse Étienne de Beaumont, disclosing the two ladies in their underwear, to the consternation of the packed salon. It was Success!'

According to Christian Dior's biographer Marie-France Pochna, even before the house of Dior had formally opened, his sales director Suzanne Luling was targeting Wallis as a potential client. Pochna writes that the Duchess of Windsor's orders from Dior reflected 'her firm adherence to styles she knew suited her understated elegance, simple evening suits worn to best set off her jewellery'. That said, the duchess was photographed by Cecil Beaton in 1950 wearing an elaborate strapless evening gown, the '*Noces de Figaro*'. She also owned a lavishly embellished ice-blue satin dress, christened the '*Palmyre*', from the autumn/winter 1952 collection, embroidered with pearls, sequins and gems. And in 1955, she bought the '*Surprise*' ensemble: a skirt and caftan top in pink silk brocade, woven with ivory Chinese-inspired motifs.

It is a measure of Christian Dior's vision and versatility that he was able to dress a young royal ingénue with as much success as the Duchess of

The Duchess of Windsor wearing the '*Noces de Figaro*' gown in 1950. Photograph by Cecil Beaton for *Vogue*. Opposite (top): Christian Dior with Princess Margaret during one of her visits to his couture house. (Below): The Duchess of Windsor is obliged to sit beside the stairs at a packed fashion show at Dior, February 1957.

Windsor, who turned fifty-one in 1947. However, in his memoir, Dior does not mention the duchess at all; instead, he gives a reverential account of meeting Princess Margaret and her mother the Queen, suggesting that it was their endorsement that mattered most to him. This may explain why Princess Margaret is the only one of Dior's clients identified by name in his memoir, as if her patronage represented the highest acclaim, beyond that of any film star or rich socialite.

Despite the Queen's concern about the suitability of Margaret's first Dior dress, she nevertheless accompanied her younger daughter to meet the couturier and view his latest collection when he came to London in April 1950. Dior was there for his British debut show at the Savoy hotel, an event that had been organised to raise funds for a costume museum. Tickets for the two scheduled fashion shows on 25 April sold out so quickly that a third was added for the evening; in all, 1,600 people attended, generating enormous publicity. The next day, a private show was held for members of the royal family at the French embassy, arranged by the ambassador's wife, Mme Massigli. The Queen and Princess Margaret attended, along with the Duchess of Kent and her sister, Princess Olga of Greece and Denmark. According to Dior, the entire proceedings were shrouded in secrecy. 'The huge ball dresses, with their voluminous skirts concealed by covers, were smuggled out of the service door of the Savoy,' he recalled. 'The whole operation took place amidst a tell-tale rustle of material and constant hasty "sshs".' After arriving at the embassy, a 'final, chaotic, rather emotional rehearsal' took place. The models had practised walking backwards out of the room, in accordance with royal protocol, but the Queen requested that they turn around so that she and her companions could see the garments in all their glory.

After the show, Dior was introduced to the Queen, and was smitten by her charm: 'I was instantly struck by her elegance, which I had been quite unprepared for: that, and the atmosphere of graciousness which she radiates. The mauve dress and draped hat which she wore would have been quite inconceivable on anyone else – as it was, on her they looked wonderful, and I felt that nothing else would have shown her to such advantage.'

Dior was equally enthusiastic about the other Englishwomen that he encountered, and the fulsome praise in his memoir appears to put him firmly on the side of tradition, as epitomised by Queen Elizabeth. 'I adore the English,' he declared, 'dressed not only in the tweeds which suit them so well, but also in those flowing dresses, in subtle colours, which they have worn inimitably since the days of Gainsborough.' Indeed, what he termed his 'Anglomania' extended even further: 'there is no other country in the world, besides my own, whose way of life I like so much. I love English traditions, English politeness, English architecture, I even love English cooking! I dote on Yorkshire pudding, mince pies, stuffed chicken, and above all I worship the English breakfast of tea, porridge, eggs and bacon.' In this and other matters, his tastes would appear to be more in line with the motherly Queen than the pin-thin Duchess of Windsor.

In fact, Dior had been an anglophile long before he encountered British royalty, having first visited the country in 1926. 'I persuaded my parents to allow me to spend several months in Great Britain to perfect myself in my study of the language,' he wrote. 'Was it because I was just twenty-one? Was it because I was, for the first time in my life, absolutely free? I felt far enough from my family to be independent and at the same time near enough to them to summon their aid, if need be. Or was it simply because in that year London was more beautiful than ever? Whatever the truth, I cherish an unforgettable memory of my visit.'

For all Dior's warm appreciation, it was by no means certain that a British royal could be dressed by a Paris couturier. However, Dior came to fame just as Princess Margaret was emerging into the post-war spotlight; and much had already been done in the decade since the abdication to re-establish a powerful visual mythology for the Crown. As the younger daughter, Margaret was able to distinguish herself from the future queen, with a glamour that also contained a streak of rebellion. It would have been perceived as unpatriotic for a queen, or the heir to the throne, to appear in French couture, but Margaret was allowed to choose a Dior dress for her twenty-first birthday, and to wear it in Cecil Beaton's memorable portrait of her at Buckingham Palace in July 1951. Amongst the most romantic of Dior's ball gowns, it was made of white silk organza, the seven layers of the full skirt ingeniously gathered into a twenty-one-and-a-half-inch waist, and embroidered with floral motifs that formed the perfect frame for a fairytale English rose. The dress exemplified the Parisian expertise of Dior's ateliers, yet it also resembled the gowns in Winterhalter's nineteenth-century court portraits that her father had commended to Norman Hartnell. Therein, perhaps, lies a clue to Dior's instinct for sartorial diplomacy.

★

When the Victoria & Albert Museum staged its immensely popular Dior exhibition in 2019, Princess Margaret's birthday dress proved to have lost none of its original appeal, drawing the crowds as a star attraction in the show. I went to look at it on several occasions, including one evening when I was allowed to visit after closing time and wander through the galleries alone. The V&A is one of my favourite places in London, and I've been going there ever since I was a child, but this was the first occasion I'd had the freedom to enjoy its treasures in solitude. Not that one is ever entirely alone in an exhibition of clothes; they seem to murmur to one another, beneath the constant hum of the air conditioning, and whenever I turned my back on a group of mannequins, I imagined them moving imperceptibly closer towards me, as if in a secret game.

The birthday gown took pride of place, displayed in a vitrine opposite Beaton's picture of the radiant princess. In the photograph, the material remains a pristine and virginal white, while in reality it has faded to a soft ivory, and is yellowing in places. After Beaton photographed Margaret in her new Dior dress, he noted in his diary that she said she liked the golden embellishment 'because it's got bits of potato peel on it'. In fact,

Princess Margaret in her Dior gown, greeting Lady Diana Cooper at a ball
in Paris, 21 November 1951.

Queen Elizabeth II and Princess Margaret at Royal Ascot, June 1952.
The princess wears a Dior dress from the spring/summer 1952 collection.

its most unusual feature was the incorporation of raffia and straw into the intricate embroidery, combined with the gleaming mother of pearl, sparkling sequins and rhinestones.

The princess wore the dress to her birthday party at Balmoral in August 1951, and again on 21 November that year, when she returned to Paris to attend a charity ball. This was held at the Cercle Interallié, a club founded in 1917 to welcome France's British and American military allies, in an eighteenth-century *hôtel particulier* on Rue du Faubourg Saint-Honoré. The morning after the event, a report ran on the front page of *Le Figaro*, enthusing about the beautiful princess in her white Dior gown, and pictures of her dancing at the ball appeared in newspapers around the world. Later that day, after lunch at the Elysée Palace, she visited Dior again to watch a presentation of the autumn/winter 1951 couture collection, and was reported to have chosen the '*Topaze*' afternoon dress, with a pleated skirt in silvery grey Aleutian gauze.

However, the next Dior dress that Princess Margaret was photographed wearing was the '*Rose Pompon*', from the spring/summer 1952 collection, which she wore to Ascot that summer. The dress had first appeared in the Dior couture collection on 5 February 1952, in a pink floral printed silk; Margaret subsequently ordered her own version in white.

Her father, King George VI, died peacefully in his sleep on 6 February 1952; he was just fifty-six, and had been suffering from lung cancer for some time. As Elizabeth ascended to the throne, the differences between the two sisters inevitably became more marked. The photograph of Princess Margaret in her white Dior dress at Ascot in June 1952 shows her walking a few steps behind her sister, the new queen. Both of them are very beautiful, but it is Princess Margaret who looks chic, her wide-brimmed hat trimmed with black ribbon to match her black gloves and sandals; her pearls the perfect accompaniment to the white calf-length dress.

In December 1951, Princess Margaret had appeared for the first time in the International Best Dressed List, an annual ranking that had been started by the New York Dress Institute in 1940, and regularly featured the Duchess of Windsor. The princess was ranked at number 13, while the duchess was in the top spot. By 1953, however, Margaret had risen to number 8, two places above Wallis. The list, although frivolous and trivial, was widely reported in the international press, with no less enthusiasm than the speculation about her turbulent love life. For as *Picture Post* observed in June 1953 about Margaret's relationship with fashion, 'What she wears is News. It is seen by thousands of women in person, hundreds of thousands on newsreels, millions who read the newspapers and magazines. Her dresses, her hats, are copied, modified and sold to girls all over the country in a matter of weeks. Her whole life is a public appearance. She is known as the Princess who loves clothes.'

Hence the significance of Margaret's appearance as the guest of honour at a Dior fashion show at Blenheim Palace, on 3 November 1954. The occasion was a charity event organised by the Duchess of Marlborough in aid of the British Red Cross. Such was the duchess's allegiance to the charity that when she conducted a preparatory expedition to meet Christian Dior at his headquarters in Paris, she arrived dressed in her Red Cross uniform, an outfit admired by the couturier as setting off 'the chic of her tall figure'. Clearly, the occasion was an important one for Dior, for he refers to it in his memoir, remarking on the 'magnificence' of the surroundings, and the series of fourteen salons that the models paraded through, before an audience of two thousand. He also noted that Blenheim had originally been built for the first Duke of Marlborough 'in recognition of his great victories over the French'. 'When I saw the two flags of France and England fluttering together in the afternoon wind over the palace, I silently asked Marlborough's pardon for having set up the triumphant standard of French fashion in such a place. At any moment I expected his indignant ghost to join the line of mannequins.' No such apparition appeared; and Dior was applauded by the audience,

Top: Princess Margaret at Blenheim Palace with the Duchess of Marlborough, for a Dior fashion show in aid of the British Red Cross, 3 November 1954.
Below: A Dior model at the show, watched by a line of Red Cross nurses.

feted by the press, and presented with a Certificate of Life Membership of the British Red Cross by Princess Margaret.

When I first came across the photographs of the Blenheim Palace show in the Dior archives in Paris, I was startled to find myself looking into the eyes of my husband's mother, Lady Irene Astor, who was sitting just behind Princess Margaret, beside her husband, Gavin Astor. I never knew my husband's parents – both of them died before we first met – but their faces were familiar to me from the photographs scattered around the family home in Scotland that Philip had inherited after his father's death in 1984. A great beauty in her youth, Irene continued to look quietly elegant in later life; and when I subsequently saw some of her exquisite clothes worn by her granddaughters, Philip's nieces, it was apparent that she had been a client of Dior from the 1950s onwards.

Some years later, when the Christian Dior exhibition opened at the V&A, there was Lady Irene again, on a repeated loop of black-and-white film of the day at Blenheim Palace. In the flickering images, I searched for clues, hoping that something might be revealed by the presence of the mother-in-law whom I had never encountered in the flesh. It seemed extraordinary to me that Irene, who had been born a century before, in 1919, the youngest child of Field Marshal Haig, was a witness to some of the events that most intrigued me. She had been sent to a finishing school in Munich in 1936, and bicycled through bomb-struck London while working for the Red Cross during the war, before marrying Gavin Astor in October 1945. He, too, had experienced momentous and life-changing events, both as a British soldier in North Africa and Italy, and as a prisoner of war in Germany. I often wish that I had been able to ask his advice while researching some of the episodes of this book.

But Irene . . . she is the mysterious figure in the Blenheim photographs; eyes to the camera, almost as if she had been waiting for me to notice her. She seems so close, and I will her to whisper to me . . . but there is only silence, and an enigmatic expression on her face; the elusive Englishwoman in Dior couture.

Princess Margaret at the Dior show at Blenheim Palace, sitting between the Duke and Duchess of Marlborough. In the second row, seen between Princess Margaret and the duke, is Lady Irene Astor.

Denise Delfau (standing) and other members of the Rue de la Pompe Gestapo,
on trial before a military tribunal in Paris, November 1952.

Taking a Stand

On 22 November 1952, the trial of the 'Rue de la Pompe Gestapo' began in Paris, with fourteen people – twelve French citizens and two Germans – facing charges of war crimes. The case against them had involved more than seven years of investigation, during which time hundreds of witness statements were slowly amassed from the surviving victims, including Catherine Dior. Yet on the first day of these momentous proceedings, held in the magnificent Cour d'Assises in the Palais de Justice, the public gallery was empty. Jean-Marc Théolleyre, the journalist covering the trial for *Le Monde*, was painfully aware that his story seemed likely to be ignored. 'It doesn't interest anyone,' he wrote; but he was determined that the details should not be forgotten. For Théolleyre, too, had been a member of the Resistance during the war, and deported to Buchenwald when he was just nineteen. Although he had not fallen prey to the torturers of Rue de la Pompe, Théolleyre was outraged that France appeared to have already forgotten the evils of wartime collaboration. At the very least, he continued, the trial 'could not fail to arouse an exasperated astonishment that . . . there still remain in prison men whom we have not found a way to judge'.

In fact, a further seven of those accused in the case were being tried *in absentia*, their whereabouts unknown. Most notable by his absence was the German leader of the gang, Friedrich Berger, who had fled Paris just before the Liberation, along with a group of his French associates and Gestapo officers. Janet Flanner, who covered the trial for the *New Yorker*, described how Berger was discussed in court, 'like a horrible myth . . . [a] sadist, drug fiend, murderer and probably madman'.

As for the fourteen defendants who were present in court, they formed two rows of nondescript-looking prisoners, facing a military tribunal of eighteen uniformed army officers, presided over by a civilian judge, Robert Chadefaux, in formal scarlet robes. The witnesses were asked by Chadefaux to tell their stories and, if possible, to identify their torturers from among the prisoners, who stood just a few feet away from them. 'Day after day,' wrote Flanner, 'witnesses have related, in a court quiet as a sickroom, what they suffered or saw or heard – men beaten until their clothing became a pulp with their flesh, and women stripped naked, their wrists chained to their ankles, and flogged.'

Among the witnesses was Catherine Dior, who had already been interviewed several times by the investigating team, identifying the men who on two occasions had assaulted her and nearly drowned her in the ice-filled bath at Rue de la Pompe. One of those men was Théodore Leclercq, but when Catherine pointed him out, his lawyer suggested that she was mistaken, and that the torture had been carried out by Rachid Zulgadar and Manuel Stcherbina, neither of whom was in court, having conveniently disappeared without trace. The lawyer then put it to Catherine that she had wrongly identified Leclercq, whom he claimed looked like Zulgadar (notwithstanding that the latter was ten years younger and of Iranian ancestry). At this point Catherine could not contain her anger. According to Théolleyre, she turned to the judge and declared, '*Monsieur le president*, I know what I'm saying. This affair cost people their lives, and now here they are, wrangling on behalf of these swine!' Catherine's outburst is at odds with her consistently measured demeanour during the course of the lengthy investigation process. But if she became emotional in court, that would hardly be surprising; for she was face to face with people who had subjected her and countless others to the most egregious treatment, murdered her F2 comrade Jean Desbordes, and ensured her own deportation to Germany.

The brief mention in *Le Monde* is the only reference to Catherine that occurs in the reporting of the trial, which might seem surprising, given that at this point her brother was one of the most famous Frenchmen in the world. *Le Monde* gives her name, but refrains from saying that Catherine was related to Christian Dior. The *New Yorker* article does not refer to Catherine at all; neither does *The Times* of London, which described the scenes that had been portrayed in court as having taken on 'the aspect of an inferno such as that conjured up by Dante'. Nor does Catherine appear in a report published by *Time* magazine, which focuses mostly on Denise Delfau, Berger's former lover and the sole woman among the fourteen defendants. (Madeleine Marchand, who had infiltrated the F2 resistance network on behalf of Berger, was deemed too sick to stand trial, and did not appear in court until July 1954.) Delfau's role at Rue de la Pompe was depicted by *Time* in colourful terms: 'From her perch at the edge of a bathtub, red-haired Denise Delfau swung her pretty legs and contentedly scribbled in a notebook. It was all quite jolly, except for the water that occasionally splashed on to her clothes when the naked, groaning creature in the tub thrashed in agony.' Janet Flanner also led with her details when she introduced the defendants: 'The woman, Denise Delfau, stenographer-mistress of the Gestapo torture chief, and accused herself of burning victims with their own cigarettes, looks the worst, with a yellow, pouched face. The men look merely like crass petty criminals; it is what the witnesses say about them that makes them loom large and menacing.'

The trial lasted a month, and concluded just a few days before Christmas. Eight of the accused Frenchmen were sentenced to death; three received life sentences of forced labour, and Denise Delfau was sentenced to twenty years' hard labour. Alfred Wenzel, the SS officer who had direct oversight of Berger and his gang, received a prison sentence of five years; the more junior Walter Kley was acquitted, on the grounds that he was simply following orders. Fernand Rousseau, the treacherous French doctor who had willingly served Berger and fled Paris with him in August 1944, was called as a witness, but the prosecutors had reluctantly concluded that they did not have enough evidence to charge him. The seven missing defendants, including Friedrich Berger (who was variously rumoured to be working as a CIA informer in Germany, or for Soviet intelligence), were all sentenced to death *in absentia*. In the event, only three of the death sentences were carried out, against Ferdinand Poupet, Théodore Leclercq and Georges Favriot. They were finally executed by firing squad on 24 May 1954 at the fort of Vincennes, where on 20 August 1944 twenty-six French policemen and members of the Resistance had been shot by the departing SS and cast into a common grave.

Meanwhile, despite the press speculation that Berger had found employment as a spy in the developing Cold War, in truth, the French judicial investigators had been unable to track him down, and he appeared to have vanished like a wraith into the fog. At the end of the war, Germany had been divided into four zones of occupation – British, American, Soviet and French – and many former Nazis slipped through the cracks of the ruined cities and different administrations. The case of Friedrich Berger was but one among the hundreds of thousands that the disparate military authorities were attempting to process, at the same time as tackling the catastrophic problems of homelessness, malnutrition and disease in the civilian population, and the millions of 'displaced persons' who were living in temporary camps. The resulting sense of chaos becomes evident when one attempts to follow Berger's progress through the official files of British and American intelligence. Further confusion arose because Berger used several different aliases (including the undeservedly illustrious-sounding Von Sartorius). Nonetheless, a narrative of sorts can be pieced together from the archival records. After his reign of terror in Paris, Berger's crimes continued remorselessly as he and his motley convoy of torturers, racketeers, mistresses and Gestapo accomplices – not forgetting Dr and Mme Rousseau – made their way through eastern France in the autumn of 1944. During this period, Berger and his thugs were involved in the abduction, torture, and murder or deportation of innumerable innocent victims, on the grounds that they may have had links, however peripheral, with the Resistance. They even participated in the capture and detention of eight British paratroopers who had been dropped behind enemy lines in the Vosges (a mountainous region close to the German border) as part of an SAS operation in September 1944, and who were subsequently shot by SS commandos.

Finally, on 8 May 1945, Berger was taken prisoner by Allied soldiers in the vicinity of Milan, and questioned by a British intelligence officer in Rome. At some point while he was in British custody in Italy, Berger offered his services as a counter-intelligence agent against the Soviets; however, he was regarded as being unreliable. 'He is a torturer rather than an intelligence officer,' concluded an early report, and a series of increasingly exasperated comments appear in his British dossier: 'Berger is talking . . . through his hat,' says one, while another observes that Berger's mental instability was such that he had been moved to a military hospital, where 'like Hamlet he might escape notice in the sense that there they are all as mad as he.'

Eventually the British appeared to lose interest in Berger, and by November 1946 he had been sent back to Germany. In February 1947 he was handed over by the British to the French authorities in Baden, from where he escaped in June, and made his way to the Soviet zone. Berger was arrested in East Berlin the following month and remained in Soviet hands until 1955, serving time in a series of Siberian prison camps. After he returned to West Germany in October 1955 (the same week, coincidentally, that Christian Dior was on his German tour), the French authorities requested his extradition to Paris. However, this was turned down by the West German government, and Berger remained at liberty.

In early April 1956, he was interviewed by a CIA officer in Munich, having offered to work for the Americans against the Soviet Union in return for financial support; he proposed to 'organise a network of agents and to improve the counter-espionage efforts'. The CIA officer was unconvinced by Berger's opportunism, concluding that 'he was probably an agent of Soviet intelligence' and possibly 'on an assignment here in the West'. There the matter might have ended, but the CIA files record one final encounter with Berger, on 14 April 1957, at a small bar called the Greta that he now owned in Munich. That night, Berger began 'talking quite freely' with an undercover agent, who reported that he 'stated that he had been a Nazi and, for that matter, was still a Nazi . . . He stated that he had been a Gestapo officer during the war and had been in Paris. He then related several humorous experiences which had occurred to him in Paris.'

The CIA dossier gives no details about these purportedly 'humorous experiences', but it does reveal that Berger was deemed 'a controversial character who may or may not be of some operational interest'. History does not relate whether his career as a bar owner prospered, but at any rate, Berger died a free man in Munich on 10 February 1960, at the age of forty-eight.

★

At the same time as the Rue de la Pompe trial was taking place in Paris, Christian Dior's work schedule was busy as ever. On 25 November 1952, the annual celebration of St Catherine's Day was held at the house of Dior, as was customary in the couture business. The French tradition, which continues at Dior, is for unmarried women, known as Catherinettes, to wear fancy-dress hats. 'It is on St Catherine's day that you should really visit 30 Avenue Montaigne,' wrote Dior in his memoir. 'In our profession, this feast of our patron saint has a tremendous importance. For me, it counts a great deal. I visit all the departments and in the little speech which I address to each workroom, I try to express the sincere and tender affection which unites me to all those who join their efforts with mine – whatever their part, big or small – in order to achieve the success of our enterprise . . . I seem to lay my finger on the pulse of the whole building. There is nothing gayer than St Catherine's day. Each workroom has its own orchestra . . . there is one continuous ball.'

Christian Dior surrounded by his seamstresses during celebrations
for St Catherine's Day.

Dior's description of the gaiety of the saint's day is another expression of his firm belief in the value of *joie de vivre*. Even though he was noted for his shyness, and preferred to meet his friends and family in small gatherings at home, he made an exception for the costume balls which had been a sumptuous feature of Parisian society before the war. Come 1947, as the fashionable world welcomed the romance of the New Look, so too, as Dior observed, 'the post-war spirit inspired a series of balls. Christian Bérard organised the "Panache Ball", where the most elegant heads in the world were decorated with every kind of feather, including birds of paradise, ostrich, osprey . . .' Then followed Comte Etienne de Beaumont's 'Ball of Kings' in 1949, 'at which every celebrity in Paris appeared beneath a cardboard crown'. The comte's pre-war themed balls, held at his eighteenth-century mansion on Rue Masseran, had been highlights of the season. During the period of Occupation, de Beaumont's social life declined somewhat, although he attended receptions at the German Institute and accepted invitations from Otto Abetz, but in the late 1940s his own entertaining gathered pace again.

Christian Dior attended the Ball of Kings as the King of the Jungle, attired in a lion costume made for him by the young Pierre Cardin (a startling contrast to Dior's usual attire of soberly tailored grey suits). Christian Bérard came as Henry VIII of England; Jacques Fath appeared in a leopard-skin doublet as Charles IX, accompanied by his wife as Empress Elisabeth of Austria. Soon after the Ball of Kings, Bérard died of a heart attack on 11 February 1949, at the age of forty-six. Bettina Ballard, who had known Bérard since the 1930s, when they had worked together on assignments for *Vogue*, was aware of his debilitating addiction to opium, and the ways in which his frantic socialising had kept him from fulfilling his promise as a great artist. 'He was buried in the same elegant superficial Paris atmosphere in which he lived,' she wrote after his funeral, noting the presence amidst the mourners of his close friend, the

Christian Bérard, *Elégante au bal.*

fashionable wit Marie-Louise Bousquet, 'in whose salon he had shone and whose portrait he had painted with an unusual brush of honesty showing the sadness behind her clowning'.

The Ball of Kings was the last of the opulent parties staged by Etienne de Beaumont. But there would be one more lavish costume ball for the beau monde, hosted by the immensely wealthy Don Carlos de Beistegui at his home in Venice, the Palazzo Labia, on 3 September 1951. The palace, overlooking the Grand Canal, had been constructed in the late seventeenth and early eighteenth centuries, and its ballroom was decorated with priceless Tiepolo frescoes depicting the story of Antony and Cleopatra. During the Second World War, the building had fallen into disrepair, and its foundations were badly damaged by the explosion of a boat carrying munitions.

Beistegui (or Charlie, as he was known to his friends, who included the Duke and Duchess of Windsor) was the heir to a Mexican silver-mining fortune, and spent much of the war at his French country estate, Groussay, thirty or so miles west of Paris. Protected by his diplomatic status as an attaché to the Spanish embassy, Beistegui continued to entertain in great luxury, his château untouched by the depredations of the Occupation. In 1948, Beistegui bought the Palazzo Labia, and following its costly restoration, he invited 1,200 guests to an event that would be dubbed in the press as 'the party of the century'. According to *Life* magazine, 'the world's most blue-blooded and/or richest inhabitants' were gathering for the occasion, and its extravagance caused some debate. Susan Mary Patten admitted that she and her husband felt 'uncomfortable, torn between our Puritan consciences and our great curiosity to see the party'. Curiosity won: 'we aren't likely to see anything like it again.'

Christian Dior attended as a guest, and was also responsible for many of the costumes; hence the scene that Susan Mary Patten observed on her way to Venice with her husband. 'We first encountered the party in the courtyard of the Beau Rivage Hotel in Lausanne, where we spent the night. At 9 am it was full of chauffeurs, strapping and restrapping

Dior boxes to the tops of Rolls-Royces in preparation for the Simplon Pass . . .'

Daisy Fellowes, however, arrived in Venice on board her private yacht, and went to the ball in a costume that was said to represent the spirit of 'America, 1750': a Dior gown of yellow satin and leopard-print chiffon, with the feathers of a lyre bird in her hair. She was accompanied by a Dior-clad retinue, including her daughter Emmeline (fully reinstated in society following her period of imprisonment for wartime collaboration) and several semi-naked young men wearing matching leopard-print costumes.

Winston Churchill had been invited to the ball, but chose not to go; Nancy Mitford also decided against it. 'I suppose it's rather dotty not to go to the Ball,' she wrote in a letter at the time. 'But a dress of the mingiest description would have been £200 . . . *hardly* worth it.' Nancy's sister Diana Mosley did go, however, as did Duff and Diana Cooper, Churchill's wife Clementine and his niece Clarissa (she had decoded ciphers at the Foreign Office during the Second World War, and in 1952 married the politician Anthony Eden). 'The ball at the beautiful Palazzo Labia in Venice seemed as fraught as some royal event at Versailles,' Clarissa recalled in her autobiography; 'people became frantic at not getting invitations. Some Americans arrived in their yachts and anchored at the Lido, waiting and hoping they would get to the party. As far as I was concerned they needn't have worried. The Palazzo Labia was so subtly lit that all the exquisite costumes the guests had slavishly created seemed colourless. Only Diana Cooper shone, as Cleopatra, in a sort of pageant held in the great vestibule and backed by the Tiepolo frescos . . .'

Jacques Fath made another grand entrance, dressed in gold as the eighteenth-century Sun King, accompanied by his glittering wife as *la Reine Soleil*; the effect, according to Susan Mary Patten, was 'like an oversweet dessert'. Beistegui himself loomed over his guests, transformed from his normal height of five foot six to a towering figure in sixteen-inch platform heels, wearing a powdered eighteenth-century wig and the scarlet robes of a procurator of the Venetian Republic.

Daisy Fellowes poses in her Dior gown at the lavish ball held at the Palazzo Labia in Venice, 3 September 1951. Photograph by Cecil Beaton

Carlos de Beistegui, the owner of the Palazzo Labia and host of the ball, in costume as a procurator of Venice. Photograph by Cecil Beaton

Perhaps the most unusual costumes of the night were those of Salvador Dalí, Christian Dior and Marie-Louise Bousquet, who came dressed in long white robes and black masks as 'the Phantoms of Venice'. In a photograph of them at the ball, they are unrecognisable, their faces entirely obliterated; they are strangely haunting figures, like ghosts at the feast. Yet Dior's own recollection of the occasion was one of magical enchantment. 'This was the most marvellous spectacle which I have ever seen, or ever shall see,' he wrote in his memoir, and continued at some length, mounting a spirited defence of the event. 'I will not disguise the fact that the Beistegui ball is a memory that I am proud to possess. Parties like that are genuine works of art: people may be annoyed by them, by the very fact that they are on a grand scale – nevertheless they are desirable, and important in the history of our time . . . Europe was tired of dropping bombs and now only wanted to let off fireworks . . . it was reassuring to find that the coarse feasts of the black-marketeers were being gradually superseded by the more elegant entertainments of smart society.'

Rereading Dior's words, I am struck by his reference to bombs and the black market, for neither had really disappeared after the war. The devastation of many European economies, with the resulting shortages in food, fuel and drugs, meant that the black market continued to thrive, particularly in Germany and Austria. Indeed, it is easy to imagine those members of the Rue de la Pompe Gestapo who had evaded justice returning to their previous activities, as crooked dealers in rationed goods. This shadowy world of subterfuge and corruption emerges vividly in *The Third Man*, Carol Reed's classic film noir, shot on location in the streets and sewers of bombed-out Vienna in the winter of 1948. (Orson Welles, who played Harry Lime, the amoral racketeer in the film, was one of the most high-profile guests at the Beistegui ball.) Graham Greene, the writer of *The Third Man*, would also draw on his own experience as a British spy to explore the illicit trade in state secrets that was central to the espionage dramas of the Cold War. Perhaps it was no coincidence that Greene's friend and former supervisor in MI6, the double agent Kim Philby, was accused of being 'the real Third Man' in the 1950s.

The most dangerous of all the clandestine manoeuvres related to the development of nuclear weaponry, for on 29 August 1949, much to the alarm of the West, the Soviet Union exploded its first atomic bomb, on a test site behind the Iron Curtain. As geopolitical tensions escalated, so did the arms race, with the Soviet Union and the United States each carrying out a series of successful tests of nuclear warheads and expanding their arsenal of weapons of mass destruction. On 13 August 1953, Jean Cocteau confided to his diary his astonishment that the newspapers were giving an equal amount of space to Dior 'shortening skirts by four centimetres' as to the Soviets' development of the H-bomb: 'I think any sense of proportion has disappeared,' he wrote, irritably. In the same week as Cocteau's complaint, a picture of Christian Dior appeared on the front cover of *Paris Match*; the couturier is holding a tape measure next to a cropped picture of a model wearing a slightly shorter skirt. Inside, the magazine announced that 'Dior has launched the battle of the skirts,' while another story in the issue drew attention to recent events in East Berlin, where people were protesting against food shortages and price increases. (These demonstrations were quashed by Soviet troops in tanks.)

In fact, Christian Dior did not ignore global politics, as is evident in his commitment to post-war reconciliation and European unity. As a young bohemian, he had even undertaken a study tour of the USSR in the early 1930s, in what he described in his memoir as a 'desperate search for a new solution for the problems that [the] crisis of capitalism had rendered acute'. There his youthful idealism had been replaced by a growing dismay about the censorship, repression and 'hideous poverty' he encountered. And for all his enjoyment of costume balls, Dior was also well aware that fashion had to be attuned to political shifts: '1952 was a serious year from the first,' he wrote; 'the year when the Iron Curtain was heavily clamped down, fires were lit in Indo-China and Korea, and Arab nationalism was reviving . . . away with the euphoria of the New Look, and the fripperies of yesteryear. The new essential of fashion was that it should be discreet.'

Dior's words might seem anomalous, given that his version of sartorial discretion did not preclude dramatic red evening gowns and floral chiffon cocktail dresses; after all, his clientele would always include socialites, to whom the notion of momentous party politics applied to guest lists, rather than events of national government. Yet his dedication to the art of couture arose from a sincere belief that it represented the finest aspects of a civilised French identity. As he wrote in his memoir, 'True luxury needs good materials and good workmanship; it will never succeed unless its roots are profoundly embedded in sober influences and honest traditions.' In this sense, an apparently frivolous party dress could be the manifestation of a genuinely important endeavour. And aside from outfits for light-hearted occasions, Dior's couture collections always offered exemplary tailoring: in 1952, for example, these included a dignified grey 'dinner dress', neat herringbone wool coats, and 'afternoon ensembles' in dark broadcloth or black jersey.

In December that year, when Catherine was appearing in court as a witness at the Rue de la Pompe trial, Christian was in the midst of creating his spring/summer 1953 collection, which he christened the *Tulipe* line. This, too, featured a tailored grey wool day dress, with a demure collared neckline and neatly belted skirt: an elegantly restrained outfit that would have been just as acceptable for the Cour d'Assises as a diplomatic mission in a foreign embassy. Yet as always, even as he sketched his designs in midwinter, Dior's fertile imagination conjured up flowers: an exquisite sky-blue organza dress, embellished with delicate spring buds; and the star of the collection, the astonishingly beautiful 'May' ball gown, embroidered with graceful patterns of leaf-green foliage and petals in rose-pink and lilac. Which of these superb examples of his artistry did he design with Catherine in mind, I wonder. The original 'May' gown is still kept in the Dior archives, and one of the knowledgeable curators suggests that it was inspired by Catherine, as another annual tribute to her love of flowers. But instead, I picture Catherine wearing a timeless grey dress at the Palais de Justice, making her case, standing her ground.

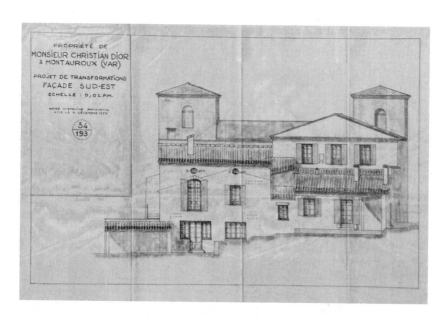

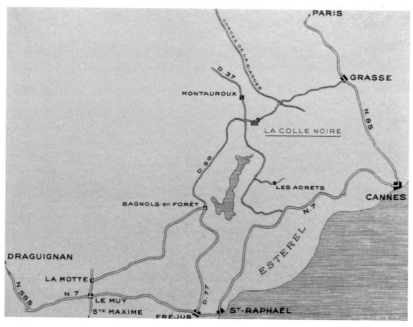

La Colle Noire

It is easy to miss the turning to La Colle Noire, on the winding road that leads through the hills of Pays de Fayence to Montauroux, but when Christian Dior bought the property in 1950, he was already familiar with the area. Just a few miles away lies Les Naÿssès, the secluded farmhouse that had been a retreat for his widowed father, Maurice, in the aftermath of his catastrophic bankruptcy and bereavement in the early 1930s, and a place that also provided sanctuary for Christian and Catherine in the early years of the war. After Catherine inherited Les Naÿssès in 1946, she continued to spend her summers there, while Christian joined her whenever he could, and still had his own bedroom in the little farmhouse.

Le Château de la Colle Noire, to give it its full name, is on a far grander scale than Les Naÿssès: a substantial manor house built in the mid nineteenth century for an eminent local lawyer, who also erected a chapel in the grounds. By the time Christian discovered that the property was for sale, it had fallen into a state of dilapidation, but its commanding position overlooking the surrounding countryside, and its ninety hectares of land, captured his imagination. Having purchased La Colle Noire, he commissioned a Russian-born architect based in Nice, André Svetchine, whose projects included a villa for Marc Chagall and the renovation of an old mill for the director of Dior's studio, Raymonde Zehnacker. However, much of the design of the house would be conceived by Christian himself, and he also oversaw the extensive replanting of its vineyards, orchards and gardens.

Top: Plan of the facade of La Colle Noire by André Svetchine, 1954.
Below: Dior's map showing the location of La Colle Noire.

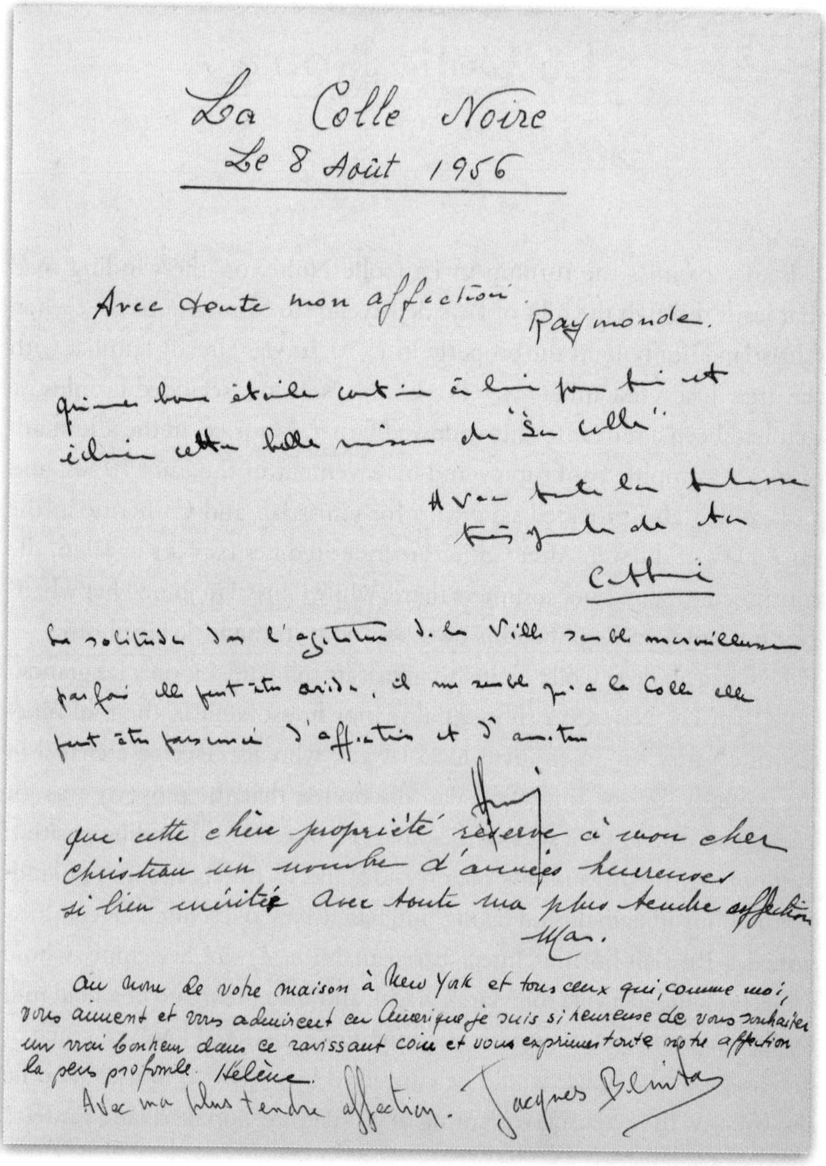
La Colle Noire
Le 8 Août 1956

Avec toute mon affection.
Raymonde.

Que ma bonne étoile continue à luire pour toi et illumine cette belle maison de "la Colle".
Avec toute la tendresse très grande de ta
Catherine

La solitude dans l'agitation de la ville semble merveilleuse parfois elle peut être aride. Il me semble que à la Colle elle peut être parsemée d'affection et d'amitié
Henri

Que cette chère propriété réserve à mon cher Christian un nombre d'années heureuses si bien méritées. Avec toute ma plus tendre affection
Mar.

Au nom de votre maison à New York et tous ceux qui, comme moi, vous aiment et vous admirent en Amérique je suis si heureuse de vous souhaiter un vrai bonheur dans ce ravissant coin et vous exprimer toute notre affection la plus profonde. Hélène
Avec ma plus tendre affection. Jacques Benita

The visitors' book at La Colle Noire, including (above) a message written for her brother by Catherine Dior, and (opposite) a drawing by Marc Chagall.

Pour Dior   grand artiste.

Marc
Chagall

1957

The restoration of La Colle Noire took several years and vast expenditure, but the resulting effect is one of permanence and grace. Outside, the stone facade has a look of quiet nobility, rather than ostentatious grandeur. Tall cypress trees stand like sentries on either side of the gravelled drive that leads to the front entrance. Inside, Christian's vision is immediately apparent in the pebbled mosaic of a compass rose in the hall, an evocative version of the motif that was such an important feature of his childhood home, Les Rhumbs, in Granville. The guest book is open on a table in the inner hall; as I leaf through it, I admire a drawing and message from Marc Chagall, who wrote, 'To Christian Dior, a great artist.' But most moving of all are the words on the first page, written by his youngest sister: 'Wishing that a lucky star continues to shine for you and lights up this beautiful house of "La Colle". With all the greatest tenderness, from your Catherine.'

Along the corridor, in Christian's private quarters, his emblematic lucky star appears in chalky-white plaster above his alcove bed. And it feels almost as if he might have just slipped out for a moment. His battered straw hat rests on his monogrammed Louis Vuitton suitcase; a vase of May roses is on the bureau, picked from the garden, mingling with the faint scent of his own choice of cologne, Eau Fraîche. Next to the bedroom is Christian's study, containing the mahogany desk where he wrote the final chapter of his memoir. It was here that he described his hopes for the future, and his voice remains resonant, long after his death. La Colle Noire, he wrote, 'is simple, ancient, and dignified. I hope its dignity conveys the period of life which I am entering. I think of this house now as my real home, the home to which, God willing, I shall one day retire, the home where perhaps I will one day forget Christian Dior, couturier, and become the neglected private individual again . . .'

I reread the chapter, sitting at Christian's desk, and then look out of the open window, with its view towards the hilltop village of Callian. Catherine's fields of roses are hidden, and so is her house, concealed within the woods and natural contours of the land. Earlier today, over lunch in the garden, I met Laurent des Charbonneries, the grandson of Catherine's partner Hervé, who used to visit them at Les Naÿssès. Laurent explained that Catherine was just as much a grandmother to him as Lucie, Hervé's wife. He portrayed Catherine as reserved, discreet, and possessed of strength and great dignity. She rarely spoke of the war, he said, but she was always willing to discuss politics and current affairs: Catherine was a Gaullist, as was his grandfather Hervé. They were patriots with a shared belief in what General de Gaulle described as 'a certain idea of France'.

Laurent himself has a military career as a doctor; he thought that Catherine was pleased about this, but she never told him so directly. She was not a woman given to physical expressions of affection – although he felt that she cared deeply about the people she loved. One of Laurent's lasting memories of Catherine is her scent, for she always wore Miss Dior – every day, whether she was working in the garden or harvesting her roses. On her dressing table, she kept a bottle of Miss Dior perfume and several Dior lipsticks. She was not a *'femme de fashion'*, but she was always elegant, said Laurent; always poised and well dressed.

As for Christian, he died before Laurent was born, but he says his father Hubert remembered him for his kindness and courtesy, and for the close relationship he had with Catherine. Her presence is still visible in La Colle Noire, not least in a collection of photographs that hang along a passage at the far end of the house. There are pictures of Catherine as a child in Granville and as a young woman in the garden at Les Naÿssès, and on the terrace there, wearing a simple yet chic Dior cotton dress, smiling, a glass in her hand.

Another sign of the connection between Christian and Catherine is evident in the study, where his original black Bakelite telephone stands on the desk, with a direct line marked to his sister in Callian. I try it now, but of course the line is dead . . . although how can it be dead, I think, when

Overleaf: La Colle Noire, 1957. Photograph by Willy Maywald

the house feels so alive? Electricity seems to pulse through the room as I write; my hair is filled with static, and so is my laptop; I feel tiny electric shocks as my fingers tap on the keyboard. I pick up the receiver again, and listen intently. There is a soft humming within the silence, like the sound of the sea in a shell, or an echo of lost time. The clock is ticking on the mantelpiece, its golden pendulum steady. On the wall is a barometer, pointing to a change in the weather. Outside, a gentle rain has started to fall and a breeze rustles through the trees, the leaves whispering in the wind. A peacock cries from somewhere in the garden, and a fountain plays on the long pool beyond the terrace. I return to Christian's own words, written at this desk. 'I am in fact at Montauroux as I write these last lines: fate has brought me into the calm and peace of the Provençal countryside to put the finish to my work. Night is falling and, with it, infinite peace. The avenue Montaigne seems far away, for I have spent the day among my vines, inspecting the future wine harvest. The first stars have come out, and are reflected in the pool opposite my window . . .'

I continue to sit at the desk, waiting for darkness, hoping to see the same stars that Christian saw. At last the clouds clear, and the night sky glimmers in moonlight, before it is obscured again, as if in black velvet. Opposite the desk is a card table, complete with two decks of playing cards, still ready for a game of canasta, which Christian adored. There are several other packs of cards in a cupboard; one looks as if it dates back to Christian's childhood, for it depicts decorous figures in nineteenth-century clothing. Then there is a set of his fortune-telling cards, anno-tated with handwriting; could these have been given to Christian by Mme Delahaye, his favourite clairvoyant? If only Mme Delahaye would mani-fest herself now, to provide a clue and point me in the direction of Dior. I shuffle the cards, casting around in the ether for guidance, and pick out a single one: the letter J is in the top right-hand corner; the two of clubs in the top left-hand corner, with the word *Fortune* handwritten above it. The picture shows a group of six women. One is pointing to the sky, where a constellation of seven stars (the Pleiades?) is connected by a series of lines, forming an arcane astronomer's drawing. Beneath the women is another drawing: a bouquet of flowers, set between two rocky outcrops or cliffs. A bird sits atop the rock on the left-hand side; on the right, another bird appears to be landing at its base. The handwriting at the bottom of the card says: '*titres renomée*'. (I'm still puzzling over how to translate these words in the cryptic context of tarot reading: a prophecy of Dior's fame and fortune, perhaps?)

Legend has it that Mme Delahaye warned Christian Dior not to go to Italy in October 1957, for she had seen inauspicious omens in the tarot cards. But for once he ignored her advice, and travelled to the Tuscan spa town of Montecatini, where he hoped to lose some weight. He was accompanied on the trip by Raymonde Zehnacker and by his seventeen-year-old god-daughter, Marie-Pierre Colle (whose father Pierre, Christian's friend and former partner in an art gallery, had died in 1948). The plan had been for Christian to relax and unwind in the course of a rejuvenating retreat. He was already suffering from heart problems, exacerbated by weight gain and mounting levels of stress, all of which he tried to keep hidden. To the outside world, Dior continued to present a calm and businesslike demeanour, yet Cecil Beaton's perceptive description of the couturier in 1954 suggests the turbulent anxiety that lay beneath the stolid exterior. 'In appearance Dior is like a bland country curate made out of pink marzipan,' wrote Beaton in *The Glass of Fashion*. 'His apparent composure is a deception that belies an innate nervousness and tension, which result in almost total prostration after each new collection has been created.'

Beaton was aware of the pressures that drove Dior, not least the sense of responsibility that he felt towards his employees, who now numbered more than a thousand. But Beaton also believed that in an industry filled with divas and drama queens, Dior was a thoughtful man who was better than most at maintaining a sense of perspective, and therefore at no risk of becoming one of fashion's sacred monsters: 'A bourgeois with his feet well planted in the soil of reality, he has remained as modest as a sugar violet in spite of the eulogies that have been heaped upon him. His egglike head may sway from side to side, but it will never be turned by success. Dior does not make the mistake of believing in his own publicity, though when he arrived in New York he received as much newspaper space as Winston Churchill. He is grateful that when fashion tires of him (and even the greatest can hold the throne for no more than several decades) he has been lucky and wise enough to save a nest egg on which to retire to his farm and cultivate his gardens.'

In fact, there was another secret that not even a fashion insider such as Beaton was aware of: Dior owed a large amount of money in unpaid government taxes. According to his biographer, Marie-France Pochna, by 1957 his outstanding tax bill was 40 million francs, or close to a million dollars. That Dior was in debt may seem implausible, given the company's astonishing success; in 1956, for example, it was reported to be responsible for generating half the total French exports to the United States. But Christian was spending more than he should: firstly, on the grand Parisian townhouse that he had bought in 1950, after moving out of his rented apartment in Rue Royale. The mansion, at number 7 Boulevard Jules-Sandeau, in the sixteenth arrondissement, had been expensively refurbished and decorated by Victor Grandpierre and Georges Geffroy. It was furnished with eighteenth-century French antiques, crystal chandeliers and Aubusson rugs; a Matisse drawing hung next to a Gothic tapestry. The household's smooth running required a domestic staff of six, including a butler and a chef. Then there was the additional cost of La Colle Noire: Christian's pursuit of architectural perfection did not come cheap, nor did his ambitious plans for the garden. The natural-looking pool was Olympic-sized. An extensive irrigation system was installed for the newly planted orchards of almond trees, olive groves, grapevines, and enormous quantities of jasmine, iris, lilies and roses. He was generous, too, whether towards his staff in Paris, or local causes in Provence: for example, he paid

Christian Dior at his Paris home, January 1957. Photograph by Loomis Dean

for the renovation of the historic chapel dedicated to St Barthélemy in the nearby village of Montauroux, and gave it to the community in 1953.

The more that Christian's appetites increased – for rich food, fine wine, exquisite homes, luxurious living – the greater his tensions, and the less he seemed to like himself. Marie-France Pochna quotes a sad observation that he made in a letter to an old friend, saying that when he saw himself in the mirror, his reflection shamed him: 'your old couturier growing fatter as he withers away'. In 1956, Christian had fallen in love with a handsome young man, a Moroccan-born singer named Jacques Benita; but this relationship appeared not to assuage his anxieties, or his constant pursuit of perfection at work. As a consequence, when Christian arrived at the Grand Hotel in Montecatini on 20 October 1957, his worries came with him.

The plan had been for him to rest, but he spent much of the following day on the telephone to his office in Paris. Nevertheless, when he did leave his room, he behaved with his characteristic politeness, and members of the hotel staff were charmed by his good manners. On the evening of 23 October, Christian played card games with Raymonde and Marie-Pierre, and then retired to his bedroom for an early night. Raymonde decided to check on him a little later – she said afterwards that she had 'a premonition' – and found him unconscious on the bathroom floor. Doctors were summoned, but Christian was pronounced dead, just after midnight, as a result of a heart attack. Raymonde rang Catherine straight away, and she set off directly for Italy. She arrived at Montecatini in time to see the body of her brother, dressed in black, laid out on the bed, before it was transferred to a coffin and flown back to Paris on Marcel Boussac's private plane.

The news of Christian Dior's sudden death at the age of only fifty-two broke swiftly, making international headlines; and there was a genuine sense of shock that he could have died just a decade after his transformation of the couture industry. Dior had appeared on the front cover of *Time* in March 1957, holding a giant pair of scissors, as if he wielded the ultimate power over fashion. Some observers believed that he would be irreplaceable, and that 'the fall of the house of Dior' was inevitable. In fact, his brilliant successor was already in place – the young Yves Saint Laurent, who had been working for Dior since 1955 – but even so, his death marked the dramatic end of an era. Several of his contemporaries had also died comparatively young – Robert Piguet in 1953, at the age of fifty-four; Jacques Fath in 1954, aged forty-two; Marcel Rochas in 1955, at fifty-three – leading commentators to question the high toll that the industry took on its practitioners.

Catherine Dior would later suggest, in an interview with Stanley Garfinkel, that her brother's inexorable workload may have contributed to his early death: 'My brother worked a lot, and that's probably one of the reasons why he couldn't endure this perpetual competition, which is that of fashion designer, for more than ten years. His health was quite fragile, and he gave himself fully in his profession, in creation, in the supervision of his fashion house, in his business and various presentations that he made in the United States: all this was very tiring for him . . .' As Christian's professional schedule became ever more relentless, she continued, 'we could not see each other as often as before, although our bonds of affection and tenderness were very strong.'

Clearly, the demands of fashion had grown consuming; yet the demise of Christian Dior seemed to represent a loss that went far beyond the world of couture. His friend Pierre Bergé, who would subsequently become Saint Laurent's partner, described Dior's death as 'a national event. It was as if France had ceased to live.' The funeral, which took place on 29 October at the church of St Honoré d'Eylau, had the air of a state occasion, with huge crowds gathering outside, and two thousand mourners inside. The Duchess of Windsor attended the ceremony, as did Jean Cocteau, Carmel Snow and the majority of Dior's fellow couturiers: Lucien Lelong, Jacques Heim, Jean Dessès, Pierre Cardin, Hubert de Givenchy and Cristóbal Balenciaga. Coco Chanel did not come, but sent a wreath of red roses. Indeed, there were so

Opposite: Christian Dior's funeral, held at the church of St Honoré d'Eylau in Paris on 29 October 1957. Above: Floral tributes arranged by Catherine to be laid beside the Tomb of the Unknown Soldier at the Arc de Triomphe. Photographs by Loomis Dean

many flowers – including Christian's favourite lily of the valley – that they filled the church and spilled out into the street. Catherine had taken care that these floral offerings should be moved afterwards to lie beneath the Tomb of the Unknown Soldier at the Arc de Triomphe. It was Catherine, too, who made the arrangements regarding her brother's final resting place in the cemetery at Callian and accompanied his coffin there on the overnight journey from Paris, her face hidden in a black mourning veil.

Pierre Bergé was among the small group of friends who travelled south in the funeral convoy, and recalled his astonishment at seeing 'all the women of the villages coming out of their houses, to throw flowers' as the hearse drove towards Callian. Another funeral mass was conducted there by the local priest, before the coffin was finally laid in its grave, with Catherine watching, her head bowed down in grief, her eyes masked by the traditional veil. 'You feel sorrow, my dear brethren,' said the priest. 'But remember that if God called Dior to Him, it was because He needed him to dress the angels . . .'

It took a more worldly man, Jean Cocteau, to provide an alternative perspective. 'His kindness was matched by that delightful genius with which he transcended the frivolous dictates of fashion,' wrote Cocteau in a memorial tribute to Dior. 'This prince of light knew and respected the princes of darkness . . . The sudden death of Christian Dior testifies to the rule that states that after the fireworks, the night must send everyone back home.'

★

Midnight approaches, and all is silent within the walls of La Colle Noire. I climb the stairs, up to Catherine's sanctuary at the top of the house, where I am to sleep tonight. In 1958, she lived here for six months with Hervé des Charbonneries, while Les Naÿssès was being modernised (up until then, the farmhouse had no electricity and only rudimentary

Catherine Dior (on the left, in a black veil) at her brother's burial in Callian, 30 October 1957, accompanied by Hervé des Charbonneries and Marthe Lefebvre.

plumbing). Her brother's will had been simple – he left everything to Catherine and Raymonde Zehnacker, the two women who represented the different sides of his life: the seasonal rhythms of rural Provence and the frenetic business of Paris fashion. But such were his debts that La Colle Noire would have to be sold, along with his townhouse in Paris. Catherine was named the 'moral heir', responsible for preserving Christian Dior's artistic heritage; a task that she took on with her characteristic loyalty, ensuring that his autobiography remained in print, and that his couture creations would be preserved in various archives, as well as supporting the establishment of the Dior museum in Granville.

After Christian's death, Catherine gave up her cut-flower business in Paris and decided to move permanently to Callian, where she would concentrate on the cultivation of roses and jasmine. But first, her brother's estate had to be settled and his affairs put in order. La Colle Noire took some time to sell, and passed through several hands before it was bought in 2013 by Christian Dior Parfums (now part of the mighty LVMH group, as is the Dior fashion business). Fortunately, its original contents had been kept safe by Catherine – even Christian's decks of playing cards – and these were reinstated in the property, along with other mementoes that were acquired by LVMH.

Such is the loving care that has gone into the restoration of La Colle Noire that it does not feel like a pastiche or a set design, as is evident in Catherine's rooms. Her bedroom has two windows overlooking the garden and the hills beyond, and on another wall a little porthole, as if on board a ship. It is discreetly feminine, decorated in charmingly old-fashioned chintz, with butterflies and birds woven between garlands of yellow and pink flowers. A spiral staircase is tucked away neatly in the corner of the bedroom, leading to another room above, an eyrie perched at the top of one of the château's two towers.

The windows are open to the May night, and the sound of the fountain below is soothing, as I lie awake in Catherine's bed. Her initials are on the wrought-iron frame; the same letters as her brother's name, although I remember that in her own copy of his memoir, preserved in the Dior archives in Paris, there is a handwritten dedication, in which he signed himself 'Tian'. ('To my Catherine, from your brother, with the greatest of devotion and the deepest tenderness, Tian'.) I await ghosts, but none are forthcoming; I sleep deeply, dreamlessly, waking at sunrise to a joyful dawn chorus of birdsong. The sky is washed clear after last night's rain, but the surrounding hills remain drenched and dark – the black hills that gave La Colle Noire its name.

For all the beauty of this terrain, it still bears the scars of the war, in the form of the local memorials to those who died in the cause of the Resistance. In early July 1944, at the same time as Catherine was arrested in Paris, the hilltop villages of Callian and Montauroux were surrounded by the Germans and searched, house by house, resulting in fifteen members of the Resistance being captured, interrogated and imprisoned. One of them, Henri Bourguignon, was deported to Dachau, where he died on Christmas Eve in 1944; a plaque in his honour has been placed on the wall of the church in Callian. The names of another seventeen local resistants are commemorated in Montauroux, three of whom sacrificed their lives for their cause, including Justin Blanc, who was also transported to Dachau, where he too died on 19 March 1945. Directly opposite the gates of La Colle Noire stands a prominent stone memorial in honour of a twenty-year-old local shepherd called Justin Ramonda, who had joined the Resistance in 1943 and was in charge of his unit's machine gun. On 15 August 1944, the same day that Allied troops landed on the nearby Mediterranean coast, and Catherine was deported from Paris to Ravensbrück, Ramonda took part in an operation to hold back a German convoy until the United States Army Air Forces could intervene. He was captured and shot on the spot, and awarded a posthumous Croix de Guerre. Less gloriously, but all too representative of the bitter divisions that existed in France during the war, Justin's elder brother had been a member of the SS security police, and was sentenced by a military tribunal to life imprisonment with hard labour.

This history is as integral to the landscape that surrounds La Colle Noire as the timeless fields of roses, the soaring steeples, ancient stone walls, tall cypress trees and immense Provençal skies. And Christian Dior's domain does not – cannot – exclude the knowledge of the wartime past. Certainly, it is a place that holds the promise of enchantment; to be here, safe within its solid walls, or wandering through its verdant gardens, protected from the outside world by evergreen hedges and encircled by trees, is to feel that one has stepped into a magical realm. Yet the vestiges of Catherine's presence remain as a powerful reminder of the importance of freedom, and why it is worth fighting for. In 1954, Christian Dior said that 'Miss Dior was born of those Provençal evenings, alive with fireflies, where young jasmine plays a descant to the melody of the night and the land.' But the perfume was created less than two years after the end of the war, and its ingredients were grown in the earth where blood was shed and lives were lost.

When Christian considered the duality of his life, in the closing lines of his memoir, he did so at La Colle Noire. 'It is the moment to bring the two Christian Diors face to face, myself and this Siamese twin of mine to whom I owe my success. It is fitting that we should meet here among the vines and the jasmine, for I am always more self-confident when I feel near to soil.' If he did indeed feel split in two – as a public and private figure, a couturier and a countryman – one can understand how this divided self might be the cause of illness and instability. That is, perhaps, Dior's tragedy, as well as the source of his greatness: a prince of light who knew the power of darkness; the tender brother who could not forget his sister's suffering and sacrifice, even as he swathed her in floral silks and the scent of love.

Handwritten dedication by Christian to Catherine in his memoir.

CHRISTIAN
DIOR
ET
MOI

pour
ma catherine
son frère, avec
tout ce que ce mot
comporte d'attachement
et de profonde tendresse

tian

No Rose without a Thorn

The scent of roses is all around me as I write, a vase of rose de Mai on the wooden table beside me. They are Catherine's roses, grown from the original bushes that she planted here at Les Naÿssès. I can see her meadow of roses through the open window, where two women are gathering the flowers in the morning sunlight.

Les Naÿssès is surrounded by fields of flowers, fringed with wild poppies and sheltered by cypress trees, tucked away beneath the hilltop village of Callian. It is a hidden domain, unmarked on the map, reached at the end of a narrow lane, after you have crossed a ford in the river that would be impassable during the storms of midwinter. Even in the gentle month of May, the river is deeper than I'd expected, and it forms another barrier between Les Naÿssès and the outside world. But Catherine liked it that way; she let the pine trees grow higher, and the hedgerows taller, the needle-sharp thorns of the briar roses forming another deterrent to unwanted visitors.

When Catherine and Hervé lived here together, after Christian's death, Hervé's three children would stay during the holidays, and her godson Nicolas came twice a year, too, at Easter and in July, for the jasmine harvest; so they were not completely inaccessible. Catherine remained very close to Nicolas's mother, Liliane, her former comrade in the Resistance, and she and Hervé kept in touch with other people who had longstanding links to the F2 network. Their guests visited during the summer months, when the heady perfume of the roses and jasmine was at its

Catherine in the garden at Les Naÿssès after her return from Germany, summer 1945.

Above: Catherine Dior and Hervé des Charbonneries in the garden and rose meadows of Les Naÿssès. Opposite: The rose harvest at Les Naÿssès.

height, and the garden was filled with flowers. It is still beautiful today. Little yellow butterflies dance over the lavender bushes; the fragrance of rosemary and thyme mingles in the air; a grove of olive trees casts a dappled shade, and the grapevines and wisteria are flourishing, just as they did in the days when Christian sat on the terrace, learning to draw fashion illustrations.

Those few surviving friends and neighbours who knew Catherine tend to use the same word when they describe her: *forte* (strong). I hear it so often that I begin to think of Les Naÿssès as a fortress: her stronghold. 'She worked very hard in her fields,' recalled one of Catherine's neighbours. 'She was completely absorbed by her roses and her vines. And she was a very strong character, but complicated, and isolated for the most part from the local community.' Catherine didn't attend services at the local church, but did go to an annual service on 24 August at the chapel of St Barthélemy in Montauroux, in honour of her brother Christian. In later life, she accepted an invitation from a local school, to talk to the children about the Second World War. And she would never miss the yearly commemoration of those who died for the cause of the Resistance. A former soldier who came to Callian on one of these occasions told me how he hadn't met Catherine before, but he introduced himself as a veteran of a more recent war, and asked her about her own experiences. She looked taken aback, he remarked, but did not turn away from him. 'She simply said, "*Aime la vie, jeune homme . . .*"' Love life . . .

Catherine's own love of life is evident in her garden, for to plant olive trees, vines and meadows of roses is to express a hope for the future. Not every rose bush will survive the winter storms, and those that do will still bear thorns. Yet to tend her land, as Catherine did for more than half a century, suggests a devotion born of a lifetime's understanding. Indeed, in this sense, Catherine's approach to gardening is not dissimilar to Christian's philosophy of couture. 'The maintenance of the tradition of fashion is in the nature of an act of faith,' he wrote in the final page of his memoir (those lines that I return to again and again). 'In a century

Top: Catherine Dior at the annual commemoration in Callian for those who fought and died for a free France. Above: Catherine's membership card of the Association of Deportees, which records the details of her imprisonment in Germany.

which attempts to tear the heart out of every mystery, fashion guards its secret well, and is the best possible proof that there is still magic abroad.'

To witness the shimmering sunrise and sunset in Catherine's garden is indeed a source of wonder. I can well understand why she fought so hard to stay alive in Germany, so that she could see these incandescent skies again. Yet there was no magician's wand that could wave away the scars of her torture and the evil of concentration camps; Catherine's medical records show that she continued to suffer the effects for the rest of her life. But such was her fortitude that she stayed at Les Naÿssès until the age of ninety, living there alone after Hervé's death in September 1989. She died on 17 June 2008, having continued to work in her garden almost until the end.

Catherine outlived the people that she was closest to: Christian, Hervé, and her friend Liliane, who died in February 1997. Those who knew her say that after these losses, she was sustained by her love of Les Naÿssès, as well as her own remarkable strength of character. Liliane's son Nicolas told me that Catherine was the person that his mother 'trusted most in her life', and that he himself admired and loved Catherine. But he also admits that as a child, he was 'a little afraid of her': 'When she rang the bell for dinner, you had to be there in two minutes. There was no physical tenderness; but she always knew what to do if there was a problem. I cut my finger badly one day when I was staying there, and she was the one who knew how to take care of it.'

Like Hervé's grandson Laurent, Nicolas remembers Catherine's signature scent, and the way in which Miss Dior seemed to be an integral part of her. Catherine's former dressing room at Les Naÿssès has been redecorated, but I have seen a picture of how it appeared in her day: the walls covered with the same floral pattern as in her bedroom at La Colle Noire, and a flask of Miss Dior standing on the dressing table. There was also a large wardrobe filled with the couture outfits that Christian had given her from each of his collections. Nicolas told me that Catherine had once shown them all to his father, Jean-Paul Crespelle, who was a renowned art critic and author; she had been proud of her brother's artistry, and recognised that his greatest work transcended the passing whims of fashion. Yet Catherine would never boast of her own achievements, nor the medals she had been awarded for her courage, including the Légion d'Honneur that she received in 1994.

★

On my last day at Les Naÿssès, where I've been fortunate to stay for a week during the annual harvest of the roses, I climb up a circuitous path to the cemetery where Catherine is buried close to Hervé, and beside Christian, Maurice, and Marthe Lefebvre. It is quiet here, except for the call of the swallows that are flying above the graves, swooping and weaving as if for the sheer joy of being alive. Watching the birds in flight, I feel a bubbling of hope and happiness, and it stays with me as I walk back down to Les Naÿssès. When I reach it, and open the gate into the garden, the church bells in Callian strike the hour; a dog barks, as if in response, and an unseen child is singing nearby. I sit down at a wooden table on the terrace outside the house; a mother hen scratches in the long grass, a trio of chicks following her.

There is a soft murmur of conversation from the rose field, where the harvest is continuing today. These flowers will be sent straight to Grasse, and once their precious essence is distilled, they will become the key ingredient of the Miss Dior perfume. The scent of the roses growing at Les Naÿssès blends with the fragrance on my skin; the voices of the women who are picking the flowers rise and fall, accompanied by a blackbird's song. The climbing roses that cover the stone walls of the farmhouse are in full bloom; for every bruised petal that falls to the ground after last night's rain, another new bud is unfurling in the warmth of today's sunshine. Clouds pass, obscuring the sun, then patches of blue sky appear again.

I wait, hoping to hear the words of Catherine Dior as a whisper inside my head. I close my eyes, but she is silent; wordless like my sister Ruth whenever she appears in my dreams. Yet I see Catherine's face in my mind's eye, and she is smiling: a young girl, a courageous and resilient woman who lived life on her own terms . . . The enigmatic smile remains the same, and she seems to raise one eyebrow quizzically, just as my sister does. '*J'aime la vie*,' I say, beneath my breath, in answer to the unasked question.

And yes, I treasure life all the more, after the journey that I have undertaken; after those moments of despair, in search of the echoing footfall of a disappearing girl, even when I thought that I was lost, and that she had vanished forever. Having looked into the darkness, the light becomes miraculous. And roses have marked the way, from the garden at Granville, on the granite cliffs above the untamed sea, to the 'Résurrection' roses planted in the ashen earth beside the lake at Ravensbrück. They flower, they fade, they die; yet, if we find the strength not to lose hope, we will continue to grow and cherish them. So now, I vow to create my own rose garden, faithful to the spirit of Catherine Dior, in honour of the people I love, and for the generations that will follow, long after I too am gone.

One of the final portraits of Catherine Dior.

Fédération Nationale des Déportés et Internés patriotes
10, Rue Leroux — PARIS (16°

AMICALE DES DÉPORTÉS POLITIQUES DE

RAVENSBRÜCK N° *64*
ET DES COMMANDOS DÉPENDANTS

DÉPORTÉ Carte d'Adhérent 1946

Nom : *Melle DIOR*

Prénoms : *Catherine*

Date et lieu de naissance : *2 8 1917*

Adresse : *10 rue Royale Paris 8°*

Commando :

N° Matricule : *57813*

Le Titulaire,   Le Secrétaire,   Le Président,

Catherine's membership card of the Association of Ravensbrück Deportees, 1946.

Acknowledgements

This book could only have been written with the help of very many others. Catherine Dior's godson Nicolas Crespelle and her friend Anne Zylinska were generous in sharing their personal memories and insights, as were Gaby Dior, Laurent des Charbonneries and Zahava Szász Stessel. I am also immensely grateful to Maria Grazia Chiuri, the creative director of Dior, for her inspiration and friendship; to Jérôme Pulis, Director of International Communications at Parfums Christian Dior, for his consistent understanding and support; and Olivier Bialobos, Chief Communication Officer at Christian Dior Couture, for sharing the benefit of his invaluable knowledge. I am greatly indebted to all those who helped me at Dior while I was researching this book: in particular, François Demachy, Mathilde Favier, Florence Ferracci-Letac, Rebecca Filmer, Gaia Pace, Rachele Regini and Perrine Scherrer. Sydney Finch has given me boundless encouragement and precious friendship. Frédéric Bourdelier, Vincent Leret, Sandrine Damay Bleu and Soizic Pfaff were endlessly patient in providing answers to my queries, as they guided me skilfully through the Dior archives, both in Paris and at Granville.

Oriole Cullen, the curator of the Christian Dior exhibition at the V&A, has been a longstanding source of expertise and advice; so too has Liz Pearn at *Harper's Bazaar*, whose knowledge of the magazine's archives is unrivalled. My sincere gratitude is also due to Gregory Klein at Société René Gruau; and to Lillian Bassman's son Eric Himmel.

I am truly grateful to Guillaume Garcia-Moreau for his warmth and thoughtfulness on my visits to Provence; Julien Decharne and his family for their hospitality and kindness at Les Naÿssès; Dr Sabine Arend and Monika Schnell for their assistance in my research at Ravensbrück; Wolfgang Oleschinski for his guidance at Torgau; Marie-France Cabeza-Marnet for her help at the Amicale de Ravensbrück; and Maya Slater for her brilliance in deciphering handwritten French documents.

I could not have been better served by the magnificent editorial team at Faber, under Alex Bowler's committed direction: so special thanks to Laura Hassan for her remarkable sensitivity and insight; Kate Ward, for her faultless eye for design; Eleanor Rees, for meticulous copy-editing; Donna Payne, for her imaginative art direction; and Amanda Russell, for painstaking picture research. I am equally grateful to Ileene Smith, my editor at Farrar, Straus and Giroux in New York, and Jonathan Galassi, president of FSG, who believed in the book from the start.

My peerless agent, Sarah Chalfant, has guided me throughout the process with her unerringly good judgement, supported by her outstanding colleagues at the Wylie agency, in particular Alba Ziegler-Bailey.

I owe many thanks, too, for perceptive suggestions to the following: Jessica Adams, Caroline de Guitaut, Gilles Dufour, Prosper Keating, Anna Murphy, Nicolas Ouchenir, Adam Phillips, Clare Waight-Keller; and for sisterly solidarity, Lydia and Sasha Slater. To my dear sons, Jamie MacColl and Tom MacColl, and their respective partners, Isabel Perry and Isa Brooks, thank you always and for everything.

Finally, to my beloved husband, Philip Astor, who led me through the labyrinth of the Rue de la Pompe investigation, and on whose shoulder I wept in Berlin; a rigorous critic, wise source of counsel, and my constant companion on a life-changing journey . . . *Je t'embrasse très, très fort.*

A Note on Sources

Christian Dior's own inimitable writing has been an essential resource for this book. His memoir, *Christian Dior et moi*, written in 1956, was translated into English by Antonia Fraser, and first published by Weidenfeld & Nicolson in 1957. The current edition, *Dior by Dior*, is published by the V&A, as is *The Little Dictionary of Fashion*, Dior's 'guide to dress sense for every woman'. An earlier book, *Talking about Fashion* (Hutchinson, 1954), is no longer in print, but I was able to acquire a rare vintage copy. Based on Dior's conversations with two writers, Elie Rabourdin and Alice Chavane, the book provides an insight into his working methods and his profound commitment to the art of couture.

I have also been given full access to the comprehensive Dior archives in Paris, and have relied on the expertise of the dedicated staff who work there, notably Frédéric Bourdelier, Vincent Leret and Sandrine Damay Bleu.

Into the Rose Garden

I have been fortunate to visit La Colle Noire on several occasions, and benefited from the Dior archives that trace the history of the house and its inhabitants. The first biography of Christian Dior, written by Marie-France Pochna, is also a vital source: published by Flammarion in France in 1994, it appeared in English in 1996 under the title *Christian Dior: The Man Who Made the World Look New* (translated by Joanna Savill, Arcade Publishing).

The Garden Maze

The Dior family home in Granville is now a museum, and I received help from its knowledgeable staff on various visits, as well as perceptive observations from Vincent Leret, who came to know Catherine Dior while he was working at the museum. I also drew on research by Frédéric Bourdelier into Raymond Dior's traumatic experiences as a soldier in the First

World War; and Frédéric and Vincent helped to track down the medical records of Bernard Dior, which trace his unhappy life, from the time of his first breakdown to his death in 1960.

Through the Looking Glass

Original source material on the lives of Christian and Catherine Dior, and the series of crises that engulfed their family, came from the Dior archives.

My description of fashionable society in Paris in the 1930s was based in part on extensive reading in the archives of *Harper's Bazaar* and *Vogue*. Janet Flanner's 'Letter from Paris' columns for the *New Yorker* were another invaluable source, as were the following memoirs: *In My Fashion* by Bettina Ballard (Secker & Warburg, 1960); *Shocking Life* by Elsa Schiaparelli (V&A, 2007); *The World of Carmel Snow* by Carmel Snow with Mary Louise Aswell (McGraw-Hill, 1962); *DV* by Diana Vreeland (Knopf, 1984). In addition, Sir Francis Rose's memoir, *Saying Life* (Cassell, 1961), gives a lively account of French bohemia in the late 1920s and early 1930s, when he encountered the young Christian Dior.

There are many excellent books that examine the speed with which France fell to the Germans in 1940, and the establishment of the autocratic Vichy regime. This short list comprises those that I found particularly helpful in explaining the historical, military and political context: *To Lose a Battle: France 1940* by Alistair Horne (Penguin, 1990); *France: The Dark Years* by Julian Jackson (Oxford University Press, 2001); *Occupation: The Ordeal of France* by Ian Ousby (John Murray, 1997); *Vichy France: Old Guard and New Order* by Robert O. Paxton (Columbia University Press, 2001); *Assignment to Catastrophe* by Major-General Sir Edward Spears (2 vols, Heinemann, 1954); *The Unfree French: Life under the Occupation* by Richard Vinen (Penguin, 2007).

Janet Flanner's book on Philippe Pétain remains as evocative now as it must have been when she wrote it during the war years: *Pétain, The Old Man of France* (Simon & Schuster, 1944). So, too, is Simone de Beauvoir's *Wartime Diary* (University of Illinois Press, 2009). I have also quoted from Jean-Paul Sartre's letters to de Beauvoir: *Quiet Moments in a War* (Scribner, 1993), and Sartre's *War Diaries: Notebooks from a Phoney War, 1939–40* (Verso, 2012).

Shadowland

I interviewed both Laurent des Charbonneries, the grandson of Hervé des Charbonneries, and Catherine Dior's godson, Nicolas Crespelle, whose mother Liliane served alongside Catherine in the F2 intelligence network. I was also fortunate to meet one of Hervé's surviving relatives, Anne Zylinska, whose late husband was a member of F2; both Anne and her husband maintained a deep and lasting friendship with Hervé and Catherine.

The French National Archives contain a dossier of informative documents on the organisation and work of F2, written by one of its leaders, Léon Sliwinski. (*Réseau franco-polonais F2*, Reference code: 72AJ/52, Archives du Comité d'histoire de la Deuxième Guerre; Archives Nationale.)

Gitta Sereny's account of F2, and the involvement of Liliane and Catherine in this group, is included in her book of essays, *The German Trauma: Experiences and Reflections* (Allen Lane,

2000). Further material on F2 can be found in *Les Réseaux de renseignements franco-polonais* by Jean Medrala (L'Harmattan, 2005). The important role of the Polish Resistance in France and elsewhere during the Second World War is explored by a former Polish commander and intelligence officer, M. K. Dziewanowski, in his book *War at Any Price* (Prentice-Hall, 1987).

I obtained background information from the following works, all of which provide scholarly detail and authoritative analysis: *The Resistance* by Matthew Cobb (Simon & Schuster, 2009); *Fighters in the Shadows* by Robert Gildea (Faber & Faber, 2015); *The Riviera at War* by George G. Kundahl (I. B. Tauris, 2017); *The French Resistance* by Olivier Wieviorka (Harvard University Press, 2016).

I was also very moved by *Jacques and Lotka: A Resistance Story* by Aude Yung-de Prévaux (Bloomsbury, 2000); the author recounts the courage and suffering of the parents she never knew, both of whom served in F2 and died for the cause of the French Resistance in 1944.

Rue Royale

Aside from my original research in the Dior archives, I relied on Pierre Balmain's vivid memoir, *My Years and Seasons* (Cassell, 1964); and Philippe de Rothschild's autobiography *Milady Vine* (Jonathan Cape, 1984).

I used the following secondary sources to trace how the couture industry adapted to German control: *Nazi Chic: Fashioning Women in the Third Reich* by Irene Guenther (Berg, 2004); *Paris Fashion and World War Two: Global Diffusion and Nazi Control*, edited by Lou Taylor and Marie McLoughlin (Bloomsbury Visual Arts, 2020); *Fashion under the Occupation* by Dominique Veillon (Berg, 2002).

Susan Ronald, the author of *A Dangerous Woman: The Life of Florence Gould* (St. Martin's Press, 2018), generously shared with me the relevant archival material covering Gould's activities in Paris during the Occupation, including the US intelligence reports that relate to Marie-Louise Bousquet.

Maureen Footer, the author of *Dior and His Decorators* (Vendome, 2018), offered her thoughtful personal insights into Georges Geffroy, and others in his social circle.

For contemporary descriptions of life in Occupied Paris, I drew on the candid diaries of Ernst Jünger: *A German Officer in Occupied Paris* (Columbia University Press, 2018).

The writing of Jean Cocteau is equally important to this chapter, in particular his *Journal, 1942–1945* (Gallimard, 1989). Additional information about Cocteau came from two major biographies: *Jean Cocteau: A Life* by Claude Arnaud (Yale University Press, 2016); and *An Impersonation of Angels* by Frederick Brown (Longmans, 1969).

Sir Francis Rose's account of Hermann Goering's love of jewels is contained in his memoir, *Saying Life*. (Rose, who was a friend of Goering's, and stayed at his home before the outbreak of war, also makes the startling claim that 'Goering loved playing with make-up at an enormous and resplendent dressing-table.')

The reference to Catherine Dior staying at Rue Royale, and her activities with other members of the Resistance, appears in Henri Sauguet's memoir, *La Musique, ma vie* (Séguier, 1990).

I collected further material from *Paris in the Third Reich* by David Pryce-Jones (Collins, 1981), which includes a series of significant first-person interviews with collaborationist writers, French fascists and German officials. My quotes from Gerhard Heller are taken from his interview with Pryce-Jones. It is also thanks to this important book that I became aware of the photography of André Zucca, whose images of Occupied Paris (shot for the German propaganda magazine *Signal*) present another perspective on the era.

Finally, there are four exceptional books that have influenced this and other chapters: *And the Show Went On: Cultural Life in Nazi-Occupied Paris* by Alan Riding (Duckworth, 2011); *Les Parisiennes* by Anne Sebba (Weidenfeld & Nicolson, 2016); *The Shameful Peace: How French Artists and Intellectuals Survived the Nazi Occupation* by Frederic Spotts (Yale University Press, 2008); and *Max Jacob* by Rosanna Warren (W. W. Norton, 2020).

Rue de la Pompe

The majority of the information in this chapter, and subsequent references to Friedrich Berger and his gang, come from the judicial investigation into the Rue de la Pompe Gestapo, launched after the Liberation of Paris. This lengthy investigation eventually resulted in a trial, held before a military tribunal in 1952. The witness statements and other legal documents are stored in the French archives of military justice. (Dépôt Central d'Archives de la Justice Militaire: DCAJM, Le Blanc, France.) These amount to about fifteen thousand documents in fourteen boxes of files, many of them hand-written, and neither indexed nor in any chronological order. My husband, a former barrister, devoted several months to reading the documents and assembling them into a coherent form, thereby enabling me to piece together a narrative.

I was able to compare notes on the case with the writer Prosper Keating, and with Marie-Josèphe Bonnet, the author of *Tortionnaires, truands et collabos: La bande de la rue de la Pompe* (Editions Ouest-France, 2013). Further background information about the nefarious activities of various other French collaborators came from *Hunting the Truth* by Beate and Serge Klarsfeld (Farrar, Straus and Giroux, 2018); *La Gestapo française* by Philippe Valode and Gérard Chauvy (Acropole, 2018); and *The King of Nazi Paris: Henri Lafont and the Gangsters of the French Gestapo* by Christopher Othen (Biteback Publishing, 2020).

Darkness Falls

Aside from Catherine Dior's slim file in the French military archives that I refer to in this chapter, I depended on accounts written by women in the Resistance who had suffered similar experiences. Of particular importance is the diary and memoir of Virginia d'Albert-Lake: she was imprisoned at Fresnes and Romainville at the same time as Catherine, and deported alongside her on the train from Paris to Germany. D'Albert-Lake died in 1997, and her wartime journal was subsequently published as a book, *An American Heroine in the French Resistance* (Fordham University Press, 2006).

Another essential source was Jacqueline Fleury-Marié, who was arrested with her mother in 1944 and remembered Catherine Dior, as they were locked into same train wagon, and subsequently endured the same series of slave labour camps. She tells her story in *Résistante* (Calmann-Lévy, 2019). Two other vital memoirs were *Résistance* by Agnès Humbert (Bloomsbury, 2009); and *La Grande Misère* by Maisie Renault (Zea Books, 2014).

For further reading about Suzanne Emmer-Besniée, whose drawings appear in the book, I would recommend Pierre-Yves Cordel's essay on her work (www.cnap.fr/le-temoignage-graphique-de-suzanne-emmer-besniee-deportee-ravensbrueck). Her set of twenty-five drawings is held at the Musée de la Résistance et de la Déportation in Besançon; these powerful images deserve to be far better known. The museum also contains extensive archives and artworks relating to the French experience of the war and the Holocaust, which have influenced my chapters on the deportees.

The description of how Christian Dior attempted to save his sister from deportation comes from Suzanne Luling's memoir, *Mes années Dior* (Cherche Midi, 2016). I learned more about the negotiations undertaken by Raoul Nordling from *Eleven Days in August* by Matthew Cobb (Simon & Schuster, 2013); *Is Paris Burning?* by Larry Collins and Dominique Lapierre (Simon & Schuster, 1965); and *The Blood of Free Men* by Michael Neiberg (Basic Books, 2012).

The remarkable story of Marie-Hélène Lefaucheux and her husband Pierre surely deserves to be told at greater length; both of them were leading figures in the Resistance, and she eventually managed to rescue him from Buchenwald. A footnote in *Is Paris Burning?* records that Pierre, who became the chairman of Renault after the war, died in a car accident in 1956, and Marie-Hélène – a member of the French delegation to the United Nations – was killed in a plane crash in 1964.

The Abyss

I visited Ravensbrück twice while researching this book, and have benefited from direct access to its archives, along with the permanent exhibitions and collection of objects held at the memorial museum.

The diaries and memoirs written by some of the French women who survived Ravensbrück were again of crucial value to this chapter. I list them respectfully as follows: Virginia d'Albert Lake, *An American Heroine in the French Resistance*; Jacqueline Péry d'Alincourt, *Témoignages sur la Résistance et la Déportation* (L'Harmattan, 2008) and *Surviving Ravensbrück* (https://liberalarts.utexas.edu/france-ut/_files/pdf/resources/Pery.pdf); Geneviève de Gaulle Anthonioz, *God Remained Outside* (Souvenir Press, 1999); Denise Dufournier, *Ravensbrück* (George Allen & Unwin, 1948); Jacqueline Fleury-Marié, *Résistante*; Micheline Maurel, *Ravensbrück* (Anthony Blond, 1959); Maisie Renault, *La Grande Misère*; Germaine Tillion, *Ravensbrück* (Anchor Press, 1975).

A fundamental secondary source is *If This Is a Woman* by Sarah Helm (Little, Brown, 2015). Sarah and I used to work together as journalists at the *Sunday Times*, and her meticulous investigation into the crimes committed at Ravensbrück has resulted in a truly momentous book.

I was also inspired by another profoundly moving book: *The Journey Back from Hell: Conversations with Concentration Camp Survivors* by Anton Gill (HarperCollins, 1994). This includes an interview with Denise Dufournier, from which I have quoted.

The other important books that contributed to my understanding of Ravensbrück are *Heinrich Himmler* by Peter Longerich (Oxford University Press, 2012); *A Train in Winter* by Caroline Moorehead (HarperCollins, 2012); *Ravensbrück* by Jack G. Morrison (Markus Wiener, 2000); *The Jewish Women of Ravensbrück Concentration Camp* by Rochelle G. Saidel (University of Wisconsin Press, 2006); *KL: A History of the Nazi Concentration Camps* by Nikolaus Wachsmann (Abacus, 2016).

Further information on Himmler and his relationship with his mistress, Hedwig Potthast, comes from a fascinating book by his great-niece, Katrin Himmler: *The Himmler Brothers* (Pan Macmillan, 2008).

I have derived considerable benefit from catalogues that accompanied previous or permanent exhibitions at the Ravensbrück Memorial Site: *The Ravensbrück Women's Concentration Camp: History and Memory*, edited by Alyn Bessmann and Insa Eschebach (Metropol Verlag, 2013); *Trains to Ravensbruck* by Karolin Steinke (Metropol Verlag, 2009); *The Roses in Ravensbrück: A contribution to the history of commemoration* by Meggi Pieschel, Insa Eschebach and Amélie zu Eulenburg (Metropol Verlag, 2015).

Additional information on the clandestine drawings of Jeannette L'Herminier and the manuscripts of Germaine Tillion comes from the catalogue to an exhibition held in 2011 at the Médiathèque André Malraux in Strasbourg: *Les Robes Grises* (Bibliothèque nationale et universitaire, Strasbourg, 2011).

Marie-France Cabeza-Marnet, from the Amicale de Ravensbrück, provided information about the 'Résurrection' rose and the associated poem by Marcelle Dudach-Roset.

The Underworld

I have relied heavily on the diary of Virginia d'Albert Lake and the memories of Jacqueline Fleury-Marié for this chapter. Jeannie Rousseau's conversation with Sarah Helm about the events at Torgau was another important source (*If This Is a Woman*). So, too, was Rousseau's interview with David Ignatius, published in the *Washington Post* on 28 December 1998.

Details of the SOE agents at Torgau are contained in their files at the National Archives in Kew: the HS 9 series on the Special Operations Executive, including the personnel files of individual agents. Eileen Nearne's records are particularly relevant, as she was in the same contingent as Catherine Dior, travelling from Ravensbrück to Torgau, Abteroda and Markkleeberg (HS 9/1089/2).

Additional information relating to SOE agents was gleaned from the following books: *The Heroines of SOE* by Squadron Leader Beryl E. Escott (The History Press, 2012); *SOE in France* by M. R. D. Foot (Routledge, 2006); *A Life in Secrets* by Sarah Helm (Little, Brown, 2005); *Sisters, Secrets and Sacrifice* by Susan Ottaway (HarperCollins, 2013); *Lonely Courage* by Rick Stroud (Simon & Schuster, 2017).

Zahava Szász Stessel, who survived Auschwitz, Bergen-Belsen and Markkleeberg, shared her memories with me. Zahava has conducted her own extensive research into the Nazi slave labour system, and the experiences of female prisoners at Markkleeberg and elsewhere; this appears in her remarkable book, *Snow Flowers* (Fairleigh Dickinson University Press, 2013).

Zahava's account of the death marches, and the rape of survivors by Red Army soldiers, was crucial to this chapter. So, too, were the memoirs of Micheline Maurel and Jacqueline

Fleury-Marié; both reveal the widespread rape of women in the final days of the war, and at the time of the Liberation.

Further context comes from an exceptional work of scholarship, *Reckonings: Legacies of Nazi Persecution and the Quest for Justice* by Mary Fulbrook (Oxford University Press, 2018).

The Homecoming

Frédéric Bourdelier's interviews with Hubert des Charbonneries, Hervé's son, have been a key source for this chapter. I was also given access to the family letters and documents in the Dior archives that relate to Catherine's return to France.

For contemporaneous reports on the Ravensbrück survivors who arrived in Paris in April 1945, and the post-war trials of Pétain and Laval, I referred to Janet Flanner's 'Letter from Paris' columns in the *New Yorker*.

Denise Dufournier's account of her return appears in *The Journey Back from Hell* by Anton Gill; I also spoke to her daughter Caroline McAdam Clark. Once again, I drew on the memoirs and journals of Virginia d'Albert-Lake, Jacqueline Fleury-Marié and Micheline Maurel. Simone Rohner's report of being mistaken for a collaborator is quoted by Debra Workman in her essay 'Engendering the Repatriation: The Return of Political Deportees to France Following the Second World War' (*Proceedings of the Western Society for French History*, Vol. 35, 2007). The quotes from Philippe de Rothschild come from his autobiography. Another vital source for this chapter was Malcolm Muggeridge's memoir: *Chronicles of Wasted Time*, Vol. 2: *The Infernal Grove* (Collins, 1973).

I also learned much from the following books: *To Marietta from Paris* by Susan Mary Alsop (Doubleday, 1975); *Paris after the Liberation* by Antony Beevor and Artemis Cooper (Penguin, 2007); *Paris Journal 1945–1955* by Janet Flanner (Harcourt Brace Jovanovich, 1965).

Palais de Glace

Past issues of *Harper's Bazaar* have been productive sources for this chapter; the magazine was launched in 1867, and regularly contained illustrated reports about Worth, Poiret, Chanel, Lelong, Marcel Rochas, Jacques Fath and other Paris couture houses.

Further details on the post-war investigation of collaboration in the couture industry come from Dominique Veillon's *Fashion under the Occupation*; and *Paris Fashion and World War Two*, edited by Lou Taylor and Marie McLoughlin.

I also consulted the following memoirs and diaries: *In My Fashion* by Bettina Ballard; *My Years and Seasons* by Pierre Balmain; *The Glass of Fashion* by Cecil Beaton (Weidenfeld & Nicolson, 1954); *The Happy Years: 1944–48*, by Cecil Beaton (Weidenfeld & Nicolson, 1972); *King of Fashion* by Paul Poiret (V&A, 2009); *Shocking Life* by Elsa Schiaparelli; *The World of Carmel Snow* by Carmel Snow; *It Isn't All Mink* by Ginette Spanier (Robert Hale, 1959).

For the section on the social circle that surrounded the British embassy, I returned to the memoirs of Bettina Ballard and Malcolm Muggeridge, and the letters of Susan Mary Alsop. I also, of course, relied on the following books: *The Duff Cooper Diaries*, edited by John

Julius Norwich (Phoenix, 2006); *Paris after the Liberation* by Antony Beevor and Artemis Cooper; *Diana Cooper* by Philip Ziegler (Hamish Hamilton, 1981).

The primary source for the section on the Théâtre de la Mode is the Maryhill Museum of Art, which has a permanent display of miniature mannequins (www.maryhillmuseum.org). The museum has also published an informative book, *Théâtre de la Mode: Fashion Dolls: The Survival of Haute Couture* (Palmer/Pletsch, 2002), with photographs of the original dolls and sets.

Magical Thinking

Christian Dior's belief in clairvoyance is evident throughout his autobiography. Pierre Balmain's memoir also refers to Dior's 'passionate' belief in fortune-telling.

For the section on ghosts in Paris, I was influenced by two intriguing books: *The Other Paris* by Luc Sante (Faber & Faber, 2015); and *Paris Noir: The Secret History of a City* by Jacques Yonnet (Dedalus, 2006). Yonnet's book originally appeared under the title *Rue des maléfices: Chronique secrète d'une ville* in 1954, and is one of the strangest and most compelling chronicles of Occupied Paris that I have ever read.

Chanel's sense of the uncanny emerges in *The Allure of Chanel* by Paul Morand (Pushkin Press, 2008). The memoirs of Carmel Snow and Elsa Schiaparelli are similarly revealing on the subject of the supernatural; further details come from Snow's biography, *A Dash of Daring* by Penelope Rowlands (Atria Books, 2005); and *Elsa Schiaparelli* by Meryle Secrest (Fig Tree, 2014).

References to the significance of Dior's designs for Lucien Lelong appear in the memoirs of Bettina Ballard and Carmel Snow. Dior's memoir gives a comprehensive account of the establishment of his own couture house, and the roles of Raymonde Zehnacker, Marguerite Carré and Mizza Bricard. Also useful was *Monsieur Dior: Once upon a Time* by Natasha Fraser-Cavassoni (Pointed Leaf, 2014).

Details of the origins of the Miss Dior perfume are contained in the Dior archives, including the notes of Alice Chavane.

Jane Abdy's tribute to Mizza Bricard was published in *Harper's & Queen* in 1978. Vivid first-hand accounts of Mme Bricard appear in the memoirs of Pierre Balmain and Bettina Ballard. René Gruau's description of Mizza Bricard came from *René Gruau* (Rizzoli, 1984). Also instructive is *René Gruau: The First Century* by Vincent Leret and Sylvie Nissen (Thalia, 2010).

The New Look

Most of the research for this chapter derived from the Dior archives, including the transcript of Catherine Dior's interview with the historian Stanley Garfinkel. I was fortunate myself to interview Pierre Cardin a few months before he died. He had worked for Christian Dior in his early twenties, and still recalled the exact details of the New Look collection. Further descriptions are drawn from the memoirs of Bettina Ballard and Carmel Snow. Ernestine Carter, the fashion editor of the British edition of *Harper's Bazaar* at the time of Dior's debut, gives one of the most memorable depictions of the New Look in her memoir, *With Tongue in Chic* (Michael Joseph, 1974).

Cecil Beaton's astute analysis of Dior's aesthetic appears in *The Glass of Fashion*. Nancy Mitford's letters concerning Dior are contained in *Love from Nancy*, edited by Charlotte Mosley (Sceptre, 1994). Susan Mary Patten's correspondence was published in *To Marietta from Paris*, under the name Susan Mary Alsop. (Her first husband, the diplomat William Patten, had died in 1960, and she had subsequently married the influential American journalist Joseph Alsop.) Francine du Plessix Gray's essay about Dior, 'Prophets of Seduction', featured in the *New Yorker* (4 November 1996). A significant compilation of Dior couture can be found in *Dior by Christian Dior, 1947–1957*, text by Olivier Saillard, photography by Laziz Hamani (Assouline, 2016).

Diana Vreeland's admission that she didn't actually wear the New Look comes from her biography, *Empress of Fashion* by Amanda Mackenzie Stuart (Thames & Hudson, 2013). Vreeland's ambivalence about the New Look is also evident in an interview which appeared in *Rolling Stone*: 'A Question of Style: A Conversation with Diana Vreeland' by Lally Weymouth (11 August 1977).

Rising from the Ashes

The description of the first Ravensbrück trial comes from *Odette* by Jerrard Tickell (Headline, 2008). Tickell's book about Odette Sansom was written soon after the war (and first published in 1949); as such, it benefits from its sense of immediacy, and the author's own position as an observer at the trial. Germaine Tillion was also present at the trial, and wrote about it in *Ravensbrück*.

I consulted the legal documents and correspondence relating to the Ravensbrück trials via the National Archives in Kew. The transcripts, witness statements and other material relating to the Nuremberg trials are available online at the Harvard Law School Library (https://nuremberg.law.harvard.edu/).

Norbert Wollheim's comments on appearing as a witness at the IG Farben trial are taken from his interview in Anton Gill's *The Journey Back from Hell*. Denise Dufournier's words come from her own memoir, and from her interview with Anton Gill.

The following books have been indispensable sources about this period: *Forgotten Trials of the Holocaust* by Michael J. Bazyler and Frank M. Tuerkheimer (New York University Press, 2014); *Nuremberg Diary* by G. M. Gilbert (Eyre & Spottiswoode, 1948); *Reckonings: Legacies of Nazi Persecution and the Quest for Justice* by Mary Fulbrook; *To Hell and Back* by Ian Kershaw (Penguin, 2016); *The Arms of Krupp* by William Manchester (Michael Joseph, 1969).

While researching the section about Christian Dior's relationship with Germany, I found valuable details in a book of photographs and essays, published to accompany a Dior exhibition in Berlin in 2007: *Christian Dior and Germany, 1947 to 1957*, edited by Adelheid Rasche with Christina Thomson (Arnoldsche, 2007).

Gregor Ziemer's account of Werner Uhlmann establishing his hosiery business in a former Nazi armaments factory was published in *The Rotarian* magazine in June 1950.

The Flower Girl

This chapter was written in the Dior archives, and relies almost entirely on the records and couture outfits that are preserved there. I also returned to Jeannette L'Herminier's drawings, and studied those held in Paris at the Musée de l'Ordre de la Libération.

Princess Dior

Original source material for this chapter comes from my research at the Dior archives in Paris and the V&A archives in London. I have been particularly influenced in this chapter by my innumerable conversations with Oriole Cullen, the curator of the superb V&A exhibition held in 2019, 'Christian Dior: Designer of Dreams'. I have also found the book that accompanied the exhibition a most useful resource: *Christian Dior* (V&A, 2019).

I discovered more information about the relationship between Princess Margaret and Christian Dior from an article by Beatrice Behlen, who is the Senior Curator of Fashion and Decorative Arts at the Museum of London. This appeared in *Costume* (Vol. 46, no. 1, 2012). Princess Margaret's remarks about her Dior dresses were published in *The Englishwoman's Wardrobe* by Angela Huth (Century Hutchinson, 1986).

Along with the diaries of Cecil Beaton and Duff Cooper that are cited in this chapter, I consulted the following books: *Elizabeth the Queen* by Sally Bedell Smith (Penguin, 2017); *Princes at War* by Deborah Cadbury (Bloomsbury, 2015); *Silver and Gold* by Norman Hartnell (Evans Brothers Ltd, 1955); *The Duchess of Windsor* by Diana Mitford (Gibson Square, 2012); *That Woman: The Life of Wallis Simpson, Duchess of Windsor* by Anne Sebba (Phoenix, 2012); *Queen Elizabeth the Queen Mother* by William Shawcross (Vintage, 2010); *Cecil Beaton: The Royal Portraits* by Roy Strong (Thames and Hudson, 1988); *Elizabeth, the Queen Mother* by Hugo Vickers (Arrow, 2006); *Behind Closed Doors* by Hugo Vickers (Arrow, 2012); *King Edward VIII* by Philip Ziegler (HarperCollins, 1990); *George VI* by Philip Ziegler (Penguin, 2014).

The late Duke of Marlborough gave me access to the Blenheim Palace archives, in order to research the Dior show that was presented there in 1954, and shared his own memories of the occasion, as did the Duke's sister, Lady Rosemary Muir.

Taking a Stand

My sources for the Rue de la Pompe trial are from reports of the court case in *Le Monde*, *Combat*, the *New Yorker*, the *New York Times*, *Time* and *The Times* of London. I obtained background information from *Tortionnaires, truands et collabos* by Marie-Josèphe Bonnet, and *Gender and French Identity after the Second World War* by Kelly Ricciardi Colvin (Bloomsbury Academic, 2017).

The section on Friedrich Berger was drawn from a variety of archival sources: primarily, the declassified CIA intelligence files (which contain hundreds of pages on Berger, including documents from the Vichy era and others relating to his post-war life in the Soviet Union and West Germany); and the National Archives in Kew (references: WO 204/12797; WO 204/12797/1; KV 2/1739).

The details of post-war parties and balls were gathered from the following memoirs, letters and diaries: *To Marietta from Paris* by Susan Mary Alsop; *In My Fashion* by Bettina Ballard; *The Duff Cooper Diaries*; *Clarissa Eden: A Memoir* (Weidenfeld & Nicolson, 2007); *Love from Nancy: The Letters of Nancy Mitford*; *Second Son* by David Herbert (Peter Owen, 1972). Background information came from *Bals: Legendary Costume Balls of the Twentieth Century* by Nicholas Foulkes (Assouline, 2011).

Jean Cocteau's comments on Dior in August 1953 are contained in his journals: *Le Passé défini*, Vol. 2 (Gallimard, 1985).

La Colle Noire

For this chapter, I drew extensively on archival research at La Colle Noire, as well as the Dior archives in Paris.

Cecil Beaton's description of Christian Dior is taken from *The Glass of Fashion*.

Background information on the financial and emotional strains affecting Christian Dior in the last year of his life came from Marie-France Pochna's biography of the designer.

The following books were also of significant value: *Dior: A New Look, a New Enterprise* by Alexandra Palmer (V&A, 2009); and *Christian Dior* by Diana de Marly (Batsford, 1990).

No Rose without a Thorn

The current owners of Les Naÿssès kindly gave me access to photographs and documents relating to the history of the property, including the period when Catherine Dior lived there.

Bibliography

Memoirs, Biographies and Studies of Christian Dior

Cullen, Oriole, and Connie Karol Burks, *Christian Dior* (V&A, 2019)

Dior, Christian, *Dior by Dior*, trans. Antonia Fraser (V&A, 2018)

———, *The Little Dictionary of Fashion* (V&A, 2008)

———, *Talking about Fashion*, as told to Elie Rabourdin and Alice Chavane, trans. Eugenia Sheppard (Hutchinson, 1954)

Footer, Maureen, *Dior and His Decorators* (Vendome, 2018)

Fraser-Cavassoni, Natasha, *Monsieur Dior: Once upon a Time* (Pointed Leaf, 2014)

Luling, Suzanne, *Mes années Dior* (Cherche Midi, 2016)

Marly, Diana de, *Christian Dior* (Batsford, 1990)

Palmer, Alexandra, *Dior: A New Look, a New Enterprise* (V&A, 2009)

Pochna, Marie-France, *Christian Dior: The Man Who Made the World Look New*, trans. Joanna Savill (Arcade Publishing, 1996)

Rasche, Adelheid, ed., with Christina Thomson, *Christian Dior and Germany, 1947 to 1957* (Arnoldsche, 2007)

Saillard, Olivier, *Dior by Christian Dior, 1947–1957*, photography by Laziz Hamani (Assouline, 2016)

Further Reading

Albert-Lake, Virginia d', *An American Heroine in the French Resistance* (Fordham University Press, 2006)

Alsop, Susan Mary, *To Marietta from Paris* (Doubleday, 1975)

Arnaud, Claude, *Jean Cocteau: A Life*, trans. Lauren Elkin and Charlotte Mandell (Yale University Press, 2016)

Ballard, Bettina, *In My Fashion* (Secker & Warburg, 1960)

Balmain, Pierre, *My Years and Seasons*, trans. Edward Lanchbery with Gordon Young (Cassell, 1964)

Bazyler, Michael J., and Frank M. Tuerkheimer, *Forgotten Trials of the Holocaust* (New York University Press, 2014)

Beaton, Cecil, *The Glass of Fashion* (Weidenfeld & Nicolson, 1954)

———, *The Happy Years: 1944–1948* (Weidenfeld & Nicolson, 1972)

Beauvoir, Simone de, *Wartime Diary*, trans. Anne Deing Cordero (University of Illinois Press, 2009)

Bedell Smith, Sally, *Elizabeth the Queen* (Penguin, 2017)

Beevor, Antony, and Artemis Cooper, *Paris after the Liberation* (Penguin, 2007)

Bonnet, Marie-Josèphe, *Tortionnaires, truands et collabos: La bande de la rue de la Pompe* (Editions Ouest-France, 2013)

Brown, Frederick, *An Impersonation of Angels* (Longmans, 1969)

Cadbury, Deborah, *Princes at War* (Bloomsbury, 2015)

Carter, Ernestine, *With Tongue in Chic* (Michael Joseph, 1974)

Charles-Roux, Edmonde, Herbert R. Lottman, Stanley Garfinkel and Nadine Gasc, *Théâtre de la Mode: Fashion Dolls: The Survival of Haute Couture* (Palmer/Pletsch, 2002)

Cobb, Matthew, *Eleven Days in August* (Simon & Schuster, 2013)

——, *The Resistance* (Simon & Schuster, 2009)

Cocteau, Jean, *Journal, 1942–1945* (Gallimard, 1989)

——, *Le Passé défini*, Vol. 2 (Gallimard, 1985)

Collins, Larry, and Dominique Lapierre, *Is Paris Burning?* (Simon & Schuster, 1965)

The Duff Cooper Diaries, ed. John Julius Norwich (Phoenix, 2006)

Dufournier, Denise, *Ravensbrück* (George Allen & Unwin, 1948)

Dziewanowski, M. K., *War at Any Price* (Prentice-Hall, 1987)

Eden, Clarissa, *A Memoir*, ed. Cate Haste (Weidenfeld & Nicolson, 2007)

Escott, Squadron Leader Beryl E., *The Heroines of SOE* (The History Press, 2012)

Flanner, Janet, *Paris Journal 1945–1955* (Harcourt Brace Jovanovich, 1965)

——, *Paris Was Yesterday: 1925–1939* (Virago, 2003)

——, *Pétain, The Old Man of France* (Simon & Schuster, 1944)

Fleury-Marié, Jacqueline, *Résistante* (Calmann-Lévy, 2019)

Foot, M. R. D., *SOE in France* (Routledge, 2006)

Foulkes, Nicholas, *Bals: Legendary Costume Balls of the Twentieth Century* (Assouline, 2011)

Fulbrook, Mary, *Reckonings: Legacies of Nazi Persecution and the Quest for Justice* (Oxford University Press, 2018)

Gaulle Anthonioz, Geneviève de, *God Remained Outside*, trans. Margaret Crosland (Souvenir Press, 1999)

Gilbert, G. M., *Nuremberg Diary* (Eyre & Spottiswoode, 1948)

Gildea, Robert, *Fighters in the Shadows* (Faber & Faber, 2015)

Gill, Anton, *The Journey Back from Hell* (HarperCollins, 1994)

Guenther, Irene, *Nazi Chic: Fashioning Women in the Third Reich* (Berg, 2004)

Hartnell, Norman, *Silver and Gold* (Evans Brothers Ltd, 1955)

Hastings, Max, *Overlord: D-Day and the Battle for Normandy 1944* (Pan, 1999)

Helm, Sarah, *If This Is a Woman* (Little, Brown, 2015)

——, *A Life in Secrets* (Little, Brown, 2005)

Heminway, John, *In Full Flight* (Knopf, 2018)

Herbert, David, *Second Son* (Peter Owen, 1972)

Himmler, Katrin, *The Himmler Brothers* (Pan Macmillan, 2008)

Horne, Alistair, *To Lose a Battle: France 1940* (Penguin, 1990)

Humbert, Agnès, *Résistance*, trans. Barbara Mellor (Bloomsbury, 2009)

Huth, Angela, *The Englishwoman's Wardrobe* (Century Hutchinson, 1986)

Jackson, Julian, *France: The Dark Years* (Oxford University Press, 2001)

Jeffery, Keith, *MI6: The History of the Secret Intelligence Service, 1909–1949* (Bloomsbury, 2011)

Jünger, Ernst, *A German Officer in Occupied Paris: The War Journals, 1941–1945*, trans. Thomas S. Hansen and Abby J. Hansen (Columbia University Press, 2018)

Kershaw, Ian, *To Hell and Back: Europe 1914–1949* (Penguin, 2016)

Klarsfeld, Beate, and Serge Klarsfeld, *Hunting the Truth*, trans. Sam Taylor (Farrar, Straus and Giroux, 2018)

Kundahl, George G., *The Riviera at War* (I. B. Tauris, 2017)

Leret, Vincent, and Sylvie Nissen, *René Gruau: The First Century* (Thalia, 2010)

Longerich, Peter, *Heinrich Himmler* (Oxford University Press, 2012)

Mackenzie Stuart, Amanda, *Empress of Fashion* (Thames & Hudson, 2013)

Manchester, William, *The Arms of Krupp* (Michael Joseph, 1969)

Maurel, Micheline, *Ravensbrück*, trans. Margaret S. Summers (Anthony Blond, 1959)

Medrala, Jean, *Les Réseaux de renseignements franco-polonais* (L'Harmattan, 2005)

Mitford, Diana, *The Duchess of Windsor* (Gibson Square, 2012)

Mitford, Nancy, *Love from Nancy: The Letters of Nancy Mitford*, ed. Charlotte Mosley (Sceptre, 1994)

Moorehead, Caroline, *A Train in Winter* (HarperCollins, 2012)

Morand, Paul, *The Allure of Chanel*, trans. Euan Cameron (Pushkin Press, 2008)

Morrison, Jack G., *Ravensbrück* (Markus Wiener, 2000)

Muggeridge, Malcolm, *Chronicles of Wasted Time*, Vol. 2: *The Infernal Grove* (Collins, 1973)

Neiberg, Michael, *The Blood of Free Men* (Basic Books, 2012)

Othen, Christopher, *The King of Nazi Paris: Henri Lafont and the Gangsters of the French Gestapo* (Biteback Publishing, 2020)

Ottaway, Susan, *Sisters, Secrets and Sacrifice* (HarperCollins, 2013)

Ousby, Ian, *Occupation: The Ordeal of France* (John Murray, 1997)

Paxton, Robert O., *Vichy France: Old Guard and New Order* (Columbia University Press, 2001)

Péry d'Alincourt, Jacqueline, *Témoignages sur la Résistance et la Déportation* (L'Harmattan, 2008)

Picardie, Justine, *Coco Chanel: The Legend and the Life* (HarperCollins, 2017)

Poiret, Paul, *King of Fashion* (V&A, 2009)

Pryce-Jones, David, *Paris in the Third Reich* (Collins, 1981)

Renault, Maisie, *La Grande Misère*, trans. Jeanne Armstrong (Zea Books, 2014)

Ricciardi Colvin, Kelly, *Gender and French Identity after the Second World War* (Bloomsbury Academic, 2017)

Riding, Alan, *And the Show Went On: Cultural Life in Nazi-Occupied Paris* (Duckworth, 2011)

Ronald, Susan, *A Dangerous Woman: The Life of Florence Gould* (St. Martin's Press, 2018)

Rose, Sir Francis, *Saying Life* (Cassell, 1961)

Rothschild, Philippe de, with Joan Littlewood, *Milady Vine* (Jonathan Cape, 1984)

Rowlands, Penelope, *A Dash of Daring* (Atria Books, 2005)

Saidel, Rochelle G., *The Jewish Women of Ravensbrück Concentration Camp* (University of Wisconsin Press, 2006)

Sante, Luc, *The Other Paris* (Faber & Faber, 2015)

Sartre, Jean-Paul, *Quiet Moments in a War*, trans. Lee Fahnestock and Norman MacAfee (Scribner, 1993)

———, *War Diaries: Notebooks from a Phoney War, 1939–40*, trans. Quintin Hoare (Verso, 2012)

Sauguet, Henri, *La Musique, ma vie* (Séguier, 1990)

Schiaparelli, Elsa, *Shocking Life* (V&A, 2007)

Sebba, Anne, *Les Parisiennes* (Weidenfeld & Nicolson, 2016)

———, *That Woman: The Life of Wallis Simpson, Duchess of Windsor* (Phoenix, 2012)

Secrest, Meryle, *Elsa Schiaparelli* (Fig Tree, 2014)

Sereny, Gitta, *The German Trauma: Experiences and Reflections* (Allen Lane, 2000)

Shawcross, William, *Queen Elizabeth the Queen Mother* (Vintage, 2010)

Snow, Carmel, with Mary Louise Aswell, *The World of Carmel Snow* (McGraw-Hill, 1962)

Spanier, Ginette, *It Isn't All Mink* (Robert Hale, 1959)

Spears, Major-General Sir Edward, *Assignment to Catastrophe* (Heinemann, 1954)

Spotts, Frederic, *The Shameful Peace: How French Artists and Intellectuals Survived the Nazi Occupation* (Yale University Press, 2008)

Strong, Roy, *Cecil Beaton: The Royal Portraits* (Thames and Hudson, 1988)

Stroud, Rick, *Lonely Courage* (Simon & Schuster, 2017)

Szász Stessel, Zahava, *Snow Flowers* (Fairleigh Dickinson University Press, 2013)

Taylor, Lou, and Marie McLoughlin, eds, *Paris Fashion and World War Two* (Bloomsbury Visual Arts, 2020)

Tickell, Jerrard, *Odette* (Headline, 2008)

Tillion, Germaine, *Ravensbrück*, trans. Gerald Satterwhite (Anchor Press, 1975)

Valode, Philippe, and Gérard Chauvy, *La Gestapo française* (Acropole, 2018)

Veillon, Dominique, *Fashion under the Occupation*, trans. Miriam Kochan (Berg, 2000)

Vickers, Hugo, *Behind Closed Doors* (Arrow, 2012)

———, *Elizabeth, the Queen Mother* (Arrow, 2006)

Vinen, Richard, *The Unfree French: Life under the Occupation* (Penguin, 2007)

Vreeland, Diana, *DV* (Knopf, 1984)

Wachsmann, Nikolaus, *KL: A History of the Nazi Concentration Camps* (Abacus, 2016)

Warren, Rosanna, *Max Jacob* (W. W. Norton, 2020)

Wieviorka, Olivier, *The French Resistance*, trans. Jane Marie Todd (Harvard University Press, 2016)

Yonnet, Jacques, *Paris Noir: The Secret History of a City*, trans. Christine Donougher (Dedalus, 2006)

Yung-de Prévaux, Aude, *Jacques and Lotka: A Resistance Story*, trans. Barbara Wright (Bloomsbury, 2000)

Ziegler, Philip, *Diana Cooper* (Hamish Hamilton, 1981)

———, *George VI* (Penguin, 2014)

———, *King Edward VIII* (HarperCollins, 1990)

Index

Colle, Carmen, 259

Colle, Marie-Pierre, 381, 384

Colle, Pierre, 28, 259, 381

Colle Noire, La (Provence), *378–9*; C lives at, 1, 388–91; CD buys, 1, 373; CD on, 376; Christian Dior Parfums acquires, 390; garden, 2, 382; renovation, *372*, 373–6, 390; study, 377–81; visitors' book, *374–5*, 376

Combat (Resistance paper), 78, 105

Cooper, Lady Diana, 220–1, 222, 262, 266, 327, 340, *347*, 365

Cooper, Duff, 220–1, 222, 263, 327, 332, 340, 365

costume balls, 363–8, *366–7*

'couture ration cards', 73, 217

Crespelle, Anne, 55

Crespelle, Jean-Paul, 400–1

Crespelle, Nicolas, 57–9, 106–7, 143, *317*, 395, 400

Cripps, Sir Stafford, 280

Dachau concentration camp, 127, 130, 136, 169, 292, 293

Dalí, Salvador, 28, 35, 327, 368

Dannecker, Theodor, 91

Darnand, Joseph, 61, 122, 205

Dautry, Raoul, 226, 233

Dean, Loomis, *264–5*, *277*, *386–7*

Delahaye, Mme, 183, 238, 240, *241*, 266, 380, 381

Delfau, André, *212–13*

Delfau, Denise, 96, 100, 103, 105–6, *107*, 108, 207, *354*, 357

Delfau, Hélène, 96, 106

Delporte, Jacques, 119

Desbordes, Eliette, 99

Desbordes, Jean, 85–8, *87*, 99, 103–4, 356

Desbordes, Madeleine, 99, 126

Dessès, Jean, 323, 385

Dietlin, Liliane, 54–7, 59, 101, 395, 400

Dietrich, Marlene, 305, *309*

Dincklage, Hans Günther von, 223

Dior, Bernard (brother), 6, 9, 13, *14–15*, *22*, 23, 25, 27, 260

Dior, Catherine

DEPORTATION AND CAPTIVITY: at Abteroda, 168; Association of Deportees card, *399*; bracelet from Hervé's mother, 250; CD attempts to halt, 113–14, 122; death march escape, 178, 179; deported to Ravensbrück, 116–17, 122–3; family awaits return, 183, *184–5*, 228; at Fresnes, 100, 101, 111–12; homecoming, 187–9, *191*, 196, *197*, 225, 236, 238, 245, 320; at Markkleeberg, 171, 173, 175, 186; military decorations, *182*, 195–6, 250, 401; official record, *188*; post-war loathing of Germany, 295, 304; psychological and physical injuries, 198, 400; at Romainville, 112–14, 116; silent about camps, 143, 179, 198, 248, 377; surviving the camps, 143, 177; at Torgau, 159, 160

GARDENING AND FLOWERS: cut-flower trade, 196–8, 248–50, 314, *316*; at Les Naÿsèes, x, 46, 314, *396–7*, 390, *394*, 395–8, *396–7*; at Les Rhumbs, 11, 12, 18, 20; mother inspires, 2, 13, 29

HOUSE OF DIOR: 1953 *Tulipe* line, 370–1; and CD's vision of beauty, 245; godson's christening outfit, 314, *317*; leopard-print coat, 314; Les Naÿsèes wardrobe, 400–1; 'Miss Dior' dress, 313, 315; Miss Dior scent, 2, 8, 248–50, 377, 392, 400; museum, 2, 11, *268–9*, 390; at New Look show, 270, 271

LIFE: CD relationship, 8, 9, 18–19, 385, 391, *393*; CD's death and funeral, 384, 385, *387*, 388; education, 11; father's funeral, 260; as Gaullist, 377; grave, 401; inherits Les Naÿsèes, 314, 373; joins CD in Paris, 28–9; and La Colle Noire, 1, *374*, 376, 388–9; *maison de mode* job, 29; modelling, *33*, 34; on mother, 18, 274; Rue Montorgueil move, 313–14; wartime in Les Naÿsèes, 35, 41, 46–7

PHOTOGRAPHS: aged 30, *5*; Association of Deportees card, *399*; CD's burial, *389*;

Dior, Catherine, PHOTOGRAPHS, (cont.)
on CD's lap, *22*; childhood, *6, 14–16, 26*;
godson's christening, *317*; with Hervé,
316, 396–7; in later life, *403*; at Les
Naÿsèes, *x, 197, 394*; modelling for CD,
33; Ravensbrück Deportees card, *404*; at
Resistance commemoration, *399*; in
Resistance uniform, *182*; smiling, *31*;
wartime, *58*
RESISTANCE: arrested in Paris, 99–100,
250; Callian commemoration, 398, *399*;
de Gaulle broadcasts, 49–53; Hervé
relationship, 47, 49, 54; leaves Provence,
62; photo-IDs Rue de la Pompe Gestapo
gang, 207; Rue de la Pompe torture,
100–2, 105, 106–8; Rue de la Pompe trial,
356–7; at Rue Royale, 66, 77, 88; saves
resistants' lives, 59, 101; tasks in F2, 54,
60, 88; in uniform, *182*
Dior, Charlotte, 8
Dior, Christian
DESIGNER: C models, *33*, 34; 'Café Anglais'
dress at Piguet, 34; on christening dresses,
311; on couture post-Liberation, 225,
260; design process, 312–13; on dresses
as blooms, 312; fashion illustration, 29,
42; on French collaborator customers, 74;
hem lengths, 369; Miss Dior look, 34; on
New Look show, 270; on obsession with
clothes, 315; on padding and corsetry,
314; philosophy, 398–400; Snow predicts
fame, 242; Théâtre de la Mode outfits,
228, *229*, 243; *see also* Lelong, Lucien
LIFE: on 1939, 34–5; on 1952, 369–70;
'Anglomania', 345; on the Armistice,
38; art gallery ventures, 27–8, 274–6;
attempt to stop C deportation, 113–14,
122; Beaton on, 381–2; Boulevard Jules-
Sandeau house, *241*, 382, *383*; burial,
388, *389*; buys La Colle Noir, 1, 373–6;
C relationship, 8, 9, 18–19, 385, 391,
393; costume balls, 363, 364, 368; death,
1, 384–5; on Dior fertiliser, 12; duality
of, 260, 376, 392; education, 11; on

family disasters, 25; father's funeral, 260;
forbidden Riviera parties, 42–3; fortune-
telling, 183, *234*, 235–8, 240, *241*,
380–1; funeral, 385–8, *386–7*; gardening,
2, 11, 12–13, 19; homosexuality, 32–4,
46; generosity, 377, 382–4; German tour
(1955), 300, 302, 304–8; grave, 401;
homecoming dinner for C, 189; on Jacob
circle, 84–5; on Les Rhumbs, 9, 11, 13;
letter on C's survival, *184–5*, 186; lucky
star, 236, *237*, 376; on mother, 23; Rue
Royale apartment, 65, 75–7; Strecker
portrait, *30*, 295; taxes and debts, 382,
390; US tour (1947), 283–4; USSR visit
(1930s), 369; wartime farm-labouring, 35,
42, 46; as wartime target, 46, 77; wealth
and spending, 382–4; will, 390
PHOTOGRAPHS: at Avenue Montaigne,
264–5; Bernard's wedding, *16*; at
Boulevard Jules-Sandeau, *241, 383*;
with C, *22*; childhood, *6, 15*; with Mme
Delahaye, *241*; drawing, *267*; funeral and
burial, *386–7, 389*; at Les Naÿsèes, *197*; at
Les Rhumbs, *24*; with Princess Margaret,
343; with Mizza Bricard, *246*; at Rue
Royale, *76*; St Catherine's Day, *361*
see also Christian Dior, House of
Dior, Jacqueline (sister), *6*, 9, *15, 22*, 260
Dior, Lucien, 8
Dior, Madeleine (mother), *6, 15, 17, 22*:
C on, 18, 274; character, 18, 23; death,
23, 25, 27; forbids CD Dior name, 274;
gardening, 2, 7, 11–12, 13; inspires New
Look, 1–2, 271; marriage, 8; muse to CD,
274; and Parisian fashion, 65, 274; portrait
on CD's desk, 271–4
Dior, Maurice (father), *6, 16–17, 22*:
bankruptcy, 25, 27, 28; CD letter on C's
survival, *184–5*, 186; death, 260; fertiliser
business, 2, 8; grave, 401; homecoming
letter to C, 189, *191*; at Les Naÿsèes, 41,
373; marriage, 8; Paris homes, 11, 28
Dior, Raymond (brother), 1, *6*, 9, *15–17*,
20–3, *21*, 27, 41, 260

Meer, Fritz ter, 296
Mengele, Dr Josef, 172
Mercier, Capt. (French magistrate), 207
MI6, 221, 223
Milice, 61, 122, 205
Miss Dior, see Christian Dior, House of
    (garments); Christian Dior Parfums
Mitford, Nancy, 279–80, 341, 365
Mohr, Heinz, 308
Molyneux, Edward, 29, 32, 65, 166, 244,
    252, 323
Monde, Le, 355, 356–7
Montluc prison, 62
Morand, Hélène, 81
Morand, Paul, 81, 206, 239
Morse, Ralph, 232
Mory, Carmen, 147, 150, 287, 289,
    290–1
Mosley, Diana, 279, 280, 341, 365
Mosley, Sir Oswald, 341
Muggeridge, Malcolm, 199–202, 203–4,
    221, 222–5
Mullen, Barbara, 310

Nast, Condé, 293
Naÿsèes, Les (Callian): C homecoming
    photographs, 196, 197, 394; C inherits,
    314; C leaves in war, 62; Diors move to,
    28–9; Diors' stay in war, 35, 41, 42, 46,
    47; garden and roses, x, 395–8, 396–7,
    401; and La Colle Noire, 373
Nearne, Eileen, 118, 119, 126, 162, 164,
    166–7, 173, 178
Nearne, Francis, 167
Nearne, Jacqueline, 167
New York Times, 225
Newsweek, 283–4
Nordling, Raoul, 113–14, 117–18, 122
Nuremberg trials, 291–3, 297; see also
    Doctors' Trial; Flick Trial; IG Farben Trial;
    Krupp Trial

Oberheuser, Herta, 294–5
Ottaway, Susan, 173

Paley, Natalie, 210
Papillault, Henriette (Hervé's mother), 49,
    250
Paris: Ballard on post-war life, 215–21; black
    market, 92–6, 200; Bousquet's salon,
    77–9; C and CD at Hôtel de Bourgogne,
    29, 32, 33; as capital of luxury and style,
    210; couture under Occupation, 68–9,
    72–4; couture post-Liberation, 214–17,
    218–19, 224, 225–6; de Gaulle's victory
    speech, 198–9; Dior family apartments,
    11, 26, 28; Germans enter, 38, 40;
    Germans leave, 116–17, 119–22; Hôtel
    Lutetia repatriation, 194–5; Maxim's, 75,
    81, 252; Mizza as emblematic, 253; in
    'Phoney War', 35–6; pre-war beau monde,
    34–5; Ritz, 211, 244; Rue de Rivoli, 70–1,
    85; survivors return from camps, 186–90,
    188, 320–1; Windsors in, 340–1; see also
    Drancy; Fresnes; Romainville; Rue de la
    Pompe Gestapo; Rue Royale; Théâtre de la
    Mode exhibition
Paris Match, 279, 369
Patou, Jean, 32, 244
Patten, Susan Mary, 280, 340, 364–5
Perrault, Rosine, 65, 274
Pétain, Philippe: cult of, 42–6, 44–5, 83;
    death sentence commuted, 202–3; Hitler
    meeting, 43, 44, 203; on shell shock, 20;
    at Sigmaringen, 122; as Vichy leader, 41
Peter, Richard, 180
Pflaum, Hans, 142, 288
Philip, Prince, 339
Picardie, Ruth, 18, 134, 135, 238, 401–2
Picasso, Pablo, 28, 79
Picture Post, 350
Piguet, Robert, 29, 34, 68, 262, 385
Pochna, Marie-France, 13, 18, 23, 32, 274,
    341, 382, 384
Pohl, Oswald, 129, 133
Poiret, Paul, 210
Polish intelligence service, 52–3
Posch-Pastor von Camperfeld, Erich, 114
Potthast, Hedwig, 129

Illustration Credits

48 Photograph by Robert Doisneau/Gamma-Rapho/Getty Images.
50 Collection Christian Dior Parfums, Paris.
51 Everett Collection Inc./Alamy Stock Photo.
58 Colourised picture by Composite. Collection Christian Dior Parfums, Paris.
63 Photograph by Robert Doisneau/Gamma-Rapho via Getty Images.
64 Photograph by André Zucca/BHVP/Roger-Viollet.
67 Photograph by Robert Doisneau/Gamma-Rapho via Getty Images.
70–1 Photograph by André Zucca/BHVP/Roger-Viollet.
76 Photograph by Frank Scherschel/The LIFE Picture Collection via Getty Images.
80 Bridgeman Images.
83 (above) Fratelli Alinari Museum, Collections-Favrod Collection, Florence/Bridgeman Images; (below) Photograph by Pierre Jahan/Roger-Viollet via Getty Images.
86 Max Jacob (*c.* 1943) *Vision of the War*. Orléans, Musée des Beaux-Arts © François Lauginie. MO.66.1454
87 Jean Cocteau, *Jean Desbordes* (1928). Pen and black ink. Given in memory of Charles Barnett Goodspeed by Mrs Charles B. Goodspeed, 1947.851. Chicago IL. © 2021. The Art Institute of Chicago/Art Resource, NY/Scala, Florence. © ADAGP/DACS/ Comité Cocteau, Paris 2021.
90 De Agostini Picture Library/Getty Images.
95 © Historical Defense Service.
107 (both) © Historical Defense Service.
110 © René Saint-Paul/Bridgeman Images.
121 Suzanne Emmer-Besniée, *Voyage de Compiègne à Ravensbrück en wagon plombé*. FNAC 20345 (1). On deposit since 2016 at the Museum of Resistance and Deportation of Besançon National Center for Plastic Arts. © Rights reserved/Cnap/Photographer: Hélène Peter.
124 Ravensbrück Memorial Museum, Photo Nr. 1699.
131 Ravensbrück Memorial Museum, Photo Nr. 1624.
132 Ravensbrück Memorial Museum, Photo Nr. 2019/5.
137 Ravensbrück Memorial Museum, Photo Nr. 2008-1749.
145 United States Holocaust Memorial Museum Collection, gift of Ilya Kamenkovitch.
146 (above) Embroidered miniature heart. Ravensbrück Memorial Museum, V548 D2. Photograph: Dr Cordia Schlegelmilch, Berlin; (below) Basket carved from a cherry stone, a birthday present for Vera Vacková-Žahourková in March 1944. Ravensbrück Memorial Museum, V2194 D2. Photograph: Cordia Schlegelmilch, Berlin.
149 (above) Jeannette L'Herminier, *Deux 27000 devisent à l'étage supérieur*. 987.1032.02-42 © Musée de la Résistance et de la Déportation de Besançon, France; (below) Jeannette L'Herminier, *Mathilde Fritz ('Tilly') et Eliane Jeannin*. 987.1032.01-38. © Musée de la Résistance et de la Déportation de Besançon, France.
152–3 (all) The estate of Violette Rougier Lecoq. All Rights Reserved.
156 Card for Vera Vacková-Žahourková on her twentieth birthday, 18.3.1945. Ravensbrück Memorial Museum, V2652 F3.
158 Matteo Omied/Alamy Stock Photo.

164 (above left) Photograph by Universal History Archive/Universal Images Group via Getty Images; (above right) Historic Collection/Alamy Stock Photo; (below left & right) Private Collection.

165 (above left) GL Archive/Alamy Stock Photo; (above right) History and Art Collection/Alamy Stock Photo; (below left) PA Images/Alamy Stock Photo; (below right) Pictorial Press Ltd/Alamy Stock Photo.

170 United States Holocaust Memorial Museum, courtesy of Yad Vashem.

174 Suzanne Emmer-Besniée, *L'Appel du travail*, 1945–1947. FNAC 20345 (6). On deposit since 2016 at the Museum of Resistance and Deportation of Besançon. National Center for Plastic Arts. © Rights reserved/Cnap/Photographer: Hélène Peter.

175 Suzanne Emmer-Besniée, *Corvée de réfection des chaussées*, 1945–1947. FNAC 20345 (8). On deposit since 2016 at the Museum of Resistance and Deportation of Besançon National Center for Plastic Arts. © Rights reserved/Cnap/Photographer: Hélène Peter.

181 Photograph by Richard Peter/Getty Images.

182 Colourised picture by Composite. Collection Christian Dior Parfums, Paris.

184–5 Collection Christian Dior Parfums, Paris.

188 (above) Photograph by STAFF/AFP via Getty Images; (below) Collection Christian Dior Parfums, Paris.

191 Collection Christian Dior Parfums, Paris.

197 Collection Christian Dior Parfums, Paris.

201 Photograph by Robert Capa/Getty Images.

208 Look and Learn/Valerie Jackson Harris Collection/Bridgeman Images.

212 Dress by Lucien Lelong, hat by Janette Colombier, illustration by André Delfau (1942). Collection Gregoire/Bridgeman Images.

213 Tailored suit by Marcel Rochas, hat by Legroux, illustration by André Delfau (1942). Collection Gregoire/Bridgeman Images.

218 Photograph by David E. Scherman/ The LIFE Picture Collection via Getty Images.

219 Photograph by David E. Scherman/The LIFE Picture Collection via Getty Images.

224 Photograph by Bob Landry/The LIFE Picture Collection via Getty Images.

229 Collection of Maryhill Museum of Art.

230–1 Photograph by Robert Doisneau/Gamma-Rapho/Getty Images.

232 Photograph by Ralph Morse/The LIFE Picture Collection via Getty Images.

234 Lenormand Prophecy Cards. Grand Jeu de Mlle Lenormand by B. P. Grimaud.

237 Collection Musée Christian Dior, Granville.

241 © Association Willy Maywald/ADAGP, Paris 2021.

246 © Association Willy Maywald/ADAGP, Paris 2021.

247 Photograph by Horst P. Horst/Condé Nast via Getty Images.

249 (both) Collection Christian Dior Parfums, Paris.

255 Collection Christian Dior Parfums, Paris. © René Gruau/www.renegruau.com

256 Collection Christian Dior Parfums, Paris. © René Gruau/www.renegruau.com

257 Collection Christian Dior Parfums, Paris. © René Gruau/www.renegruau.com

258 © Christian Bérard.

261 © Christian Bérard.

264 Photograph by Loomis Dean/The LIFE Picture Collection via Getty Images.

265 Photograph by Loomis Dean/The LIFE Picture Collection via Getty Images.

267 © Association Willy Maywald/ADAGP, Paris 2021.

268–9 Catherine Dior legacy. Collection Musée Christian Dior, Granville.

272 Photograph by Eugene Kammerman/Gamma-Rapho via Getty Images.

273 Photograph by Eugene Kammerman/Gamma-Rapho via Getty Images.

275 © Archives Charmet/Bridgeman Images.

277 Photograph by Loomis Dean/The LIFE Picture Collection via Getty Images.

278 Photograph by Walter Carone/Paris Match via Getty Images.

281 © Association Willy Maywald/ADAGP, Paris 2021.

286 (above & below) Polish Research Institute, Lund. Photographer: Presse-Bilderdienst, Hans Koch.

289 Photograph by ullstein bild via Getty Images.

306 Photograph by Margaret Bourke-White/The LIFE Picture Collection via Getty Images.

307 Photograph by Ralph Crane/The LIFE Picture Collection via Getty Images.

309 Photograph by Horst P. Horst/Condé Nast via Getty Images.

310 Photograph © Estate of Lillian Bassman.

316 (above) DR/Collection Christian Dior Parfums, Paris; (below) Collection Christian Dior Parfums, Paris.

317 DR/Collection Christian Dior Parfums/Fonds Nicolas Crespelle.

319 Collection Dior Heritage, Paris.

322 Photograph by Cecil Beaton. © Victoria and Albert Museum, London.

326 Photograph by Fayer/Getty Images.

329 Photograph by Underwood Archives/Getty Images.

333 Photograph by Keystone-France/Gamma-Rapho via Getty Images.

334 Photograph by Popperfoto via Getty Images.

337 Photograph by Fox Photographs via Getty Images.

338 Photograph by Popperfoto via Getty Images.

342 Photograph by Cecil Beaton/Condé Nast via Getty Images.

343 (above) Photograph by Bettmann/Getty Images; (below) Photograph by Keystone/Getty Images.

347 Photograph © AGIP/Bridgeman Images.

348 PA Images/Alamy Stock Photo.

351 (above) Photograph by Keystone-France/Gamma-Rapho via Getty Images; (below) Photograph by Popperfoto via Getty Images.

353 Photograph by KEYSTONE-FRANCE/Gamma-Rapho via Getty Images.

354 akg-images.

361 Photograph By Tony Linck/The LIFE Premium Collection via Getty Images.

362 Illustration by Christian Bérard. Photograph © Christie's Images/Bridgeman Images.

366 Photograph by Cecil Beaton/Condé Nast via Getty Images.

367 Photograph by Cecil Beaton/Condé Nast via Getty Images.

372 (above) André Svetchine, Luc Svetchine collection; (below) Collection Christian Dior Parfums, Paris.

374 Collection Christian Dior Parfums, Paris.

375 Illustration by Marc Chagall from the visitors' book at La Colle Noir. Collection Christian Dior Parfums, Paris. © ADAGP, Paris and DACS, London 2021.
378–9 © Association Willy Maywald/ADAGP, 2021.
383 Photograph by Loomis Dean/The LIFE Picture Collection via Getty Images.
386 Photograph by Loomis Dean/The LIFE Picture Collection via Getty Images.
387 Photograph by Loomis Dean/The LIFE Picture Collection via Getty Images.
389 Collection Christian Dior Parfums, Paris.
393 Collection Christian Dior Parfums, Paris.
394 Collection Christian Dior Parfums, Paris.
396–7 Collection Christian Dior Parfums, Paris.
399 (all) Collection Christian Dior Parfums, Paris.
403 Collection Christian Dior Parfums, Paris.
404 Collection Christian Dior Parfums, Paris.